THE
MODERN
EXPLORERS

EDITED BY ROBIN HANBURY-TENISON
AND ROBERT TWIGGER

268 illustrations, 256 in color

Thames & Hudson

THE MODERN EXPLORERS

CONTENTS

First published in 2013 in hardcover in the United States of America by
Thames & Hudson Inc., 500 Fifth Avenue, New York, New York 10110

thamesandhudsonusa.com

Library of Congress Catalog Card Number 2012956321

ISBN 978-0-500-51684-3

Printed and bound in Singapore by Tien Wah Press Ltd.

EXPLORATION:

AN ALLIANCE WITH ADVENTURE

Half-title Robert Twigger pulls his supplies on a trolley across the Great Sand Sea in Egypt.

Title pages The Kum Tagh desert in northwestern China is a trackless labyrinth of sand dunes. Here, John Hare's camel caravan threads its way along the ridge of one, as many more stretch away into the distance.

Page 4 Lorenzo Ricciardi and Richard Bonham, an experienced hunter, follow a crocodile's blood trail through reed marshes.

Opposite Karen Darke made the bold decision to return to the rock face having been paralysed in a rock-climbing accident. She reached the summit of the mighty El Capitan in Yosemite by pulling herself up, in over 4,000 pull-ups.

EXPLORATION IS ALIVE AND WELL and never more popular than today. The glib assertion that, apart from the deepest oceans and outer space, there is nowhere left to explore is instantly refuted by the facts. The expedition advisory centre at the Royal Geographical Society gives advice, help and support to over a thousand expeditions each year. The word explorer itself has, however, become controversial. It is applied without irony to people looking for oil and gas, even in well-mapped areas, but woe betide an adventurer who has the temerity, after treading where no one has trod before, to call himself or herself an explorer. One thing we were sure of when we collaborated on this project was that it should provide inspiration for those drawn to the world of exploration. We hope that, having read the accounts by these international modern explorers about their marvellous exploits in many different fields, you, too, will feel the urge to join in.

The world is not fully explored, nor can it ever be, but neither were parts of it 'discovered' when a European was deemed to have seen them for the first time. In the nineteenth century David Livingstone and Richard Burton followed old existing trade routes – slave routes in many cases – established by the Arabs. And yet they are considered great explorers. They brought back news of 'unknown' terrain, though it was not news to the people whose countries they travelled through. From this we can derive a simple definition: explorers make difficult, and often dangerous, unique journeys to bring back news from distant lands. It may be scientific news, or news about topography. It could be cultural or even psychological news. The account by Jason Lewis, the first person to circumnavigate the globe by human power alone, gives ample evidence that such news also includes the personal challenges and strange delusions one is prey to on risky solo voyages.

In this book we have selected some of the finest modern living explorers and most of them are still exploring. Some are well known; others deserve to be. They also come from many nations. For instance, Wong How Man was the first to locate the exact source of the Yellow River in his native China, while Michel Peissel came from France to explore Tibet and the many rivers originating there, especially the Mekong. Sadly, Michel Peissel died in October 2011 after agreeing to write his contribution to this book, now completed by Sebastian Guinness, who travelled with him. Børge Ousland and Liv Arnesen continue the Norwegian tradition of polar exploration, just as Ranulph Fiennes and Pen Hadow continue the British one. Desert explorers include Arita Baaijens from the Netherlands, Bruno Baumann from Austria, Jon Muir from Australia, and Michael Asher and John Hare from Britain. Their modes of travel range from Bactrian and dromedary camels, to foot-slogging over harsh terrain dragging a light-weight cart.

While much of the planet may have been mapped and has been photographed from satellites, we are only now beginning to realize how little we know about how it works, and that the great majority of species on it are yet to be identified – even as many are fast disappearing. It is often explorers who reveal such mysteries to us and make them widely accessible. Among them are Sir Ghillean Prance, the great plant hunter and ex-Director of Kew Gardens in London, as well as the intrepid pioneer of rainforest canopy investigation, Meg Lowman, and, by far the youngest contributor, Martin Holland, who exemplifies all that is best about modern young explorers. And explorers also have an important part to play in protecting and conserving what is under threat, as reported from central Africa by J. Michael Fay.

Below Bactrian camels are well adapted to desert conditions and are frequently used to carry heavy loads, but even they found it difficult to cope with the treacherous sands of the Kum Tagh on John Hare's expedition in 1999.

Opposite left Pen Hadow set out to measure the thickness of the Arctic sea ice cover by manually drilling through it – and that meant hauling all the team's equipment across the ice. Disintegrating ice floes are often invisible and are a source of real danger when sledging.

Opposite right Brazil has the most uncontacted tribes in the world, and specialists, called *sertanistas*, were empowered to make first contact with them. Of these experts, Sydney Possuelo is the last, seen here with a group of Korubo in the Amazon.

Vast numbers of mountains in Central Asia remain unclimbed, and being the first to stand on a peak where no one has trod before must be a great moment of achievement and discovery. The indefatigable Sir Chris Bonington describes one such exhilarating climb. Other mountaineers writing about their experiences include Stephen Venables, whose evocative descriptions of mountains have few equals, and Rebecca Stephens, the first British woman to climb Everest. Mountains can also be some of the most precarious environments. Our shared terror at Haraldur Sigurdsson's close encounter with an active volcano changes to awe when we read about the truly breathtaking courage and tenacity of the paralysed Karen Darke as she pulls herself up an endless, sheer cliff face.

As well as many mountain peaks, large stretches of desert and polar land have yet to feel human footprints. Swathes of the great jungles, as Wade Davis's traverse of the notorious Darien Gap shows us, are 'untrodden', though within some of them, still today, live uncontacted peoples. In Amazonia, Sydney Possuelo's life and explorations have been devoted to contacting such tribes and protecting their land and rights. In these remote and sparsely inhabited places, where people have lived their lives for centuries, significant discoveries can still be made. Mikael Strandberg describes his epic Siberian journey and the lessons he learnt from local people, both about how they cope with the extreme conditions they experience every day and about his own attitude to exploration.

The essence of exploration is the desire to find out what is over the other side of the hill, across that river, through that forest. The first explorers were Palaeolithic nomads, who desired to find new and better sources of game. These early hunter-gatherers would have followed animal paths

'High-altitude archaeology': Johan Reinhard's work focuses on Inca sites on the tops of mountains. Here he examines a well-preserved mummy on the summit of Llullaiaco, at 6,739 m (22,110 ft). Because such remains are frozen, they yield an immense amount of information about the Inca and their world.

and noted terrain, flora and fauna, and brought back accounts of what they saw. The activity of the explorer may have changed a great deal in many ways, but in others it has changed hardly at all. Exploration can take many forms and use different means, each yielding its own set of sensations and observations, and this is reflected in the range of personal accounts in this book. The sense of walking over new land is a real part of exploration. To fly over a mountain chain is a very different experience from conquering its peaks. Driving fast over a desert results in completely contrasting perceptions to crossing it on foot or riding a camel. Even the same journey or route at different times can produce a variety of impressions.

The world never stands still, and explorers record this. Ecosystems, land use, human and animal species density – all change, all the time, and always have. Scientists such as the discoverer of dinosaur remains, Mark Norell, who has conducted his researches over many years in the Mongolian deserts and has identified numerous new species, study these things. Explorers also bring back reports, the anecdotal stories that are the raw material of hard science. They are researchers as well as searchers, with a desire to find the truth behind myths, or the reasons why things are as they are. Tahir Shah, while seeking for King Solomon's Mines, encountered scenes that could have come from the Old Testament. Johan Reinhard, high in the Andes in search of sites built by the ancient Inca, found remarkably preserved mummies of the people themselves.

Adventure is to exploration what story is to the novel. When exploration loses touch with adventure it strays into the realm of something more commercial and pedestrian. Explorers make dangerous journeys, and in the danger lies the adventure. By maintaining an alliance with adventure,

exploration remains an activity in which all aspects of being human are tested. Courage, intelligence, persistence, imagination – all make being a modern explorer as complete an activity as exists today. In a world where increasingly people are required to spend all day staring at a computer screen, it is a thing to be celebrated. However, when exploration tips too far towards adventure it runs the risk of bringing no news back. It becomes in the words of Wilfred Thesiger 'a meaningless penance'. If you travel through a different culture or note your own reactions to a uniquely experienced journey, that 'penance' may be justified, but only if your conclusions change the world or our perception of it. Mirella and Lorenzo Ricciardi have revealed the wonders of Africa to us through their writings and photographs, while George Bass and Franck Goddio unveil the marvels of the oceanic deeps and the archaeological treasures lying there through their

Above There is an abundance of crocodiles on Lake Rukwa in Tanzania, as encountered by Mirella and Lorenzo Ricciardi on their journey across Africa by boat on their African Rainbow Expedition.

Right The remote and uninhabited islands of Patagonia contain some extraordinary cave features that have not been well explored. Jean-François Pernette and his team have mounted several expeditions to investigate these caves and made some spectacular discoveries.

own very different perspectives. Similarly, the great British caver Andy Eavis and his French colleague, Jean-François Pernette, describe the astonishing underworlds they probe and the spectacular discoveries they make.

The open oceans are vast, trackless spaces, with no landmarks or features, just the horizon. Jon Turk, paddling alone in the Pacific in his kayak acquires clarity and enlightenment through solitude; while Henk de Velde pushes the limits and gains understanding as he sails alone around the world on his never-ending voyage. Tim Severin makes long sea voyages using historically accurate reproductions of ancient craft. In the Brendan Voyage he also followed an ancient text, the apparently mythological tale of an Irish saint. The news he brought back animates and expands the dry pondering of historians. It is an exploration of the past, certainly, but it is also an exploration of the present: travelling in an historical craft forces the crew to view the world through different eyes, through the eyes of ancient men.

Jeff MacInnis was not the first person to traverse the Northwest Passage, Amundsen was, but he was the first to do it by sail power alone, and, even more impressively, he used a Hobie Catamaran – an open 'sport' boat. MacInnis was thus able to experience the land, sea and weather of the extreme north in a way impossible for someone using a more robust craft. By getting into close proximity with the elements he travels through,

the explorer discovers a whole realm of new experiences that inform the way we relate to the planet we live on. And if it is possible to make such journeys we may begin to question our unthinking reliance on fossil fuels. In this sense the explorer brings back new cultural models for the rest of us to consider and adopt.

John Blashford-Snell, now in his mid-seventies, is still making expeditions. He characterizes the indomitable spirit of British exploration, and also perhaps its eccentricities. His journeys down the Blue Nile and the Congo, among others, demonstrate both immense organizational skill and courage. They have also served as encouragement to many through the Operations Drake and Raleigh schemes for young adventurers, which he initiated. This serves to remind us of the huge educational impact explorers have always made. Not only do they inspire through the epic quality of their achievements, they also open up areas of the world to the attention of the young. Many of our explorers decided at an early age on their future course after hearing or reading the stories of their illustrious predecessors.

Exploration may, today, serve its greatest purpose not just through its value to science and commerce, as it has always done, but for what it brings to humanity as a whole. We live in a world where pessimism is rife, where big decisions about the way the planet should be run are based on a dangerously narrow life experience. By encouraging exploration we are encouraging the acquisition of a far wider life experience than is generally available through, for instance, the modern conventions of school, university and some kind of professional job. By visiting other countries not as a consumer, which is the tourism model, but as someone there to learn, which is the explorer's role, we are providing a wonderful mechanism for curbing first-world arrogance as well as first-world ignorance. By putting ourselves under trying conditions on difficult and dangerous journeys (the risk of which we seek to control through acquired skills rather than negate through blindly applied safety regulations), we are learning how to deal with anxiety, pressure, the demands of leadership, resourcefulness and many other utterly necessary human skills you cannot find by staying at home and watching television.

Robin Hanbury-Tenison
Robert Twigger

Jeff MacInnis completed a traverse of the Northwest Passage by sail power alone in a small catamaran. One advantage of this craft was that, when needed, he and his companion, Mike Beedell, could drag it over the ice that blocked their way – though it was very heavy.

POLAR

Since the beginning of the modern age of exploration something has drawn people to the extremes of climate, and of geography. The Poles represent these extremes in every sense: they are colder and more remote than anywhere else. The polar regions, too, like the tops of high mountains, are often still truly virgin territories.

In their sub-zero pristine clarity, the Poles remain the purest exploration ambition, the zenith for many would-be explorers, where they may test their strength and courage against the most inhospitable climate on Earth. There is an utter simplicity in that super-cold environment lacking in more varied regions. But what may appear monotonous is in fact an infinite variety within heavily prescribed limits. The very curtailment of the explorer's view becomes an impulse to look deeper and harder at the surroundings. Hence the almost mystical accounts of people travelling to the Poles, as the true majesty of their isolation strikes home day by day.

With the use of sledge dogs now excluded by law in the Antarctic, new methods of travel – manpower and sail power – have extended the limits of what was thought possible in terms of human capacity. Using only individual strength, and the force of the gales that blow across the polar landscapes, new records of endurance and endeavour have been set at both Poles.

The Poles are uninhabited, vastly so; and though we know much of their broad geography, there are still huge areas where no people have ever been. For many years to come they will remain a favoured destination for all who seek adventure and new discoveries.

Børge Ousland was the first person to walk solo across Antarctica from coast to coast via the South Pole. As he describes in these pages, while an expedition with others is a great adventure, a journey completely alone, with no one else to rely on, is a very different experience, bringing an added element of meditation.

RANULPH FIENNES

FROSTBITTEN FINGERS

IN THE MILLENNIUM YEAR THERE WAS CONSIDERABLE ENTHUSIASM to knock off the Arctic journey that most polar pundits considered the only true challenge that still remained: the final grail of reaching the North Pole solo and unsupported specifically by the North American or direct route, which involves travelling against the prevailing currents. At fifty-five and after some thirty expeditions, including being the first, with Charlie Burton, to reach both poles by surface travel and the first, with Mike Stroud, to cross the Antarctic continent unsupported, I thought I should give it a try. So, on 14 February 2000 I was flown in a Twin Otter from Resolute Bay to the edge of the Arctic Ocean and the conical hill at the north end of Ward Hunt Island that is the starting point of most North Pole attempts.

My morale was high, for the two sledges I was pulling in relay ran well, whatever the surface – far better than any previous design. My mental arithmetic raced ahead and I estimated a Pole arrival in only seventy days. Then, on a dark night, at -49°C (-56°F), and still within the chaotic belt of broken ice floes that swirl and grind together for some 48 km (30 miles) north of the Canadian coast, disaster struck.

I had been travelling for well over the intended ten hours and making good progress, but was tired and cold. I ate a chocolate bar every two hours to ward off hypothermia, but was very weary and decided to camp on any surface that looked solid. I came to a zone of interlacing fractures. The moon had vanished and, whenever I stopped, I heard the grumble of ice on the move. I tried to avoid a trench of black water and mounted a bridge of 30-cm (12-in) thick slabs, buckled by floe pressure. I had the small sledge with me and had left the big one some 500 m (500 yd) to the south. I clambered over the slabs with my skis on. The sledge followed easily in my wake.

There was no warning. A slab tilted suddenly under the sledge, which responded to gravity and, unbalancing me, pulled me backwards. I fell on my back and slid down the slab. The noise that followed was the one I most hate to hear in the Arctic: a splash as the sledge fell into the sea.

I kicked out with my skis and flailed at the slab with both hands. One ski boot plunged into the sea and one gloved hand found an edge of the slab. Taking a firm grip, I pulled my wet foot and ski out of the water. I unfastened the man-haul harness. I was already beginning to shiver. I squirmed around until I could sit on a flatter slab to inspect the sledge in the gloom. It was under water, though still afloat. I hauled on the traces, but they were jammed under the slabs. Seventy days worth of food and thirty of fuel were on that sledge – and the communications gear. Without it, the expedition was over. A nearby slab crashed into the sea: the ice was moving. I had to save the sledge quickly. Soon I would be dangerously cold.

With my feet (skis off) hooked around a slab, I lay on my stomach and stretched my left arm under the slab to free the sledge trace. I took off my mitt so that I could feel where the rope was snagged. For a minute or so I could not find the underwater snag. Then, by jiggling the rope sharply, it came free. I pulled hard and the sodden sledge rose to the surface. My wet hand was numb, but I could not replace the mitt until the sledge was out of the sea. Gradually, its prow rose on to a slab and water cascaded off its canvas cover.

Minutes later the sledge was on 'dry land'. I danced about like a madman. Both my mitts were back on and I used various well-tried cold

One way of crossing open leads between ice floes is with 'amphibious' sledges.

Standing in the freezing darkness of the polar night.

hands revival techniques to restore life to the numb fingers. Usually this works and the blood returns painfully to all my fingers; this time it did not.

I took the wet mitt off and felt the dead hand. The fingers were ramrod stiff and ivory white. They might as well have been wooden. I knew that if I let my good hand go even partially numb, I would be unable to erect the tent and start the cooker – which I needed to do quickly for I was shivering in my thin man-haul gear. I returned to the big sledge. The next thirty minutes were a nightmare. The cover zip jammed. With only five usable but increasingly numb fingers, precious minutes went by before I could free it and unpack the tent. By the time I had eased one tent-pole into its sleeve, my teeth were chattering violently and my good hand was numb. I had to get the cooker going in minutes or it would be too late. I crawled into the partially erect tent, closed its door zip and began a twenty-minute battle to start the cooker. I could not use the petrol lighter with my fingers, but I found some matches I could hold in my teeth.

Starting an extremely cold petrol cooker involves careful priming so that just the right amount of fuel seeps into the pad below the fuel jet. The cold makes washers brittle and the priming plunger sticky. Using my teeth and a numb index finger, I finally worked the pump enough to squirt fuel on to the pad but was slow in shutting the valve; when I applied the match a 1-m (3-ft) flame reached to the roof. Luckily I had had a custom-made flame lining installed, so the tent was undamaged. And the cooker was alight – one of the best moments of my life.

Slowly and painfully some feeling came back into the fingers of my right hand. An hour later, with my body warm again, I unlaced my wet boot. Only two toes had been affected. Soon they would exhibit big blood blisters and lose their nails, but they had escaped true frostbite. All around the tent cracking noises sounded above the steady roar of the cooker. I was in no doubt as to the fate of my bad hand. I'd seen enough frostbite in others to realize that I was in serious trouble. I had to get to a hospital fast to save some fingers from the surgeon's knife. I had to turn back.

I hated the thought of leaving the warmth of the tent. Both hands were excruciatingly painful. I battered ice off the smaller sledge, unloaded anything not essential and hauled it back to the big sledge. I set out in great trepidation. Twice my earlier tracks had been cut by newly open leads, but fortunately only small diversions were needed to detour the open water. Five hours later I was back on the ice-shelf. I erected the tent properly and spent three hours massaging my good hand and wet foot over the cooker.

I drank hot tea and ate chocolate. I felt tired and dizzy, but the wind was showing signs of rising and I knew I should not risk a high wind chill.

I HATED THE THOUGHT OF LEAVING THE WARMTH OF THE TENT.

The journey to the hut on Ward Hunt Island took for ever. Once, I fell asleep on the move and woke in a trough of soft snow well away from my intended route. Hypothermia is a danger at such times. When I feared its onset I often spoke to myself aloud, trying to enunciate the *My Fair Lady* lines about the rain in Spain, because an un-slurred voice was about the only reliable assurance that I was not on the slippery path to hypothermia and, on a solo expedition, death.

When at length I came to the old hut, I prepared the communications gear and arranged to be evacuated the following day. The fingers on my left hand began to grow great liquid blisters. The pain was bad so I raided my

The journey back to the hut on Ward Hunt Island hauling the sledge took for ever.

medical stores for drugs and some forty-eight hours after my arrival at the hut I was on my way to try to save my left hand.

Media barbs the week after I returned home from Ottawa about my age and this failure were easily kept in perspective by the more immediate worry of what to do about my damaged fingers. They throbbed most of the time and complained loudly with needle-sharp pain when brought into contact, however lightly, with any object, even clothing material. To avoid this, especially when trying to sleep, was often difficult.

After checking the records of a number of specialists, my wife Ginny found a surgeon in Bristol, Donald Sammut, with a history of brilliant treatment of damaged fingers. Under no circumstances, he warned, should I undergo any amputations until at least five months after the date of the accident.

After four months of living with grotesque, witch-like talons, purple in colour, sticking out of my stumps, I could take it no longer and, with another month to go before Donald Sammut was due to cut

THE ANSWER WAS OBVIOUS. them off, I decided to take the matter into my own hands.

Each and every time over the previous sixteen weeks that my fingers had hit or merely brushed against anything, never mind something hot, I had sworn at the pain. Ginny suggested that I was becoming irritable. Throughout this period I took penicillin to keep gangrene from developing in the open cracks where the damaged but live flesh met the dead and blackened ends.

The answer was obvious. The useless finger ends must be cut off at once, so they could no longer get in the way and hit things. I tried tentatively to cut through the smallest finger with a new pair of secateurs, but it

DIY digital surgery.

hurt. So I purchased a set of fretsaw blades at the village shop, put the little finger in my Black & Decker folding table's vice and gently sawed through the dead skin and bone just above the live skin line. The moment I felt pain or spotted blood, I moved the saw further into the dead zone. I also turned the finger around several times to cut it from different sides, like sawing a log. This worked well and the little finger's end knuckle finally dropped off after some two hours of work. Over that week I removed the other three longer fingers, one each day, and finally the thumb, which took two days.

My physiotherapist congratulated me on a fine job, but Donald Sammut was not so happy. He later recorded my visit: 'Ran appeared one day on a routine appointment and calmly told me he'd chopped off his fingertips. We had quite a heated exchange over this. He risked making it worse.' I apologized to Donald, but felt secretly pleased with myself since life improved considerably once the gnarled, mummified ends no longer got in the way. Ginny agreed that I had done the right thing. She no longer had to tie my tie for me, nor put in my cufflinks before I gave a conference talk.

Ranulph Fiennes (British, b. 1944) was the first person to circumnavigate the world along its polar axis, making him the first to reach both Poles on foot (with Charles Burton), and also the first to cross both the Antarctic and Arctic oceans (with Charles Burton). In 1992/93 he achieved another world first by completing the first unsupported crossing of the Antarctic continent (with Mike Stroud); this was also at the time the longest unsupported polar journey in history. In March 2007 he climbed the North Face of the Eiger, raising £1.8 million for Marie Curie Cancer Care's Delivering Choice Programme. In May 2009 he successfully summited Everest, raising a further £6.3 million for Marie Curie Cancer Care. He is the author of numerous books, including an autobiography *Mad, Bad & Dangerous to Know* (2007).

LIV ARNESEN

SKIING SOLO TO THE SOUTH POLE

From the crossing of Greenland in 1992: note the size of the GPS in my hand. This was the first hand-held GPS and we took a sextant as a backup.

THERE IS A BOOK IN MY LIFE which has led me to where I am today. As an eight-year-old I visited the home of the Norwegian explorer, scientist and Nobel Peace Prize Laureate Fridtjof Nansen. Back at home my father gave me Nansen's book about his traverse of the Greenland icecap. Its language was too hard for a child of my age, but I was inspired to find out more about polar explorers. In the school library I found a book for kids about Roald Amundsen's expedition to the South Pole. Ever since I got my first pair of skis I have loved skiing, and that book created my childhood dream: to ski to the South Pole. It also opened my eyes to the fact that books could take me everywhere and teach me everything I wanted learn.

Many years later I read in the local newspaper about a man who had completed a demanding solo ski tour across Greenland – and he was fifty-eight years old. It was like a revelation. He was a seasoned traveller, but I knew I was a reliable skier with plenty of stamina! I remember that day so well. I was sitting at the kitchen table with a cup of coffee and the paper in front of me. My partner sat directly opposite, immersed in local news, but I was already on my way across Greenland. I was bubbling over with enthusiasm. How could I have ignored the classic route across Greenland, and only wandered around dreaming of following in Amundsen's footsteps to the South Pole? Who could I persuade to accompany me? My partner didn't even look up. He had no taste for camping, and was definitely not fired by the thought of an expedition of this kind.

LIFE ON THE GREAT WHITE OPEN SPACES IS WONDERFUL, AND I REMEMBER THAT AT THAT MOMENT MY THOUGHTS FLEW TO AN ICECAP EVEN BIGGER THAN THE ONE WE HAD JUST CROSSED.

During the days that followed, it was as if I was possessed by Greenland. The more interest I showed in the project, the quieter my partner became. As the weeks passed, he began to understand that my dream would become reality, and not long after I was alone – again.

Two years later, in 1992, I succeeded in crossing the Greenland icecap with Julie Maske. It took us twenty-three days to cover 570 km (355 miles) and we became the first women to cross from one side of the inland ice to the other unsupported. Life on the great white open spaces is wonderful, and I remember that at that moment my thoughts flew to an icecap even bigger than the one we had just crossed. But Julie said that, unlike me, she was finished with the great white open spaces. She would not be coming with me to the South Pole. That was a setback. One has to be extremely careful in choosing companions for such an enterprise. Three weeks after returning home, I heard that Erling Kagge was planning to go to the South Pole alone. Perhaps the only way of skiing to the South Pole was to do it solo.

Reaching Isortoq on the east coast of Greenland after the crossing in 1992.

The hunt for sponsors turned out to be much harder than I had imagined. The reactions indicated that it must have been considerably more difficult for me than for the men who had made the rounds before me. 'Have you ever hauled a sledge?' was a constantly recurring question. I wondered if the same question had been put to the boys – certainly, I'm sure they didn't have to sit through all the stories of military service. In the end, I heard enough tales of winter manoeuvres to fill a whole book. Having been told all those dramatic episodes, I could only marvel at how many Norwegians managed to survive military service in winter.

I was taken aback by these reactions. I had sensed them in private life for many years, but I believed that contemporary industrialists were more tolerant and open-minded. In Norway, we had a woman prime minister at the time, and there are many female politicians and cabinet ministers, and women in the armed forces and most of the professions. Business and industry actively encourage women, don't they? My generation is one of transition, in which everything is fundamentally open to all. Nonetheless, there's often something or someone holding us back. Was I intruding on territory that belonged to men alone? Eventually, I realized that to plan an expedition to the South Pole was treading on male preserves. Girls don't go to the South Pole – at least, not alone.

EVENTUALLY, I REALIZED THAT TO PLAN AN EXPEDITION TO THE SOUTH POLE WAS TREADING ON MALE PRESERVES. GIRLS DON'T GO TO THE SOUTH POLE – AT LEAST, NOT ALONE.

The constant question, both before and after such an enterprise, is always 'why?' Was it a craving for publicity, something to do with feminism, or an urge to prove how strong I was? Why go to the North or South Pole when it's been done before? Why on earth climb Everest when nearly

six hundred people already have? Why write poems when so many have already been written? Why compose music? Why do people work to the point of exhaustion in order to acquire status symbols and heart disease?

Every age has its own particular form of expressing the creative urge and giving vent to vitality. Those of us who aren't artists must try to make something else out of life. What we do and why we do it has as many variations as there are human beings. What drove me was a combination of upbringing, childhood surroundings, social influences and my way of life in adulthood, to which must be added my old dream of the South Pole, a taste for testing myself mentally and physically, enjoying long tours and, above all, the fact that I love skiing.

At last, the day had arrived that I had been looking forward to, consciously or unconsciously, for nearly thirty years. On 2 November 1994, I was let off at Hercules Inlet at the Rønne Shelf. It had been a long and tortuous path; now there were few ways back and only one course to my goal, 1,200 km (745 miles) straight ahead.

The weather was fine, with good visibility, and the terrain rose in a succession of terraces. I passed some narrow crevasses now and then. In the distance I could see blue ice and huge open chasms, luckily they lay to the east of my course. After 10 km (6 miles), with a vertical climb of 420 m (1,378 ft), I was satisfied with the day's work and made camp. It was impossible to find a level tent site, so I had to make do with a night on a slope. It had been a trying day with many a heavy heave, and I fell asleep on my way into my sleeping bag. That first night, I slept deeply for twelve solid hours.

I often thought of Amundsen, Shackleton and Scott and, with the sufferings of the old heroes at the back of my mind, I tramped on towards the

Opposite Our first camp on the crossing of Greenland in 1992.

Right On my way to the South Pole in November 1994.

South. I had food enough and also proven equipment and navigational systems. I had prepared myself mentally in advance by assuming that it would be horribly cold and unpleasant. I had absorbed all the sufferings of the old polar explorers into my subconscious, where they had been churning around for many a year. Psychologically, I was prepared for my own expedition to turn out just as badly. So what happened to the suffering? Of course it was cold, but I was expecting it to be colder. It began to dawn on me that I was on the ski tour of my life.

In the small hours of 19 December, I woke up with a feeling that something was awry. It was silent, exactly as if I had ear plugs in. Carefully, and a little anxiously, I opened the zip fastener and looked out. It was dead calm, with an unbelievable, deafening silence. It was my first day in the Antarctic without wind.

I opened the tent door and for a long time sat in my sleeping bag staring out at a still, white expanse and a blue sky. Huge snow crystals were glittering in the sun. I crawled back into the sleeping bag and felt happy, rested and content.

The final few days were like a fairy-tale. The wind had almost completely vanished. The silence seemed overwhelming, almost oppressive. For the first time I had a feeling of being completely alone.

It is Christmas Eve 1994. The Amundsen-Scott base has been visible for five hours. The dome grows bigger, and more and more buildings appear. I cross the landing strip and, for the first time on the whole tour I feel my skis gliding, and make my first double heave on the sticks.

It has been a wonderful experience to be a lonely nomad in Antarctica. The fifty days have gone incredibly quickly. I do remember the overwhelming fatigue and emptiness of the first few days. But I sense another kind of emptiness now, as if something has been lost. Mentally, I feel as if I still have enormous reserves. I feel privileged to have gone through this experience; above all to have realized a dream. I feel loaded with an incredible energy and I make one promise to myself; I will go back to teaching and inspire my pupils to search for and chase after their dreams!

However, I never went back to being a high school teacher. After the solo trip I was invited around the world to give talks with such titles as 'Good girls do not ski to the South Pole' or 'From dream to reality'. I started my own company and make my living giving motivational lectures and running team-building programmes.

IN THE SMALL HOURS OF 19 DECEMBER, I WOKE UP WITH A FEELING THAT SOMETHING WAS AWRY. IT WAS SILENT, EXACTLY AS IF I HAD EAR PLUGS IN.

Christmas Eve 1994 –
reaching the South Pole after
fifty days, my best Christmas
present ever.

But once a teacher always a teacher. After teaming up with the American educator and explorer Ann Bancroft in 1998, I have used expeditions as an educational tool. Our biggest success so far is the crossing of the Antarctic continent in 2000–01 with three million kids in 116 countries following us. Our mission is to inspire and promote the achievement of dreams by empowering youth to explore issues that affect their world.

Liv Arnesen (Norwegian, b. 1953) is an internationally recognized leader and role model for women and girls. A self-proclaimed 'keen' but not fanatical outdoors enthusiast, Arnesen is most interested in the development of adults and children. Through her rich life experiences, both on and off the ice, and her diverse roles as a polar explorer, educator and motivational leader, Arnesen ignites passions in others to reach beyond their normal boundaries and achieve their dreams by sharing her own stories about exploring some of the most remote places on Earth.

BØRGE OUSLAND

ALONE ACROSS ANTARCTICA COAST TO COAST

IN 1994 I BECAME THE FIRST PERSON to reach the North Pole alone and without support, setting out from Cape Arktichesky in Siberia and arriving at the Pole fifty-two days later. This was a huge achievement for me, and following a series of Arctic expeditions I decided that it was time to look south. In 1995, I walked over 1,000 km (620 miles) to the South Pole on my first attempt to cross Antarctica, but then had to stop. I had suffered so much from frostbite and infected blisters that it was impossible to go on. Only a few days after reaching the Pole, I was forced to give up. Instead of reaching my destination on the other side, I had to hitch out by plane halfway through the expedition.

I don't like giving up. So the question was: dare I try again? Should I risk having to abandon the next attempt as well? When I got home, I shuddered at the thought of starting a new round of preparations, training by pulling car tyres and carrying heavy backpacks, all the work of finding a sponsor, and, not least, another family separation. But by the end of March 1996 I had made my decision. It was obvious that the way forward was via the Antarctic. I knew that I would be sorry if I didn't try and if I was to do it at all, it had to be now.

What made this year particularly special was that two other solo explorers were setting out to do the same thing. One was the Englishman Ranulph Fiennes and the other Marek Kaminsky from Poland. Both were experienced polar explorers. In addition, there was a Korean group of six. The plan for all of us was to cross Antarctica from coast to coast via the South Pole, alone and without outside support. We all saw this expedition as one of the last classic challenges left and were all gripped with a burning desire to be the first to complete the journey.

Opposite Arriving at New Zealand's Scott base, 17 January 1997, the first to have crossed Antarctica from coast to coast unsupported.

Above A rare warm day on the Ross Ice Shelf: a self-portrait taken just down from Axel Heiberg Glacier.

On 15 November 1996 I stood on the northeastern corner of Berkner Island. Behind me lay the pack ice of the Weddell Sea and before me a gently rising landscape of ice that seemed to have no end. Fiennes had set out a couple of days earlier, while Marek and I had shared a plane to save money and we had dropped Marek a few miles further west.

The beginning of these solo trips is almost the hardest part of the whole expedition. This is a paradox, since it is entirely voluntary, and I work long and hard to get to the start point. But watching that plane vanish above my head, taking those first steps on a trip that no one has succeeded in completing, is a shock to the system. In some ways, it's much easier at the North Pole. There something is happening all the time, but the Antarctic is so desolate, with so little external stimulation, that I think a solo expedition in Antarctica is an even greater mental challenge than at the North Pole.

It generally takes about ten to fourteen days to really get into an expedition and fall into the routine and inner harmony that are needed to survive in such a cold and unforgiving world. But when it all comes together, being so totally alone is also a good experience; in fact, the best part of the whole expedition. Precisely because there is no one else to lean on, I have a different dialogue with myself and the world around me. An expedition with others is a great experience, but it is more of a physical journey from A to B. A long solo trip, on the other hand, has the added element of meditation to it.

Going to the South Pole once is probably understandable. But going the same way two years in a row is beyond what most people could grasp

Shaped by wind and driving snow, this sastrugi on the polar plateau catches light from the December sun, not far from the South Pole.

in terms of the motivation and patience needed for such a monotonous journey. So this time I chose a slightly different route up through the Dufek Massif, one that I had not taken before. I had decided on this way based on aerial photos, and it turned out to be a good choice, without the many crevasses that normally form when the ice flows through mountains.

Massive peaks carved the horizon into jagged, unpolished landmarks: Washington Mountains to the west, Forrestal Range with Saratoga Table to the east, and there in front of me, the plateau stretching out all the way to the South Pole. It meant a steady climb of about 50 m (165 ft) a day, but the worst thing is the ice-cold hurricane-like winds that whip through bone and marrow. There are no trees or land formations for shelter. The only variations in this endless landscape are the numerous belts of so-called sastrugi – hard snowdrifts formed by the wind constantly blowing from the same direction, some as much as 2 m (6½ ft) high.

From time to time the task just seems too big, and a large part of coping with this kind of expedition lies in being able to change perspective. On good days I can raise my eyes to the horizon and think far ahead, but on difficult days I draw my perspective right back to the tips of my skis and only consider the next hour ahead. Even in this uniform world I can always choose, and it is important to remember that. I can look around me and see how white, desolate and exhausting this is, how godforsaken and hopeless. Or I can turn it around and take in all the new and positive aspects, and contemplate the beauty of nature, the nuances of light, shape and colours.

I knew that the South Pole base would be a potential trap and I decided not to stop there. I needed to keep the ice and isolation within me. If I let

Drifting snow builds up around the campsite after a blizzard close to the Pole. A high-frequency radio antenna stretched out between skis enabled me to keep contact with Patriot Hills at certain intervals.

myself go inside and feel cosy, it could be difficult to get going again. The base doctor wanted to check me out, but I declined and just kept going.

The plateau around the South Pole is cold and high, but there is not usually much wind. It isn't until you get out near the edge and the mountain ranges that the air currents begin to sweep down towards the coast. I was able to exploit this with a ski sail when the wind was in the right direction. It was fantastic to be pulled along by the wind for kilometre after kilometre. The only problem is that where there is wind there are also sastrugi. When the drifts got too big, that was the end of the ski-sailing. It was just too dangerous, and breaking a leg out there would mean certain death.

WHEN THE DRIFTS GOT TOO BIG, THAT WAS THE END OF THE SKI-SAILING. IT WAS JUST TOO DANGEROUS, AND BREAKING A LEG OUT THERE WOULD MEAN CERTAIN DEATH.

Which route should I take down between the mountain ranges? I considered the Beardmore Glacier, which is a more direct route to McMurdo, my final destination, but Beardmore is heavily crevassed and as I was alone, I opted for the Axel Heiberg Glacier. That route is about 200 km (124 miles) longer, but safer. In addition, this was Amundsen's route, and as a Norwegian it was a great experience for me to traverse the mountains and glaciers that Amundsen and his men named in 1911.

At the base of the Axel Heiberg glacier the huge Ross Ice Shelf begins. A scientist I spoke to said that this ice shelf has existed for at least 100,000 years, in other words before a country such as Denmark was formed. Some skiers claim that they have crossed Antarctica when they have reached the inner edge of the shelf ice, regarding that as the sea. But how can you call freshwater ice several hundred meters thick and thousands of years old the sea? A proper crossing of Antarctica has to be from shore to shore.

It's about 500 km (310 miles) across the Ross Ice Shelf to McMurdo, and to get there you have to go through a treacherous area of crevasses around Minna Bluff. These crevasses are often invisible, covered only by thin bridges of snow. It was a good thing I had stiff titanium bars almost 4 m (13 ft) long between me and my sled. On one occasion off Berkner Island this system had saved my life. I was crossing a snow bridge that suddenly collapsed, but the rigid titanium rods stopped me falling any further. There is always that extra risk with solo expeditions – there is no one to help if an accident occurs.

I reached Scott Base on 17 January 1997, after walking almost 3,000 km (1,864 miles) across the Antarctic without outside support. Quite by chance, I arrived in time for the celebration of the base's fortieth anniversary. Present for the event was Sir Edmund Hillary from the 1953 Everest expedition. It was fantastic for me to meet this legend, who himself had undertaken an expedition to the South Pole in 1957. In fact, I was able to fly back to the South Pole with Hillary. It took just two and a half hours to fly the same distance it had taken me more than a month to walk. At the South Pole, amazingly, I met the Korean expedition that had just arrived. They had given up after reaching the Pole, as did Marek Kaminsky, while Ranulph Fiennes had abandoned his expedition a few weeks after the start on medical grounds.

Before leaving Antarctica, I spent a few days wandering around McMurdo Station at the tip of Ross Island. On Observation Hill there is a huge wooden cross in memory of those who died on Scott's *Terra Nova* expedition in March 1912. Engraved on the cross are the following words

Below Having reached Scott Base just in time for its fortieth anniversary, I then joined Sir Edmund Hillary on a US flight back to the South Pole, where both of us were asked to sign this T-shirt belonging to one of the staff at the station.

Opposite left The inscription on the cross at Observation Hill, raised in January 1913 by the crew of the *Terra Nova*.

Opposite right Taking a snapshot of the metal ball marking the point of the geographical South Pole on my solo crossing of Antarctica.

from the poem 'Ulysses' by Alfred Lord Tennyson: 'To strive, to seek, to find, and not to yield.'

Since then, these words have inspired me. They bring to mind the first men who sailed here in their wooden ships, spending years cut off from the outside world and undertaking their expeditions without GPS or satellite phones. I believe we still have a lot to learn from their courage and strength. They are the true heroes of Antarctica.

Børge Ousland (Norwegian, b. 1962) is described by *National Geographic Adventure* as 'arguably the most accomplished polar explorer alive'. His first expedition was across Greenland in 1986; since then he has been to the North Pole nineteen times. He was the first to ski alone and unsupported to both the North and South Poles, and he is also the first and only explorer to have crossed Antarctica and the North Pole alone from coast to coast. In 2003 he crossed the Southern Patagonia icecap with Thomas Ulrich, another first. In 2006 Børge and partner Mike Horn skied to the North Pole during the dark months of winter, one of the most difficult Arctic expeditions ever. In 2007 Børge and Thomas Ulrich followed Fritdjof Nansen's footsteps through Frans Josef Land on a five-month-long expedition that began at the North Pole and ended in Oslo. Børge's most recent achievement was in 2010, when he and Thorleif Thorleifsson became the first to sail around the Arctic, through both the Northeast and the Northwest Passage, in one season.

PEN HADOW

MEASURING THE ARCTIC SEA ICE

EXPLORATION HAS PERMEATED MY EXISTENCE SINCE INFANCY. I was brought up on a mind-nourishing diet of the best stories of 'The Antarctic Boys', as I grew to know them: Scott, Amundsen, Shackleton and others. They were told to me by my nanny, Enid Wigley, who in her teenage years had looked after Peter Scott, son of Britain's most famous polar explorer, Robert Falcon Scott – Scott of the Antarctic. The seed had thus been sown of the idea of being an 'explorer' – the distinction between adventure and exploration having been skilfully drawn by Enid. That seed germinated and broke through into the light in the spring of 2004.

The year before, on 19 May, I had finally fulfilled the vow I had made to my father on his deathbed in 1993, that if I achieved nothing else with my life, I would be the first to make a solo journey from Canada to the North Geographic Pole, without resupply. It took three attempts – in 1994, 1998 and 2003. Within twelve months of reaching the North Pole I had made another polar journey, again without resupply, this time from Antarctica's continental coast to the South Pole and with a partner. Then, as I lay in the bath one evening some months later, wondering about the future, three thoughts suddenly collided to produce a dramatic realization ... I had the opportunity to become an explorer proper. Not a guide, not an adventurer, but what I had been brought up to believe was the real deal.

The first thought was that people with sea ice survival and travel expertise are in a unique position to be able to reach places and find out things in the ultra-challenging Arctic Ocean that others simply cannot – especially scientists. The second revelation came from connecting this with my awareness that to advance scientific understanding of the rapidly changing status of the sea ice required more accurate measurements than remotely sensed satellite and submarine-derived data could produce. And the third idea was about capturing and transmitting data digitally – scientific observations, photographs, audio accounts and video sequences. This would allow a more direct and immediate engagement with a large audience worldwide than previously possible in the polar regions, communicating both the extreme human effort involved in extracting the information and the significance of the dramatic changes taking place in the high Arctic. And so, in that moment, these three strands came together to produce the vision for Arctic Survey.

The objective of Arctic Survey was simple: to measure the thickness of the sea ice cover of the Arctic Ocean by manually drilling through it. Working in collaboration with our scientific partners at the University of Cambridge, this would contribute to a more confident projection of when the polar 'icecap' would cease to be a year-round surface feature of our planet. With the United Nations' greenhouse gas emissions control negotiations looking to culminate at the Conference of Parties (COP15) event in December 2009, delivering the most up-to-date scientific evidence about the status of the North Pole region – the most obvious visual manifestation of global climate change – gave special motivation and focus to our work.

A huge sum of US$5 million was secured, primarily through corporate sponsorship, with the lion's share coming from Catlin Group, gaining them the title rights to what thus became the Catlin Arctic Survey. The BBC's global online, radio and television platforms followed the Survey closely, as did other networks. Six months before our departure, over 45 people were engaged, full- or part-time, in delivering the operational and communications ambitions of the expedition.

Below left Measuring and recording ice floe thickness with a manual drill.

Below right Finding a route across a dangerous section of moving ice rubble between floes.

Using all my strength and experience, I haul my sledge carrying 140 kg (308 lb) of equipment up over the edge of an ice ridge.

Just three people, however, would form the survey team to go 'up on to the sea ice'. Ann Daniels was to be our navigator across the frozen ocean surface, her extraordinary capacity having been proved on many previous expeditions. Simply heading north is relative child's play. Ann's hour-after-hour challenge would be to plot for us, sight-unseen, the most energy-efficient route north, as we pulled our desperately heavy sledges across the drifting, disintegrating ice floes, edged by ridges of jumbled ice blocks. Martin Hartley, the world-class expedition and adventure travel photographer, would use his experience to capture the natural phenomena and human stories that occurred on the journey. And I was to be the expedition's surveyor and leader.

Traditionally, most expeditions on the Arctic Ocean seem drawn to the inescapable symbolism offered by the North Geographic Pole. Although our route, defined by the scientific requirements of Professor Peter Wadhams (of the Polar Ocean Physics Group, University of Cambridge), had an obscure start point roughly in the middle of nowhere in mid-ocean, it deliberately had the North Pole at its end. This would maximize global public interest and give us something to aim for. But our primary goal was to survey the thickness of the sea ice for the greatest possible distance in 'the travel season' (1 March to 15 May). The journey began on 1 March 2009.

I am always struck by the feeling of alarm I experience in that final drop-off by air on to the sea ice. A series of flights, from London to Ottawa (Canada), Ottawa to Iqaluit (capital of Nunavut), Iqaluit to Resolute (only settlement on Cornwallis Island), Resolute to Isachsen (abandoned weather station on uninhabited Ellef Ringnes Island), serve to create a useful phased separation from 'the other world', and a gradually tighten-

There are many risks and hardships in polar exploration, not least the extremely low temperatures that freeze even your breath.

ing focus on the mission. But the full physiological and psychological reality of what lies ahead only ever hits me in that last leg up on to the Arctic Ocean. As the pilots of the Twin Otter bring the plane round to start the descent, turning like a vulture in ever-decreasing circles around a carcass, trying to pick out a runway made by nature not man, motion sickness combines with rapidly escalating anxiety to make me feel positively sick. You see, it is in that last leg, with the inevitability of the drop-off looming, that all that dreaming, strategizing, planning and selling of 'The Vision' is absolutely and irrevocably transforming from talk to deed. Either you can or you can't. It's show-time.

I AM ALWAYS STRUCK BY THE FEELING OF ALARM I EXPERIENCE ON THAT FINAL DROP-OFF BY AIR ON TO THE SEA ICE.

Start point: 81° 40′ North, 129° 48′ West in the northern Beaufort Sea area. No sun visible through the cloud cover, so no solar navigation possible; and sufficiently close to the current position of the North Magnetic Pole to rule out the magnetic compass option to orientate ourselves north. Ann coaxes the batteries and the LCD screen of her GPS to produce information long enough in the extreme cold to derive the direction north. We observe the lightest of breezes and tie a thin strip of super-fine pantyhose (donated by an ardent supporter) to Ann's ski pole. With the wind direction indicated by the fluttering pennant kept in appropriate alignment, we at last begin to make way. And being as much an ocean voyage as a surface journey, making way is a fair description.

We then did whatever it took. My sledging partners were fearless and relentless in their determination to get the job done, and we travelled in the dark using head torches in the earlier and later parts of the opening days –

whatever it took. Within a few weeks, the sun rose above the horizon never to set again. Our routine soon became familiar: sledging for 75 minutes, stopping for 10 minutes, then sledging again. We aimed to do at least six sledging sessions each day. If we encountered open water, we could don our immersion suits over our sledging clothes and boots, lower ourselves into the inky black freezing waters, and swim, towing our sledges behind us. We had a systematic look-out system to spot any polar bears that might be attracted by our scent-trail. We pitched camp every night, cooked and slept; and every morning we packed everything back into our sledges and headed off. We didn't travel if the wind-chill fell below -75°C (-103°F) for safety reasons.

WE TRAVELLED IN THE DARK USING HEAD TORCHES IN THE EARLIER AND LATER PARTS OF THE OPENING DAYS.

Combining rigorous scientific research with long-range travel across sea ice requires operating at the margins of human tolerance. Our daily distances were roughly half those covered by adventure-only expeditions. This in itself was a useful discovery for the future. Over the course of 73 days we recorded the ice thickness of every significant surface feature we encountered on the 430-km (267-mile) route, and manually drilled 1,500 holes. This makes a total of 3 km (almost 2 miles) of ice if all the hole-depths are added together. Using a pencil on a template form attached to

a clipboard hanging from my sledge harness, over 4,500 bits of data were collected. From Professor Wadhams' subsequent analysis it emerged that the average thickness of the un-deformed flat ice floes was 1.8 m (almost 6 ft), and the average overall ice thickness, including ridges and expanses of open water, was 4.8 m (15 ft 9 in). Both values are consistent with first-year sea ice formed the previous autumn in open water – a significantly unexpected discovery for this sea area, where it would be anticipated that thicker, multi-year ice would be found.

On 14 October 2009, the Catlin Arctic Survey created a global media event ahead of COP15. Professor Wadhams was able to announce that the Survey's uniquely acquired data had provided valuable supporting evidence for the emerging consensus among scientists that there is a high probability the sea ice will cease to be a year-round surface feature of the Arctic within twenty to thirty years, likely nearer twenty. Over the course of the Survey, over 90 countries, more than 100 TV news networks, over 300 international newspapers and over 1,000 online news sites covered the changing environmental state of the Arctic Ocean's surface. We may not have reached the Pole, but, far more importantly, the ocean's story did reach the world.

Occasionally the only option was to swim. Here I watch Ann Daniels towing her sledge across open water; we are both wearing full immersion suits to counter the sub-zero temperature.

Pen Hadow (British, b. 1962) became the only person to make the journey by a route starting from the Canadian coast to the North Geographic Pole, solo and without resupply, in 2003 – a feat that has not been repeated since. Eight months later he set up a new route from Antarctica's continental coast to the South Geographic Pole, again without resupply, with sledging partner Simon Murray. Pen is the director of Arctic Survey, a pioneering international scientific research programme investigating the rates, causes and global impacts of the rapidly thinning sea ice cover of the Arctic Ocean. After the inaugural 2009 expedition, on Arctic Surveys 2010 and 2011, in addition to long-range surveys in the mid-Arctic Ocean, Pen set up and operated the only scientific research base in the world located on sea ice. He also established a specialist guide service to the North and South Poles in 1995, and subsequently has led fifteen made-for-TV, charity fund-raising and private team expeditions to the North Pole.

MIKAEL STRANDBERG

A YEAR IN SIBERIA

Johan Ivarsson and I arriving at our final destination at Ambarchik Bay in May 2005, after skiing some 3,000 km (1,865 miles) over a year.

WHEN I TURNED FIFTEEN, I FIRST SERIOUSLY STARTED THINKING ABOUT LIFE. There was one major reason for this. Books. From the day as a bored ten-year-old that I discovered Jack London, whose two books *White Fang* and *The Call of the Wild* made up two-thirds of my family's library, I spent every spare moment I had exploring the world of books. I read the likes of Franz Kafka and Hermann Hesse, but most of all books about travelling the world. Some made a huge impression on me, especially adventures set in mountains and the polar regions. So, at fifteen, I decided to become an explorer like the heroes in the books. They all seemed pretty much to look exactly the same: white men with rough, wind-hewn faces, often with icicles hanging down from their beards, staring into the distance with a stern and determined look – a gaze that said 'we will conquer anything, anywhere'.

This profound message inspired me to leave my little village at fifteen and hitchhike around Europe for a year. The books had taught me to build up knowledge and competence gradually, until the day the Big Adventure presented itself to be conquered. And I felt that a full understanding of the meaning of life would follow. A year of backpacking in South America and another year in Asia followed as part of my preparations.

At the age of twenty-four I started my life as a professional explorer. I then spent almost eight years cycling around the world. I cycled from Chile to Alaska, Norway to South Africa, New Zealand to Egypt: 90,000 km (55,925 miles). After that I spent a year exploring the unknown parts of Patagonia with twelve horses. Another year followed living with the Maasai in East Africa. Finally, I was prepared for the Big Adventure, one which would follow in the footsteps of my teenage heroes.

The venue was one of the coldest inhabited places on Earth, the Kolyma River in the northeastern part of Siberia. Together with young Johan Ivarsson, I would spend a year travelling the river by canoe and skis, hunting and fishing for survival, so far away from civilization that we couldn't even be rescued if an accident happened. Just like in the days of my heroes of adolescence, and true exploration! That heroic image lingered with me until the day in the middle of November 2004, when we left the settlement of Zyryanka and started to ski. Four weeks' skiing later, my old heroes were dead for ever. And I was terrified that we would die as well. Every little mistake created a feeling of horror. Like when Johan didn't get his glove on quickly enough.

'That's another frostbite', Johan stated through his facemask in despair. 'That means I've got one on every finger.'

Below left Temperatures in midwinter fell below -58°C (-71°F). It was impossible to tell by how much, since the scale on our thermometer stopped at that temperature, but the line continued below.

Below right We pulled 136 kg (330 lb) of supplies each. Most of it moose meat, frozen fish and reindeer.

He was having another bout of diarrhoea. It was the third time in an hour he'd had to squat down and pull his trousers off. And his three sets of gloves. On every occasion he had experienced that burning feeling followed by numbness in one of his fingers. The first stage of frostbite. I could barely make him out in the eternal darkness of midwinter and I shivered violently. The same way I had every day since we left Zyryanka.

'I think we'd better move on', I whispered.

I then exhaled, coughed and heard that familiar tinkling sound that occurs when your breath turns into a shower of ice crystals, locally referred to as 'the whispers of the stars'. It was -57°C (-70°F) and it was impossible to form a decent thought or even to daydream. Or feel any worries. By pure survival instinct, we knew we had to keep moving and not stop. So we continued with great effort in the darkness, pulling our 150-kg (330-lb) load each behind us. Even though the river was covered with only a couple of inches of snow, it felt like pulling the sledges over sand. It didn't help that we were both now walking, not skiing, since our ski bindings had broken when the temperature dropped below -50°C (-58°F), as with most metal parts of our equipment. The heavy load made us sweat profusely the whole time, but we couldn't stop and have a break. Every time we did, we seemed to pick up more frostbite on fingers or cheeks, and it felt like the liquid in our elbows and knees was freezing and we started to shiver uncontrollably. Consequently, we kept moving in complete darkness. Hour after hour. Steadily putting one foot in front of the other. The darkness didn't matter since our eyelashes were always iced up, making it hard to see anything anyway. As long as we kept moving, at least it made us aware that we were still alive. Until that dreadful moment it was time to get inside the tent.

Once we reached the Arctic Ocean I felt like I had experienced everything I wanted from life. The past year was now like one long dream.

After sixteen hours of moving it took us just a few minutes to pitch the tent, but at least an hour to get the stove going. Some nights it didn't work at all. Poor-quality Russian petrol was the problem. It froze solid. As a result, we carried the petrol bottle under our armpit for the last hour of the day to keep it warm. We always knew when it was usable, since the bottle would then leak. But the stove was still completely frozen, so we had to pour petrol in a cup and light it to defrost the stove. We both had to keep busy during these efforts in order to keep the dangerous apathy at bay. The cold made us tremble, sometimes almost hysterically. When the stove finally worked, we could momentarily form a thought, but unfortunately this relief just made us more aware of how cold it was. Once inside the sleeping bag, we knew we had at least six hours of unrelenting pain. Not from the frostbites thawing out, but because it took at least three hours to gain control over our bodies. During this terrifying time we lay on our backs, bodies arched, trying to keep the worst shivering at bay, and to rest as much as possible. We hardly slept at all. Sharing the sleeping bag with the facemask, the PDA, satellite phone, torch, spare batteries, boots, stove and gloves didn't help. It was usually dead silent outside, although at times we heard a lone howling wolf in the distance or the odd explosion when a tree detonated from the cold. Most nights we didn't thaw up completely.

AFTER SIXTEEN HOURS OF MOVING IT TOOK US JUST A FEW MINUTES TO PITCH THE TENT, BUT AT LEAST AN HOUR TO GET THE STOVE GOING.

There's only one reason we survived a full Siberian winter like this – the local people we encountered along the river. Best people I have ever met. They're extremely generous, funny, interested, and they have the right attitude to life. Two meetings stand out, which completely changed my

Cooking only became possible in late March, when it was warm enough, around -35°C (-31°F), to enjoy life in the tent.

life. The first occurred in the settlement of Srednekolymsk, where we stayed for six weeks to recover. A place where I also came across the biggest cockroaches I have ever seen. They made our lives a sleepless hell until I went to the owner of where we were staying to complain.

'Do you know what the problem with you Westerners is?' Vladimir Ivanovich asked me. 'You have the wrong attitude to life. Instead of seeing the cockroaches as enemies, why don't you look upon them as your best friends in life, like I do?'

I took his advice and ended up having a lot of very good friends!

The second meeting killed off my notion of the Western image of a true hero and explorer once and for all. We arrived, as always, in darkness at a hunters' cabin and were received with usual warmth by two Evens, Sasha and his son, Sasha. The son was holding up a freshly flayed skin of a wolverine he had caught that morning. Slowly, in the normal Siberian no-big-drama voice, he was telling us how he had trapped this elusive animal, which he admired enormously. In the light of my head torch I saw that the tip of his elongated nose was black and rotten. Suddenly, he somehow brushed his arm against his runny nose and it seemed as if the tip dropped off. I had never seen anyone lose their nose tip, so naturally I moved my beam on the ground and this upset Sasha to such an extent that he said, slightly irritated: 'Misha, this is normal. This is Siberia. Listen to what I have to say.'

FINALLY I REALIZED WHO THE TRUE HEROES WERE. LOCAL PEOPLE.

And he simply continued his wolverine story, which was far more interesting to him. Finally I realized who the true heroes were. Local people. The footnotes in most Western explorers' accounts. Local people

Below The Siberian people of the north are by far the best human beings I have ever come across. Their humour, generosity and hospitality are almost unbelievable.

Opposite left The Yakut horse is well used by the locals and is adapted to these extreme temperatures. The rider is Yakut and all his gear is made from the skins of reindeer, dog and horse.

Opposite right The life of a reindeer herder is a demanding one, but offers great freedom and a non-settled life. These are Chukchi reindeer herders near Kolymskaya.

have travelled up and down the Kolyma for possibly as much as five thousand years – almost all of them unknown, everyday heroes, who out of the necessity to survive perform some of the hardest and most demanding physical tasks known to mankind. If a Westerner does it, he becomes a hero.

Since returning from this expedition I have travelled around the Western world and lectured about my Siberian trip. Some think I am a true hero. This makes me feel very embarrassed. I have been back to Siberia twice to lecture. There I didn't dare talk about the extreme cold and how it affected us, a normal situation for everyone in the audience, so I talked about the people I met. And fishing and hunting. They loved it. And most audiences, even in the West, also prefer hearing about something other than the white man with a beard talking about his physical efforts and being the first in history to do this or that. I know that in many cases this is not true – local people throughout the ages have passed through most places today regarded as being 'firsts'. It's just that they didn't brag about it.

Mikael Strandberg (Swedish, b. 1962) is an explorer and documentary film maker. He cycled 90,000 km (55,925 miles) over 7½ years, explored unknown parts of Patagonia by horse for a year, lived with the Maasai in East Africa, and travelled by canoe and skied for a year in the coldest inhabited place on earth: Kolyma, Siberia. He has written seven books, published in Swedish, and produced three award-winning documentaries. In 2011 and 2012 he made expeditions by camel in Yemen.

DESERT

The moment before the sun rises in the desert, just a second or so before the disc breaks the distant horizon, there is an observable green flash of light, an anomaly of refraction. Strange and suggestive of the mystery of the desert, this optical display is but one of the attractions that make exploring the desert a special, even addictive activity.

The desert is dry, by definition, and the lack of water, the immense potential torment of thirst, is offset by the otherwise benign nature of the place. In the deep desert there are no flies or mosquitoes, nothing dirty, nothing stagnant; cuts heal fast as there are fewer infectious agents, and there are even very few snakes and scorpions once you leave the ambit of well and oasis for the pure desert of dunes and rock.

This is a place of light par excellence. At noon, with the sun beating down, the landscape can appear flattened and uninteresting. At dawn and dusk its full majesty is revealed. Shafts of light turn rock mounds into castles and wadis into fantastic canyons of colour and contrast. The sheer beauty revealed leaves one in little doubt why the great monotheistic religions all arose in desert countries.

Desert explorers are marked by an affection for the people of the desert – nomads, Aborigines and Bedouin, whose harsh lifestyle and traditions of generosity and courage have inspired generations to find out more about this extraordinary environment.

Bruno Baumann's camel caravan in a vast sea of desert. Ensuring a sufficient supply of water for the journey is one of the key factors in desert exploration – or having to find it when it runs out, as Baumann discovered in the Taklamakan.

MICHAEL ASHER

ACROSS THE SAHARA SIDEWAYS

ONE DAY I STOOD ON THE EASTERN EDGE OF THE SAHARA DESERT and realized that if I were to set off in a straight line from that point I could travel for day after day, week after week, and never come across a road, nor a river, nor a major city, until I reached the shores of the Atlantic Ocean, 4,828 km (3,000 miles) away. It was then that I first conceived the idea of crossing the whole breadth of the Sahara, travelling in the way desert folk had done for millennia, by camel and on foot. If I succeeded, it would be the first recorded lateral crossing of the desert by such means, but for me that was not the main goal. The real prize lay in the prospect of living beyond the industrial world, of moving within the rhythms and cycles of nature, in close harmony with the Earth.

It was several years later, in 1986, that I arrived in Nouakchott, Mauritania, with my wife, Italian photographer and Arabist Mariantonietta

In the desert, water is life. Some Moorish nomads showed us this *gelta* or rainwater-cistern, hidden in the hills, after we had marched for ten days without finding water. To desert people such sites are sacred.

Peru, to live that dream. By then, though, I had learnt to speak Arabic fluently, had travelled thousands of miles by camel, and had lived for three years with a nature-based nomad tribe, the Kababish, as one of them.

These desert nomads moved ceaselessly with their camels and goats, living as their forefathers had done for generations. At first I regarded them as 'quaint'. Soon, however, I came to see that while they had none of the 'benefits' of modern civilization, their lives were so much more satisfying and harmonious than ours. I came to understand, as they did, that humans are not separate from Nature, but part of it, and that the wilderness must be approached not in the spirit of conquest, but with humility, reverence and awe.

When Mariantonietta and I set off in early August from Chinguetti Oasis in Mauritania with three camels and a guide called Mafoudh, it was like entering a blast-furnace. In such heat, a human being could not last a day without water. On the upside, however, it was also the rainy season, and at first we were able to fill our waterskins from rain-pools scattered through the desert. We carried six skins, stitched from tanned goat-hide, which we proofed with a tar extracted from the seeds of the bitter desert melon, *Citrillus colocynthis*. The skins kept the water cool by evaporation, but thus lost moisture in the heat: after a while the tar could render the liquid barely drinkable.

We passed through a landscape of amazing diversity – vast, flat sand-sheets, rippling fish-scale dunes, endless gravel plains and surreal massifs where sand and water had bored natural arches through the stone. Our days followed the same routine, striking camp before sunrise, setting off on foot, walking behind the camels until the morning grew hot, then mounting up as the fancy took us, riding until about midday, when we would rest in the shade of a blanket.

The afternoon was the hardest time of day: the heat poured down like molten lead, and we would squint anxiously at the sun, longing for the coolness of the night. The evenings were a holy respite from the day's firewalk: we would unpack the camels and turn them out to graze. While they grazed, we cooked couscous or polenta on a three-stone nomad's fireplace, made with firewood collected during the day or with dried camel's dung. Often we baked bread in desert fashion, burying a flat loaf in the sand under the embers of the fire. Onions were our only fresh food; protein

> I LEARNED TO UNDERSTAND, AS THEY DID, THAT HUMANS ARE NOT SEPARATE FROM NATURE, BUT PART OF IT, AND THAT THE WILDERNESS MUST BE APPROACHED NOT IN THE SPIRIT OF CONQUEST, BUT WITH HUMILITY, REVERENCE AND AWE.

came from *tishtar* – a jerky we prepared by cutting goat's meat into strips and hanging it in the sun to dry.

After dinner we would bring the animals back into camp, hobble them, and surrender to sleep under the overwhelming magnificence of the stars. We brushed our teeth with sprigs of *araq* bush, and after defecating cleaned ourselves with stones. We wore nomad dress – long shirts, baggy trousers, headcloths and sandals: we never washed our clothes and rarely removed them at all.

As we made our way southeast towards Timbuktu, nomad life completely disappeared. A week passed. We saw no one, and found none of the wells shown on our maps. After failing to locate two wells in succession, Mafoudh confessed that he'd forgotten how to find them. The situation began to look serious. Mafoudh swore that he could find the next well, but when we reached it after another desperate day's march, it proved to be dry. We had no choice but to continue, plodding on painfully with cracked lips and swollen tongues, bent over with kidney pains.

I was beginning to give up hope, when we suddenly came across growths of sweet melon, *Citrillus vulgaris* – a rare desert succulent the size of a tennis ball. The liquid these fruits contained probably saved our lives. The next afternoon we spotted a curl of blue smoke in the distance – the first nomad camp we'd seen in ten days. The nomads welcomed us to their tents, made a place for us to sleep, gave us food, water and camel's milk. In the morning they showed us a *gelta* or rainwater cistern – a sacred site – hidden in the nearby hills.

Travelling through the dunes on the edge of the Aouker Valley in Mauritania, our small caravan runs into a sandstorm – the first of several fierce storms we were to encounter on our journey. Desert nomads find navigation difficult in these storms; our compass proved invaluable.

From Timbuktu we headed east across Mali towards the Niger frontier. The landscape here never varied from undulating red sand and gravel plains, but each day was a drama – a struggle for survival, a quest to find food, water, fuel and shade, to find grazing for the camels, to keep ourselves and our caravan moving. Time seemed to stand still: it was as if the journey had no beginning and no end, as if we had been wandering across these vast horizons for eternity. The civilization we had grown up in receded in our minds to the fringes of reality: this wilderness was, and had always been, our home.

From Agadez, Niger, we traversed the Ténéré erg, or sand sea, a mystic ocean of rolling sand dunes as desolate as the surface of Mars. It took us seventeen days to cross it, and in all that time we saw not a stone, not a tree, not a single blade of grass. It was on the edge of the Ténéré that the worst sandstorm of the trek hit us like a hurricane, bringing with it a wave of dust hundreds of feet high, reducing visibility to just 2 m (6 ft). The roar of the wind was shocking – it felt as if the Earth itself was trying to shake us off. Desert nomads cannot navigate through sandstorms and usually go to ground in them, frequently dying of thirst. This was not the last time my compass would prove of crucial value. We marched into the eye of the storm: when it blew out two days later, it seemed as if the whole desert world had been washed clean.

The cool season was at its height by the time we reached Chad: nights were freezing, the cold cutting right to the bone. By this stage, though, we had become perfectly adapted to our desert world: travelling on a compass bearing, now without a guide, we would often cover 50 km (31 miles) a day. We crossed into Sudan, tramped across Darfur into the vast empty

A lone tree in the wilderness might become our home for a few hours during the heat of midday. We would rig up a blanket for a square of shade, while the camels grazed on whatever sparse grasses were available. For nine months, the few possessions that are laid out here were all we needed to survive.

deserts west of the Nile. It was here that the most terrifying experience of the journey occurred: we began to lose touch with reality. We heard the chattering of demonic voices and the sound of footsteps behind us, saw eyes leering at us out of the night. We were 322 km (200 miles) from the nearest settlement and had seen no one else for days, yet it felt as if we were not alone – that some ghostly caravan was accompanying us. We had been ready to take on any challenge, but had not expected the danger to come from within ourselves. This nightmare stayed with us until we reached the camp of some nomads: once we were among real people again, the delusions passed.

We were only ten days from the Nile, but there was one well – Abu Tabara – that we had to locate on the way. It was hidden in a labyrinth of sand and volcanic blocks, and was notoriously difficult to find. We arrived in the area and spent an entire morning searching for it – in vain. For the first time we were obliged to

IT WAS HERE THAT THE MOST TERRIFYING EXPERIENCE OF THE JOURNEY OCCURRED: WE BEGAN TO LOSE TOUCH WITH REALITY.

turn back, an ironic twist of fate so close to the Nile. We had just wheeled the camels around when Mariantonietta glanced behind her and gasped. She pointed out in the distance the dark figure of a man. At first we thought it might be another illusion, but as we approached nearer we realized that not only was it a real person, but that he was standing right next to our lost well.

Six days later we saw the Nile flowing beneath us at Ed-Debba, like a brilliant electric blue streak. We had fulfilled the vision I had experienced standing on the desert's edge so many years before – albeit the opposite way round – yet our journey was not over. From here, we turned due north

Below left Mariantonietta Peru, near the end of our journey: a photographer and an Arabist, who studied at the White Fathers Institute in Rome, she became the first known woman to have crossed the Sahara from west to east, by camel and on foot.

Below right Michael Asher, on a later journey in Eritrea.

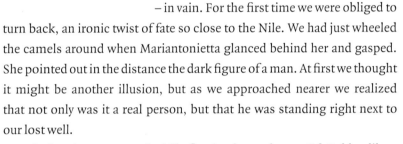

and travelled parallel with the Nile, crossing the Egyptian border several weeks later. At Abu Simbel the border police arrested us. They confiscated our camels and put us on a tourist bus under armed guard. We could not believe the journey was over. We had made the first recorded west–east crossing of the Sahara Desert by camel, traversing a total of 7,242 km (4,500 miles) in 271 days, yet there was no exhilaration; instead, it felt as if we had been sent into exile.

This was not the end of my desert travels. Three years later, I returned to Egypt to cross the entire Western Desert from north to south with a Bedouin companion. I have gone back many times to Egypt, Sudan and Mauritania, I've travelled in Algeria, Morocco, the Empty Quarter of Arabia, in Sinai, India, Pakistan, Australia and many other places, always without modern technology, covering more than 48,280 km (30,000 miles) by camel. In one way, though, our great journey across the Sahara has never ended, for the strong sense of belonging we felt there has not left me: ever since then, in this industrial society that destroys a little more of our planet each day, I have been a stranger in a strange land.

Sheltering from the heat under a great boulder at Abu Tabara, the last well before we reached the Nile at Ed-Debba, in the Sudan. There were no trees, but nomads lived here, drinking camels' milk and using camel-dung for fuel.

Michael Asher (British, b. 1953) is an author, explorer, historian and deep ecologist. Having travelled in many desert regions for more than 30 years, he has received the Ness Award of the Royal Geographical Society and the Mungo Park Medal of the Royal Scottish Geographical Society for desert exploration. A former soldier in the Parachute Regiment and SAS, he is a graduate of the University of Leeds, the author of 21 books, and an elected Fellow of the Royal Society of Literature. He ran the joint UNICEF/WHO support project among the Beja nomads of the Red Sea Hills, lived independently for three years with a nature-based nomad group in western Sudan, and with his wife, Mariantonietta Peru, made the first recorded west–east crossing of the Sahara by camel. US author Dean King has paid tribute to Asher's desert experience: 'having walked the entire breadth of the Sahara himself ... Asher understands this passion, this place, and these people, as well as any Westerner alive.'

JON MUIR

WALKING ACROSS AUSTRALIA UNASSISTED

BY SUZAN MUIR

Jon on his fourth and, finally, successful attempt at his unsupported traverse of Australia, hauling his desert cruiser across a dried-up clay pan.

IN THE LATE 1980S MANY OF THE WORLD'S EXPLORERS were focusing on unsupported polar expeditions. Jon Muir also found himself attracted to both the North and South Poles, but the complex logistics and enormous expense of polar travel made those objectives rather cumbersome. He began instead to search for something a little different. A challenge that would break completely new ground, something fresh and exciting. An expedition that would raise the question: 'Is this humanly possible?' Where to find such a quest?

By the time Jon had finished with mountaineering he'd achieved his personal best in all fields of climbing. On his return home from the summit of Everest in 1988 he sat down in front of a map of Australia and let his eyes wander. 'The challenge that leapt out at me took my breath away – an unsupported traverse of the continent. Unsupported – no assistance from pack animals or vehicles, no pre-laid depots, no re-supplies, relying entirely on my own energy. I was sure that nothing like it had been done before and wondered if it was even possible?'

So began Jon's inspiration for his attempt to march 2,500 km (1,550 miles) across the Australian continent from the Spencer Gulf in the south, to the Gulf of Carpentaria in the far north. His vision of this history-making traverse kept him resolutely focused for the next twelve years, as he immersed himself in the process of learning the fundamentals of survival in Australia's arid interior.

During this time Jon drew heavily on the experience of around 50,000 years of human inhabitation of Australia. Aboriginal people are experts on where to find bush tucker and water in the desert and some of their wisdom has been recorded in books. Jon avidly sourced as much literature as he could on the subject. He then spent time in the Australian wilderness identifying food plants and cautiously sampling wild bush foods. During his numerous two- to six-week solo forays into the desert he gained experience in tracking game and hunting using a gun. He also learned to recognize the signs that would lead him to water, as he knew that this would be critical to his survival during his march north. He would have to negotiate three deserts: the Sturt Stony, the Tirari and the Arunta (or Simpson).

HE ALSO LEARNED TO RECOGNIZE THE SIGNS THAT WOULD LEAD HIM TO WATER, AS HE KNEW THAT THIS WOULD BE CRITICAL TO HIS SURVIVAL DURING HIS MARCH NORTH.

Jon was sidetracked from his Australian journey when the perfect opportunity arose for a new route to the South Pole in the austral summer

Hunting and gathering made the 2,500-km (1,550-mile) unsupported traverse possible. Here Jon holds a handful of ducks he shot on the Eyre Creek.

Right The team – Seraphine and Jon beside an historical surveyor's cairn in the Sturt Stony Desert.

Below Jon started walking each day at dawn to maximize the cool morning hours. Seraphine was always reluctant to crawl out of the warmth of the sleeping bag.

of 1998/99. This trek to the Pole was a walk in the park compared to what he was attempting in Australia, but nevertheless it was good training.

After three unsuccessful attempts at the traverse of Australia, Jon finally set off once more for the fourth time in 2001. His wheeled cart, or 'desert cruiser' as he calls it, had undergone numerous modifications. It was attached to a hauling harness so that Jon was able to pull up to 160 kg (353 lb) of equipment, food and water along behind him, including his lightweight camping gear and repair kit, a .303 rifle and .22 rifle, and ammunition. The 40 kg (88 lb) of food he took with him consisted mostly of high-energy carbohydrates to supplement the wild meat and plant foods that were to be his main source of nutrition. He also carried maps of his entire route, and these alone weighed 1 kg (over 2 lb).

His little friend Seraphine, a Jack Russell terrier, also went along for the adventure, and Jon carried 7 kg (15 lb) of food and equipment just for her. She had some modified doggie boots as protection from prickles and a fancy rabbitskin coat that Jon had made for her to wear on the sub-zero desert mornings.

As he set off, Jon was weighed down with more than just equipment. He also carried a great deal of nervous tension, as he describes in his book *Alone Across Australia*:

> I was to revisit some of the land I had come to love, and then push beyond that land into the unknown. The exhilarating unknown, exciting but also daunting. I had prepared myself physically and had mentally readied myself the best I could for the attempt, but the size of the challenge before me made me feel small, weak and vulnerable. Could I do it?

Torrens, the world's longest salt lake, was the first big challenge, and it took Jon nineteen days to walk the length of its eastern shore. Most of the time, the surface here was too soft and he had to travel on the adjacent land. This was tortuous going as the terrain was incredibly rugged, sapping his energy and leaving him exhausted by each day's end. His previous three attempts at the traverse had already shown him that an unsupported crossing of the continent would make all his previous expeditions seem like training trips.

> Hauling everything I needed for a prolonged trip in desert country was taking me closer to my physical limits than anything I'd attempted before. At the end of most days I found myself far more worn out than the day I'd broken trail through deep snow to reach the summit of Everest alone.

Being a salt lake, Torrens provides no fresh water and Jon had to process any available salty liquid in his homemade desalinator. Every day he boiled up some water in a pressure cooker over a fire. The evaporating liquid condensed in a coil of copper pipe and dripped slowly into his drinking container – it was a foul-tasting brew, but sufficiently desalinated to keep him alive.

Heavy rains ended his steady progress up the shore. His cruiser wheels clogged with sticky red mud to the extent that they would no longer turn. Jon was forced to rest for several days until the muddy surface dried out enough to allow him to continue. While waiting, he tried to conserve his

A dead camel near Lake Torrens (a salt lake), a vivid reminder of the danger of walking through the world's driest inhabited continent.

food supplies by rationing them and by doing extra hunting and gathering to minimize his reliance on his stores.

Leaving Torrens, Jon headed into the stony country south of Lake Eyre; here he was entering the driest region of the country, where the average annual rainfall is less than 150 mm (6 in). But the pebbly plains of red gibber were a pleasant change from the broken country surrounding Lake Torrens and it was much easier to travel. From the gibber country he headed northwards to the Tirari Desert. Although this desert is Australia's driest, recent weeks of rain had collected in the shallow claypans and Jon was able to take advantage of the fresh surface water. As he barrelled his way up the interdunal corridors, or swales, the water in the claypans was evaporating fast. Carrying water would slow him down, so his preference was to rely on the surface water, but at what point would that source run

Australia's largest lakes are all salt. While providing a surreal, haunting vision, these lakes do not support human life. Jon marched over 400 km (248 miles) along the eastern borders of Australia's two largest lakes, Eyre and Torrens.

Crossing the Dingo Fence, which excludes these opportunistic predators from the sheep-grazing lands of southern Australia. Jon and Seraphine were set upon by a hungry pack of dingoes in the Arunta Desert one evening.

out? He felt like he was playing a game of dare. When should he start to fill his containers and contend with hauling the extra weight?

As he neared the northern edge of the desert the ground was yielding only just enough water to sustain him.

I got water from only three spots today. Three tiny claypans had minuscule pools in camel pad depressions. There were only about 200 to 300 millilitres in each pad print and funny things swam in the brown ooze, but I sucked it all up and then spat it into my water bottles. That water was the thickest drink I've ever had, but definitely the most satisfying and my rice tonight is chocolatey and full of protein!'

He reached the Warburton River the following day and knew that running the Tirari fast and light had indeed been the best option.

Jon had anticipated that the roughly 200 km (125 miles) along the Warburton would be relatively easy, but in reality the heaviest winter rains of the previous twelve years had turned the surrounding land into a quagmire that delayed his progress yet again, and proved to be one of the greatest challenges of the trip.

AND IF HE HADN'T HAD A GUN WITH HIM, HIS FEARS MIGHT WELL HAVE BEEN REALIZED.

He arrived at the Eyre Creek in the Arunta feeling shattered and overcome with fear that his chances of completing the continental traverse were slipping away. And if he hadn't had a gun with him, his fears might well have been realized. That evening, after cooking his dinner on a tiny fire made from the sparsely available wood he'd collected, he noticed a mob of dingoes appearing over the crest of a sand dune about 100 m

The intensity of the experience of walking across large swathes of untravelled Australian wilderness is reflected clearly in Jon's face at sunset in the central desert.

(330 ft) away. There were five or six animals in the pack and in the twilight Jon could see them fan out in an attempt to encircle him. He immediately tied Seraphine to his cart and as the pack moved in he started banging his billy and lid together and yelling in an attempt to scare them off. They must have been hungry because they weren't at all deterred, even when Jon threw the billy at them. Jon has a great love of the dingo, but at that moment he knew he would have to kill the head dog. Grabbing his gun he fired at the alpha male. It fell to the ground, instantly dead; the rest of the pack, seeing their leader go down, scattered into the night.

Jon rested on the Eyre Creek for two days, sorting his gear and trying to discard everything that he could in order to lighten his load. For the next fifty-eight days he travelled without losing a single day. Leaving the Arunta behind he followed the Mulligan River and then hooked into the Georgina River. The Georgina had dried up into a series of small puddles along the river bed, and these became scarcer as he headed higher up the river.

It was on the Georgina that he faced a critical situation. He was getting low on water and the puddles seemed to have disappeared. It was also hot – so hot that Seraphine became heat-stressed and sat down, refusing to move. In the cool of the night Jon made a hopeful trek 15 km (9 miles) due north away from the river to where a bore was marked on his map. It was dry! He then trekked due east back to the river, where he finally found water at 2 a.m. He had marched 42 km (26 miles) in sixteen hours to secure their water supply.

A few days later he abandoned his cart at Roxborough Downs Station in Queensland because the terrain ahead had too many steep ravines to continue pulling it. Now carrying everything on his back, he discovered terrible problems with his boots – the angle of his feet while hauling had moulded the inside of his shoes in a particular way. Without the cart, he was walking in a more upright position and his shoes no longer fitted: he was in agony. He staggered along under the 45-kg (99-lb) load on his back.

HE WAS GETTING LOW ON WATER AND THE PUDDLES SEEMED TO HAVE DISAPPEARED.

After crossing the one bitumen road of the trip, the Barkly Highway, he headed in the direction of the ruins of Old Morestone Station. It was here that Seraphine took a dingo bait and died, convulsing, in Jon's arms. Already at his limit physically and mentally, the loss of his brave and faithful partner so close to the end of his journey was almost more than he could bear. Only the discipline of hard marching kept him from toppling into the abyss of madness.

Constant hunger was now his main companion as he walked the last stretch of his journey down the Gregory River. He arrived in Burketown on the Gulf of Carpentaria on 20 September 2001, 128 days after setting off from Port Augusta and 30 kg (66 lb) lighter.

He felt a particular emptiness on finishing his quest, as though his spirit still roamed wild through Australia's arid interior. His body and mind did their best to acclimatize to the cultural shock of the modern world. Though even now, when he talks of his walk across the continent, he gets a strangely wild, wide-eyed, haunted expression, as though the incredible beauty and freedom of that Dreamtime landscape still holds its claim over him.

Postscript: Five months later Jon completed an unsupported walk to the North Pole. He then went back for more arid zone exploring in 2007, walking seventy days non-stop and unsupported from Port Augusta to the geographic centre of Australia, the point furthest from the sea. Although a shorter walk than the traverse of the continent it proved more challenging as the terrain was more rugged and the country was in the grip of the worst drought in recorded history.

Expedition's end: tidal salt water at Burketown, Gulf of Carpentaria. Jon contemplates the completion of his 128-day unsupported traverse, an epic journey in which Jon's spirit was irrevocably entwined with the Dreamtime landscape.

Jon Muir (Australian, b. 1961) began his life of adventure at the age of fourteen after seeing the documentary *Everest, the Hard Way*. He pioneered numerous new rock routes and made first ascents of extreme alpine and Himalayan climbs, often alone. He also made the first Sherpaless ascent of the South Ridge of Everest, reaching the summit alone in 1988. In 1998/99 he established a new route to the South Pole and in 2002 completed an unsupported trek to the North Pole. The highlights of his career thus far are his history-making unsupported Australian walks, including his traverse of Australia from the Spencer Gulf to the Gulf of Carpentaria (2001) and his march to the geographic centre of Australia (2007), which far exceeded the challenges of any of his previous expeditions. He wrote a book and made a documentary film about the traverse, both called *Alone Across Australia*. He has also travelled over 5,000 km (3,100 miles) by sea kayak and now gives talks worldwide on his lifetime of adventure.

Suzan Muir is a freelance writer and grower of organic food.

JOHN HARE

THE SAND DUNES OF THE KUM TAGH

Yuan Lei (left), head cameleer Mamuli (right) and myself, scouring the horizon for wild camels among the Kum Tagh sand dunes.

SCRAMBLING UP AND OVER SAND DUNES CAN BE RELATIVELY EASY or extremely difficult. It all depends on the firmness of the sand. Where the Kum Tagh sand dunes meet the Arjin Mountains in Xingjiang Province, China, the dunes are very soft. The Uighur people call this type of sand *yaman kum* – 'hateful sand' – and not without reason.

As we climbed, the surface shifted and sank around us. A few feet from a dune's peak, a pinnacle of sand, with its finely turned edge, would invariably collapse and I would be left floundering and threshing about in the *yaman kum*. This was tiring, as was the effect of the sand continually filling my boots. Exasperated at having to stop, unstrap and empty them, I took them off, tied them around my neck and continued the climb in bare feet. This provided some relief, but not for long. That evening the soles of my feet were blackened where the hot sand had burnt them.

Our camel caravan crossing the rolling Kum Tagh sand dunes. Even today there are blank spaces on the maps of this region.

I now understood, somewhat belatedly, why these dunes had not been crossed in recorded history. I also remembered when, in 1988, Professor Yuan Guoying and I, together with his son Yuan Lei, were planning this expedition in the professor's office in Urumqi – I had looked at a map and casually run my finger along the base of the Arjin Mountains where they were linked to the Kum Tagh. The professor, who had been instrumental in obtaining permission for me to enter Lop Nur, China's former nuclear test area, had protested that the dune crossing was too difficult. I had persuaded him it was possible and I now recalled my earlier enthusiasm. It's easy to be brave and bold when planning an expedition, but as I lay on my back for the umpteenth time gasping for breath, the reality was somewhat different.

IT'S EASY TO BE BRAVE AND BOLD WHEN PLANNING AN EXPEDITION, BUT AS I LAY ON MY BACK FOR THE UMPTEENTH TIME GASPING FOR BREATH, THE REALITY WAS SOMEWHAT DIFFERENT.

Parts of the detailed map of the Arjin Mountains' foothills had been left as small, blank, white spaces. Even in these days of satellite imagery, such white spaces can still be found in places where mountain gullies are obscured and dunes shift. Then they had inspired me, but now, as I spat out yet another mouthful of sand, doubts set in. On past expeditions it had never occurred to me that I might not get out of a particularly tight situation. On this occasion, my pounding heart and fading strength made me think again – had my bravado been foolish? In 1895, the Swedish explorer Sven Hedin was entertaining similarly gloomy thoughts while tackling sand dunes during his crossing of the neighbouring Taklamakan Desert, which lies due west of Lop Nur and absorbs the Kum Tagh sand dunes that we were attempting to cross. As he described in his book *Through Asia* (1899):

Above left Mamuli and I slither down a steep slope of one the dunes. The local Uighur people call this 'hateful sand'.

Above right One of our camels loses its footing and disappears down a dune. Luckily it was unharmed.

Otherwise I was alone, absolutely alone, in the midst of a death-like silence, with a sea of yellow sand dunes before me, rolling away in fainter and fainter billows right away to the horizon... A bewildering chaos of ridges ... were flung across one another in the strangest fashion. Our position was desperate.... We were being slowly but surely killed by these terrible ridges of sand.

Hedin continues, recounting an experience the next day similar to the one we were enduring:

That day the sand-hills were the highest of any we had yet crossed – fully 200 feet high ... It will readily be understood that over gigantic billows of sand like this we could not advance very rapidly. We were compelled to make many a detour, involving great loss of time, in order to avoid them; in fact, we were sometimes compelled to travel for a time in the exactly opposite direction from that in which we wanted to go.

It was not just our human team that was struggling. The camels, too, sank up to their hocks in the soft sand. Our Kazakh herdsmen, just like those of Hedin, had to unstrap the loads from the camels' backs and carry them themselves, staggering up the dunes. Yet even in these terrible and testing conditions, not one of the camels sat down and gave in. One by one, grunting and groaning, they clambered up and over the sheer walls of shifting sand.

'Come on, Ye Tuzi, come on', Leilei shouted to me by way of encouragement. Leilei frequently calls me Ye Tuzi – the 'mad hare'. A further encouragement was the rare sighting of the critically endangered wild camel, perched near the summit of one of the dunes in the middle distance – this must mean that the dune had a firmer surface. The higher we climbed, the harder the sand became. We had finally reached the *ighiz kum* – 'high sand'.

I sensed that the star of good fortune, which had shone so brightly on previous expeditions, was still twinkling overhead.

At last, the steeply rolling barrier of sand flattened out and spread to the western horizon. In front of us lay endless stretches of fine, yellow sand, pock-marked like the surface of the moon. To the northwest, where

**IN A LAND OF SHIFTING SAND
IT IS IMPOSSIBLE TO MARK DUNES ON A MAP.**

the Kum Tagh stretched back towards the dried-up lake of Lop Nur, the tips of the gigantic dunes peeped up one behind the other for mile after mile. This vast desert, which earlier that day had taxed our strength to the uttermost, was now laid out before us in a vast spread of undulating sand. In the unbroken stillness it was a majestic, intoxicating sight.

Some of the patterns left by the wind on the sand were extraordinary, and unlike anything I had ever seen. One design in particular was made up of immaculate, parallel zigzag lines, as if a master craftsman had rhythmically wafted a light brush over the grainy surface.

'Look over there, Ye Tuzi.' Leilei tugged at my shirtsleeve and interrupted my musing. He was pointing to the centre of one of the sand craters that were dotted about in front of us, handing me his field glasses. I raised them and immediately saw what had excited Leilei, a bull camel quietly grazing with his harem of fifteen females. Flagging spirits rose. Our domestic Bactrian camels raised their heads and sniffed the evening air.

Crossing the Kum Tagh – even this sparse vegetation is enough to sustain the wild camels.

This was compass territory. A GPS can tell you where you are, but it is the GPS's compass that tells you where to go. In a land of shifting sand it is impossible to mark dunes on a map. In three years strong winds can make them disappear or realign in a completely different area. So we fixed our compasses on a bearing to the east and walked accordingly, skirting where possible the base of the dunes and climbing up and down steep-sided surface hollows, by now firm enough to take our weight.

That evening, the blood-red glow in the sky to the west filtered through an elongated series of darkly corrugated clouds. Just as the sun was about to set, exhausted men and beasts collapsed in a convenient hollow of firm sand, surrounded by nourishing tufts of dry vegetation for our camels. Li Weidong lost no time in turning out an acceptable meal of noodles and tinned meat and the shoots of wild onions. Our camels browsed contentedly and chopsticks click-clacked on metal bowls. When these were empty, we settled down to sleep.

For a long time I lay gazing at a rising moon and stars, which seemed to shine more brightly than I had ever seen. In the dry desert air the sky becomes a beautiful backdrop for myriad brilliant stars that hang clear, without the illusion of lights twinkling through holes in a curtain as is the case in murkier climes. The Milky Way has not the whitish haze of Western skies, but is a phosphorescent shower of spots of light. As I stared up at the gigantic mass I wondered whether we all end up as a star in the Milky Way, twinkling forever in an infinite mass of light.

Lawrence of Arabia experienced similar sensations. In *The Seven Pillars of Wisdom* he wrote: 'The brilliant stars cast about us a false light, not

Below left A wild argali ram, a member of a 'naïve' population of wildlife discovered by a freshwater spring in a previously unmapped valley; we named the spring Kum Su. The animals were 'naïve' because they had never previously encountered man.

Below right 'Many Rat Hole Valley', where our camel expedition was replenished with fresh supplies during the six-week expedition.

illumination, but rather a transparency of air, lengthening slightly the shadow below each stone and making a diffused greyness of the ground.'

The moon is more self-revealing than in northern latitudes and heavier atmospheres. Rather than a mere silver cradle swinging in the void, in the desert the moon flaunts herself, hanging in space with a particular brilliance. As the moon rises the desert embraces her. During the long hours while she travels from one side of the horizon to the other she exerts her own effect on the human imagination, softening the austere outlines of the rocks and hills; even saddles, water-carriers and boxes are invested with a subtle charm.

Desert travellers plan their journeys according to the phases of the moon. My Kenyan friend, the late Jasper Evans, knew instinctively the current phase of the moon and never had to check in his diary. Whether in Africa or Central Asia, this most subtle of light infusions enables us to walk freely, even on rough ground, swinging along behind our camels under the glittering stars.

John Hare (British, b. 1934) is an explorer, conservationist and writer. In 1993 he made an expedition into the desert of Mongolia with Russian scientists and he has since undertaken six surveys riding on camels to discover the status of the critically endangered wild camel in the injiang Province of China. In 1995/96 he became the first foreigner in recorded history to cross the Gashun Gobi from north to south and to reach the ancient Silk Road city of Lou Lan from the east. He discovered an abandoned outpost of Lou Lan called Tu-ying, previously missed by earlier explorers. In 1997 he founded the UK registered charity The Wild Camel Protection Foundation (WCPF).

In 1999 John Hare discovered two previously unmapped valleys in the desert of Lop Nur with a 'naïve' population of wildlife – animals that had never encountered man. In 2001/02 he crossed the Sahara Desert from Lake Chad to Tripoli on a camel, a journey of 2,415 km (1,500 miles), to raise awareness for the wild camel, and in 2006 he made the first circumambulation of Lake Turkana in northern Kenya and Ethiopia with camels.

ARITA BAAIJENS

THE FORTY DAYS ROAD BY CAMEL

AS A CHILD I GREW UP IN THE QUIET BIBLE BELT OF THE NETHERLANDS, close to farms and woodlands, but I later escaped to study biology in Amsterdam. In 1990 I gave up my job as a consultant in environmental affairs and bought some camels – ever since I've explored the desert of Egypt and Sudan during the winter months with my small camel caravan.

To survive in the desert you must face up to some hard facts. How strong are you when there is no back-up? Can you handle fear and panic? Where do your limits lie? This is precisely what I intended to find out, more than twenty years ago, when I first set off on a solo journey across the vast and waterless Egyptian desert with two camels, an old map and a compass. At the time I had no clue why I was so obsessed with the desert. It was only much later that I realized that facing up to the challenge of death was a way of overcoming my fear of life. If I could successfully traverse a hostile

No stirrups, a rock-hard saddle, ten to thirteen hours per day in a trot. Every crew member in the trade caravan is sore the first week. I'm smiling, so this must be the second week.

desert and look death in the eye, there wouldn't be anything to be afraid of, ever again. Being completely alone in the desert I was happier than I had ever thought possible. Not that desert life is romantic; it's a harsh existence with at least as many lows as highs. And yet it is infinitely more satisfying to take on the elements than join in the frantic rat race to get ahead in your chosen profession.

My later travels on camel in the region took on a more scientific character. I explored the whole of northern Sudan, an enormous desert stretching from the Red Sea in the east to the border with Chad in the west, and discovered ancient gold mines, prehistoric petroglyphs and ruins of medieval cities. In bandit-infested Darfur I travelled with bodyguards –

NOT THAT DESERT LIFE IS ROMANTIC; IT'S A HARSH EXISTENCE WITH AT LEAST AS MANY LOWS AS HIGHS.

tawny men, their dark skin contrasting sharply with the white cloth wrapped round their heads. You could tell by their dignified demeanour, their piercing eyes and the leather charms and amulets on their forearms that these were true desert men. I befriended one of them, Yussuf Gamaa, a rather chaotic, stocky fifty-something I had first hired as a *chabir*, guide, for a 1,200-km (745-mile) trek through north Darfur. And when I joined a trade caravan of four hundred camels along the Darb el-Arbain, the Forty Days Road the year after, in 2001, Yussuf came along as well. But his presence couldn't save me from being skinned alive on that journey.

A ray of light dances over my face. A burly trader with a torch beckons and I follow him, trailing the white form of his robe to a group of camels that are standing there, grazing in the dark. They all look the same to me, but the trader instantly identifies my camel among the masses: 'That one is

Yussuf Gamaa is a desert guide from Darfur in western Sudan. His family lost a camel herd during the drought back in the 1970s. Since then Yussuf has earned a living as a desert guide. He joined me on the journey on the Forty Days Road with four hundred camels.

Below left When I purchase a camel I have a checklist, but unfortunately it's only after the deal is done that I find out whether the new acquisition is brave or timorous, lazy, or just plain full of mischief.

Below right The crew, early morning. Within an hour we drink tea, count and load the camels and are off for another gruelling day of eleven to thirteen hours in the saddle. The desert guide is the first to wake up and kindle the fire. He is also the first to saddle his camel.

yours.' He then walks off, knowing full well that I will never recognize that camel tomorrow.

The *dabouka*, trade caravan, I have joined consists of four hundred camels. The animals have to walk about 2,000 km (1,240 miles) through the merciless desert from Darfur to southern Egypt, from where they are taken by lorry or train to the meat markets in Cairo.

'Get on with it!' Yussuf snaps at me when the camel drivers are already sitting on their animals and I still fuss with my saddle. Hurry, hurry, hurry – everyone in this caravan seems to be forever in a hurry. Before sunrise, our *chabir*, Djemera, is busy making a fire with small pieces of wood and matches. When the teapot sits on top of the flames he murmurs his morning prayers and then warms his callused feet. The tiny glasses with the sweet drink are emptied in a single gulp. Sometimes we get something to eat after that, sometimes we don't.

'*Ya Arita, keef?*' At regular intervals the men shout at me, asking how I'm doing. They grin when I give them the thumbs-up because they know that in reality I am tortured by saddle pain. But what's the point of complaining about something over which you have no control? For the first few days, my back and behind are assaulted by flashes of pain. I had no idea that a human being could have aching muscles in so many places; everything, absolutely everything hurts and the worst part is my bottom, which has become completely sore from the bouncing and grating of the saddle. There is no way I can prevent being skinned alive on that sensitive spot because we are galloping eleven hours each day.

The four hundred camels have been split in three groups, each with a *chabir*, three camel drivers and two soldiers. The six *haras*, soldiers, travel

A caravan at Bab el Gasmund pass. I am descending a 300-m (985-ft) high plateau into the Egyptian Dakhla Oasis. Descending is easier than ascending. The passage was so steep that I sometimes had to blindfold my camels to trick them to keep them going.

almost without luggage and use real riding saddles, making them fast and nimble. We, however, have sacks of flour, onions and water in goatskin bags hanging from our saddle pins and have been condemned to using the stronger but unpleasant pack saddles. The *haras* gallop around all day on the lookout for suspect riders. Passing nomads and herdsmen bring them the latest news and this is how Ibrahim can tell me that a caravan behind us has been raided by seven bandits. There have been three deaths, one of whom is Ibrahim's colleague. 'Isn't it time to look for a less dangerous job?,' I enquire. After all, he has been testing fate for the past seven years. 'Allah decides on life and death. When my time has come, it has come', is his bold reply. Amulets skip perkily up and down on his chest, arms and back – apparently a little extra divine mediation is not such a bad thing.

'They smell home', is Yussuf's explanation for the insane speed with which the caravan is travelling. 'They' refers to the three *chabirs* and the rest of the crew who are all from the Dongola area, on the Nile, the caravan's provisional destination. As an old-timer, my travel companion condemns racing the camels unnecessarily, but he is wise enough to keep his opinions to himself. Caravan leaders do not like criticism. During the trek, they are all-powerful and must be obeyed without reservation.

'The knife! Yussuf, please, use the knife.' Djemera wrings his hands and walks around one female camel who refuses to get up. Number 125 I call her. Every trader who sends camels across by caravan has his number or sign burnt in the animal's neck after the purchase. I always recognize the emaciated *naga*, or female camel, by her number, and this last week by the way she limps. Now she is lying on the ground for dead. She has wounds on all four legs and her faltering step is terrible to behold. This afternoon, Djemera decided to fix the worn out soles of 125 by sowing pieces of leather on to them. Routine work. The female's legs are bound and her head is tied to her tail. While Djemera uses a few large stitches to sow the water-soaked pieces of leather over the wounds, Ali and Yussuf hold the protesting animal in check. The *naga* howls in agony. Now her mouth hangs open, without a will of its own, the pink insides of her lips covered in sand. The caravan must continue and Djemera wants to put the animal out of her misery. He walks around her, knife drawn. He hesitates. Nothing to do with faint-heartedness and everything with the dreaded trader who will want to know why his commodity has not made it. 'Yussuf, you do it!' But Yussuf was not born yesterday. For the umpteenth time the men are trying to drag the beast to her feet. Finally she rolls to her knees, sits up and slowly gets on her feet. Like a drunk she staggers away from her tormentors, looking for support among the herd.

THE CARAVAN MUST CONTINUE AND DJEMERA WANTS TO PUT THE ANIMAL OUT OF HER MISERY.

While number 125 gathers new force we are eating *asida*, a thick porridge of flour and onion sauce. '*Choudi*', 'take it', but one bite is already enough for me and I turn away from the circle. For a few days now I have had very serious diarrhoea and the prospect of many sanitary stops does

The trek across sand, grit and gravel is gruelling for the camels, and walking on worn soles is painful. Limping camels are provided with an extra patch of leather sewn on to their feet. If carried out quickly, the procedure need not cause pain.

The true professional in the desert is conspicuous not for his tools, but for the lack of them. Ingenuity is the hallmark of a master. A rope and a piece of wood are all it takes to make an *ogal* or knee hobble.

not appeal to me at all. Although the men would be decent enough to look the other way if I had to crouch on the sand of this barren expanse, the idea of having a caravan passing me by while I sit there with my pants down is not particularly attractive.

Later that night I am staring at the stars from my sleeping bag and listening absent-mindedly to the merry chatter of the men near the fire. I am not bothered by the goat they slaughtered. No, what is haunting me is an image of the day before yesterday: a little grey fluffy camel that we left to its own devices just half an hour after its birth. It had been born during the noon break and when I presented it with two fingers its sucking reflexes were immediate. But fluffyhead was not allowed to come with us, not even in a saddle bag. A nursing camel would mean too many delays, I was told.

'She's got a firm behind but her heart's made of camel's milk', one of the camel drivers said sympathetically when Yussuf told him how upset I had been. The news of my tears quickly went around. Yussuf, dependable as always, had comforted me by saying that everyone would look for a nomad family that could adopt it. But just this day, nobody came.

Three weeks after we left El Fasher on this journey of a thousand kilometres, we meet the Nile, where a fresh crew takes over the caravan. We are warmly welcomed and, like the camels, we are immediately fed and watered. Even the *naga* has made it, with death snapping at her heels. The same afternoon, having rested briefly, Djemera and his men climb aboard an empty Toyota pickup, together with the few humble things they own, and take their leave without much ado. A light handshake, a perfunctory farewell and they are gone, dissolved in a cloud of dust.

Arita Baaijens (Dutch, b. 1956), desert explorer, author and photographer, is the first Western woman to explore the Sudanese desert solo and on camel, and to travel the Forty Days Road twice. She is a Fellow of the Royal Geographical Society and a biologist. Between travels she lives in Amsterdam, the Netherlands. Her current project is the Search for Shambhala, a mythical kingdom supposedly located in a remote valley somewhere north of the Himalaya.

Right When I started my career as desert explorer in 1988 the GPS didn't exist. My navigation tools were a watch, compass and a 70-year-old map. Often days or a week would go by before I could check my position. If I didn't find the water well or the hill that I was aiming for, I never knew if the map was wrong or my navigation skill lousy.

Below It was love at first sight with Mabrouka, the female camel who accompanied me on that first solo desert journey, almost 25 years ago. Since then I've travelled with many other camels, but no one has ever been able to take her place.

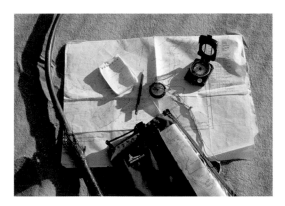

ROBERT TWIGGER
EGYPT'S GREAT SAND SEA ON FOOT

THERE IS SOMETHING SPECIAL ABOUT BEING FIRST in some way, the first to see something, the first to bring back news. For me, exploration is about being the first to bring back news of some distant and intriguing place, either by travelling in a new way or by being a rare visitor to such a place.

My childhood was spent in Warwickshire, as far from the sea as you can get in the United Kingdom. I was obsessed by the explorer Bill Tilman. Tilman had been on several Everest expeditions before the war, but it was his postwar explorations using a small yacht (once glimpsed in Lymington harbour – for me it was like seeing Nansen's *Fram*) to visit remote Arctic islands that caught my imagination. Here was a man exploring in his own way, using his own gear, refusing the carnival of sponsorship – it seemed, to me, that Tilman had distilled the essence, got to the beating heart of exploration, and was living his life by listening to its quiet demands.

Dressed for the desert: two travellers in our party, Bob and Spencer Timothy, wear appropriate headgear to protect against the sun.

How to do it though? How to get away? It wasn't obvious to me how to go about exploring; even a Tilman-type trip needed some money, and I always had none. By my late twenties I'd finally worked out how to amass the small amount needed to buy a ticket and enough extra to get to a distant location. In my case it was northern Borneo and Kalimantan. I was supposedly in search of the world's longest python – it was an idea that interested a publisher, and there was a prize of $50,000 offered by the prestigious Wildlife Conservation Society of New York for any snake caught that was longer than 9 m/30 ft. For six months this quest took me to some very remote patches of jungle and even remoter islands between Borneo and New Guinea. I learnt that a crazy quest could get you to places you would never have thought existed if you went at it straightforwardly.

As I zigzagged my way through the jungle following up leads, accompanied by local tribesmen, former headhunters, I came across, by chance it seemed, a huge menhir, for all the world like an excerpt from Stonehenge: two uprights and cross piece built on an enormous hill of large pebbles. A few kilometres further on there was another. It turned out to be a line of menhirs stretching across the border into Kalimantan that had never before been recorded. Even the hunter who came with me said very few of the tribe came this far into the montane jungle. I was hooked. Suddenly I understood what exploration was all about – be first, bring back news.

Perversely, on my next long trip I set out not to be first, but second. No one had crossed Canada by the same route as Alexander Mackenzie using a birchbark canoe since he had done it in 1793. And we discovered why. By the third season of the expedition we were already a year behind

Day after day we followed our line of camels. We almost lost one to exhaustion – on the same journey, Gerhard Rohlfs lost ten.

Modern equipment and desert gear includes plastic jerry cans and nylon feed sacks, but the camel remains the best method of transport.

the two it took Mackenzie. Though we paddled from the moment the rivers melted to the moment they began to freeze again, we were still way behind those eighteenth-century explorers, the first men ever to cross North America – twelve years before the more famous Lewis and Clark expedition. I was learning first-hand just how tough and fit the explorers of two centuries before had been.

Though we were 'second' from the beginning, it didn't feel like it. Just as Livingstone, Burton and Stanley had been 'second' behind the Arab slave traders, who in their turn followed the native routes into the interior of Africa, so the very gap, in both time and culture, made our journey into a kind of first in one sense. We had discovered how hard it must have been, and we could bring back news, expand on what Mackenzie had found, since those who had heard his news were all long dead.

If you want to go where no one has been before there is surprisingly a lot of Earth out there still waiting to be visited. Much of it is mountainous – a third of all peaks over 6,500 m (21,325 ft) in eastern Tibet are unclimbed, and there are trackless jungles and deserts and uninhabited islands – you just have to look.

In 1997 I started making trips to Egypt to explore the desert between the Nile and the Libyan border. In 2004 I moved there permanently to be able to make both long and short journeys of exploration. Parts of the Egyptian desert form the most arid spots on Earth in terms of groundwater. There are no wells for hundreds of kilometres. This is unusual in any desert, and it makes it almost impossible for nomads to exist there. Unlike many parts of the Sahara, where Berbers or Tuareg seem to pop up as if by magic whenever and wherever you stop, the Western Desert

For my first desert journeys with Steve Mann we explored the Sahara pulling everything along on a small trolley.

of Egypt is empty. In six weeks of desert travelling in 2009/10 I saw not a single human being other than those who were on the expedition travelling with me.

My early trips were made using a trolley on which I pulled all my supplies. This enabled me to see far more than if I'd taken the usual mode of modern desert travel: a Toyota Landcruiser, piled high with fuel and water. But the trolley was cumbersome, even if it was real exploration in the sense of walking over ground never before walked over. I decided to learn about using camels and started making journeys with local Bedouin in this remote arid part of the Sahara.

Its remoteness means it is still possible to reach places where no one has been for at least 5,000 years or more, when the Sahara was much wetter. Those ancient dwellers left behind vast amounts of stone tools and rock art, and it is finding these that enlivens a desert journey here. But my aim in 2009 was not to find artifacts, it was to replicate on foot the journey made in 1874 by the German explorer Gerhard Rohlfs. What interested me was that even Rohlfs didn't make the entire journey on foot. He rode a camel much of the way, sensibly probably. But riding all day on a camel means you can miss a lot on the ground. Of course, you still see far more than you do speeding along in a car, as later explorers in this region did, such as Ralph Bagnold and Lázsló Almásy (on whom the character in the novel and film *The English Patient* was loosely based).

The challenge, then, was to walk Rohlfs' route, no more than a series of points on a blank map, from the oasis of Dakhla to that of Siwa, the

ITS REMOTENESS MEANS IT IS STILL POSSIBLE TO REACH PLACES WHERE NO ONE HAS BEEN FOR AT LEAST 5,000 YEARS OR MORE, WHEN THE SAHARA WAS MUCH WETTER.

The names of members of Rohlfs' expedition carved on a pillar in the Dakhla Oasis. We followed the trail he had left.

home of the oracle sought by Alexander the Great. It seemed a fitting end to our proposed expedition, covering a distance of 700 km (435 miles).

Much of the journey was along sand and gravel corridors between dunes on either side that were hundreds of metres high. We would cross into new corridors when there was a gap in the dunes. On several occasions we found ourselves in sections with no car tracks for miles, a sure sign, on gravel, that no car had ever been through, because in such places tracks remain visible for eighty years or more. I have seen the tracks left by Almásy in his baby Ford expedition of 1932. So, no tracks, and an enormous dried-up lake surrounded by strange harpoon-like stone tools I had never encountered before. There was no vegetation, but the ground and surrounding rock was coloured green from mineral deposits, making this 'green valley' more memorable because of it.

Rohlfs lost ten of his twenty camels on his journey; we were determined to lose none of our nine. On one day, Hassan, the sixty-year-old Bedouin – a tower of energy with twenty-one children and a child's skipping gait and humour – told me that one of the female camels was going to die. Losing a camel is not like having a car breakdown. You feel you can will a camel back to life. Perhaps we did – by the next morning the camel was looking better. It survived, and so did our record at keeping our beasts of burden alive.

Walking each day in temperatures of over 30°C (86°F) with a limited amount of water means you have to be careful. We found that by covering up, walking in the shade of the camels, drinking hot tea to raise the body's internal temperature and only drinking during the cool parts of the day, we were able to keep our water consumption to a survival minimum.

Right An example of rock art in the Sahara, at a site that had been discovered in 2003.

Below The Oracle at Siwa, the end of our expedition and the place where Alexander the Great learned of his destiny and his divinity, and asked what was the cause of the Nile flood.

Which isn't to say we didn't cut it close. The only well on the entire trip had been drilled by Russian oil explorers in the 1970s. They found water, a large amount; and five years before I had seen the well and it had been gushing. When we arrived it was just a dribble. Before the dribble had been glimpsed, Ali, the Bedouin who led the camels, said, 'If that is the well we are all going to die'. It was the well, and a dribble into half an oil drum is all you need to survive.

What news did we bring back? Nothing scientific. Nothing very practical at all except that one well was nearly dry. The real news was of strange skies seen, vast stretches of sand traversed, news of a lonely place, news that such utter isolation still exists on this over-crowded planet. News indeed.

Petrified wood – the remains of a giant fossilized tree – just one of many strange sights and treasures to be found deep in the Sahara.

Robert Twigger (British, b. 1964) is a writer and explorer who has written numerous books. His first, *Angry White Pyjamas*, was an account of the three years he spent studying traditional arts in Japan: it received the William Hill Sports Book of the Year award and the Somerset Maugham award. His second, *Big Snake*, about exploring remote islands in Indonesia in search of giant reptiles, was made into a National Geographic/Channel 4 film. He then made a three-year, 4,828-km (3,000-mile) journey across northern Canada in a handmade birchbark canoe, retracing the route taken by Alexander Mackenzie in 1793, and wrote about it in his book *Voyageur*. His latest publication is *Red Nile: A Biography of the World's Greatest River*. In 2010 he was the first person to make a foot crossing of the Libyan/Egyptian Great Sand Sea.

BRUNO BAUMANN

THE TAKLAMAKAN: DESERT OF NO RETURN

LONG BEFORE I STARTED TO TRAVEL I was fascinated by the stories of men who set out into a world before Google Earth; a time when not every spot on Earth seemed mapped and known. One of the heroes of my childhood was the Swedish explorer Sven Hedin, who became the first man ever to cross the mighty sand sea of the Taklamakan Desert.

Covering an area of more than 336,675 sq. km (130,000 sq. miles), the Taklamakan is the second largest continuous sand desert in the world. It is situated in the northwest corner of present-day China – to the east it is bordered by the Gobi Desert, and on the other sides it is surrounded by the highest mountains on Earth – the Karakoram to the west, the High Pamirs to the northwest, the Tien Shan range to the north and the Kunlun Shan to the south. From glaciers high among peaks reaching 8,840 m (29,000 ft), several rivers flow down into the 'Desert of No Return', as the locals call

As he did every morning, Omarjan, the younger of our two camelmen, climbed up one of the surrounding dunes to scan anxiously the eastern horizon. However, there was nothing to see but sand, not even a single plant on which to pin our hopes.

the Taklamakan. But they all just seep into the sand and evaporate some-where out in the middle of the dunes.

The Taklamakan has always been feared for its extremely dry climate and terrifying sandstorms. As early as 130 BC, the legendary Silk Road split into two branches that skirted around the northern and southern edges of the Taklamakan, but no one had ever succeeded in penetrating the desert's interior. Hedin set out on 10 April 1895, his luggage filled with more letters of recommendation from well-meaning friends than water. His expedition turned into a veritable death march. Almost the entire caravan died.

Hedin's account of his ill-fated expedition in *Through Asia* had fasci-nated me since I laid my hands on the book as a boy. I first set eyes on the Taklamakan in 1989. Like Hedin, I travelled by camel caravan, although on this occasion I followed a more easterly course than he had. I also chose to travel at a better time of year. Maybe that's why I had the feeling during that

JUST THOSE FEW HOURS WITHOUT WATER WERE ENOUGH TO CAUSE ME TO DETERIORATE PHYSICALLY TO THE POINT OF COLLAPSE.

journey lasting twenty-one days that I had crossed a completely different desert from Hedin. Was this the infamous desert of death? I was beginning to think that he might have been exaggerating the dangers, embellishing the story for dramatic effect.

This scepticism increased all the more after my first attempted solo crossing of the Gobi Desert in 1996. That experience taught me first-hand what it really felt like to be close to dying of thirst. I had underestimated the amount of water I would need for the trek, and had already consumed the last drop while still miles away from the next water site. Just those few hours without water were enough to cause me to deteriorate physically

During a sandstorm the animals dropped to the ground. We followed their lead and snuggled up to their flanks, seeking shelter behind their massive bodies.

to the point of collapse. With my last ounce of strength, racked with kidney pains, I just about managed to drag myself to the next oasis, where I promptly threw in the towel, debilitated and exhausted.

After that experience, I re-read Hedin's accounts of his desert drama in the Taklamakan – but with different eyes. Running for his life through the desert for a full five days without a single drop of water? Impossible! It would have been a medical miracle. Burying himself up to the neck in the sand during the day and walking at night? A desert fairy tale! The time lost in making such stops would have been fatal because he would have been dehydrating just as much at rest as he would have been while walking, but he wouldn't have been getting any closer to water. How had the drama in the Taklamakan really unfolded?

I decided to re-create Hedin's expedition and uncover the truth about what had actually happened. I was also secretly hoping to find some remains of the 'camp of death'. Hedin had by his own account been forced to abandon most of his equipment, hundreds of photographic plates, priceless documents, all packed in crates that were likely to have been well preserved in the arid desert climate.

In order to reproduce the expedition as authentically as possible, I not only decided to take precisely the same route and use the same method of transportation – a camel caravan – but I also chose the exact same month of the year. Of course, I knew there was still only a limited comparison that could be made between a desert crossing nowadays and Hedin's pioneering journey. After all, unlike Hedin, I had the most modern maps and state-of-the-art satellite navigation equipment. Plus, I knew the desert much better than Hedin had when he embarked on his first major expedition.

At first the wind only swirled the sand into fountains of dust that span across the surface like rotating columns, but moments later it became dark as night and we were in the midst of a fully fledged Buran, one of the feared sandstorms.

When we entered the vast sea of sand our caravan consisted of six pack camels and two local camelmen. Roze, the more experienced one, took leadership and guided four of the heavily loaded animals, while Omarjan followed with the other two.

For these very reasons, I didn't consider my plan to be unduly difficult or dangerous, particularly since I was certain I could avoid making what was Hedin's biggest mistake – not taking enough water.

On 17 April 2000, with two drivers and six camels, I embarked on the most difficult leg of our journey – 177 km (110 miles) in a straight line across a vast sea of sand stretching all the way to the shore of the Khotan-daria (a tributary of the Yarkand River), all without a source of water. I figured we would cover about 14.5 km (9 miles per day), which would mean we could reach our destination in twelve days. We loaded up the camels with fourteen days' water for the men (we were consuming around 30 litres or over 6 gallons of water a day), and another 118 litres (26 gallons) for the animals.

But after seven days – beyond the point of no return – all my careful calculations went out of the window. The dunes were much higher and harder to navigate than any of us had expected. On top of that, we were slowed down by sandstorms. We weren't that far behind schedule, but, as it turned out, the camels needed much more water, and much sooner, than any of us had anticipated. On day eight, the first of our six camels collapsed from thirst. And then, just hours after that, we lost a second.

The whole time I was on the lookout for signs of Hedin's expedition, scanning the terrain with my binoculars, hoping to spot a weathered wooden crate or a tin canister, polished smooth by the sand, lying some-where out on top of a dune. I never found any traces of Hedin's 'camp of death' – instead, I created one of my very own.

On the next day we lost the third of our camels. In an attempt to find a way out of the crisis I increased my efforts and walked far ahead to scout

After we lost three of our six camels within two days, all our hopes turned into despair. Roze, the older camel man, was lying in the sand, unwilling to continue marching any further.

out the easiest route for the exhausted camels to follow. Behind me, the caravan had sunk out of sight in the sea of sand; when it resurfaced there were only two camels left. We marched on. Sometime later, the caravan came to a final halt. The last two camels had collapsed. Roze, the older of the two local camelmen, started shouting angrily. In his eyes it was all my fault – and he was right of course. It was my idea to follow Hedin's footsteps. The death of the animals was on my head. But there was no time to blame each other or to regret. Now we had to run for our lives. Each of us had about 4 litres (under 1 gallon) of water left – enough for a few hours, at most. Other than that, I took only the absolute necessities: the satellite navigation device, compass, binoculars and a waterproof bag with a long drawstring, in case we needed to scoop water out of a deep well.

BEHIND ME, THE CARAVAN HAD SUNK OUT OF SIGHT IN THE SEA OF SAND; WHEN IT RESURFACED THERE WERE ONLY TWO CAMELS LEFT.

'If we walk night and day,' I said to the others encouragingly, 'we can make it to the Khotan-daria by tomorrow.' We abandoned the camels, which were now too weak to follow us, and I watched them fade out of sight as we crossed over the next dune.

After about two hours we spotted a lone tamarisk bush. It was the first sign of life since we had left the last well. I knew this was the moment of truth. It was all, or nothing. If we dug here for water and failed, we would have spent the last of our water supply. We took the risk and got to work immediately. Every few inches, we checked the sand's consistency, and were happy to see that it was getting damper. Two hours and about 1 m (3 ft) later, the ground turned muddy – a bit further down and we were standing in a brown puddle. We'd made it!

Meanwhile, Roze set out to rescue the last two camels we'd left behind. Our joy knew no bounds when he showed up with them before darkness. Next day we reached the dry riverbed of the Khotan-daria.

Although I did not succeed in finding Hedin's 'camp of death', it is certain that the wreckage of his expedition is still out there somewhere, now added to by the baggage we had to jettison along the way. But finding it would take more than just retracing Hedin's old route, it would require a major technological and logistical undertaking – or a lot of luck. However, I had learnt and suffered enough to be able to say with confidence that I can separate the truth from the legend of the famous explorer's expedition.

Hedin's ambitious plan was doomed to failure from the start. Whether his men did, or did not as he claimed, actually fill the water containers is irrelevant. His own records indicate that he was transporting large quantities of additional equipment, such as blankets, furs, boots, tools and gifts for the locals, because he was planning to travel directly on to Tibet after crossing the Taklamakan. The truth is, he had loaded the camels with so much cargo that there could never have been enough room to transport the amount of water the caravan needed. And even under better conditions, the animals, emaciated and weak as they were after a long winter, would not have been strong enough to carry it – as we had had the misfortune to prove with our own caravan.

I could probably have reached many of these conclusions without having had to go through the exercise of retracing Hedin's route. One thing is certain, had I known then the price I'd have to pay to uncover

I COULD PROBABLY HAVE REACHED MANY OF THESE CONCLUSIONS WITHOUT HAVING HAD TO GO THROUGH THE EXERCISE OF RETRACING HEDIN'S ROUTE.

Khara Khoto, the 'Black City', is the most impressive of the sand-buried ruins to be found in Central Asian deserts. The walled city was once part of the ancient kingdom of Xixia, conquered by the Mongols under Chinghis Khan and finally buried by the sand of the Gobi.

Crossing the ridge of a giant dune during my solo attempt in the Gobi Desert.

the truth – four dead camels and near disaster – I would certainly have thought better of it.

In the end, the most important revelation about the legend of Sven Hedin didn't come in the desert, but in Kashgar, where we did some investigating in the surrounding villages. Several old Uighur locals told us that at least one of two men Hedin claimed had died of thirst in the Taklamakan had in fact survived, and had even gone on to become the mayor of the village. His name was Kasim Akhun. He was the native guide on the expedition, the man Hedin had accused in his book of being primarily responsible for the entire disaster.

Bruno Baumann (Austrian, b. 1955) is an award-winning writer and photojournalist living in Munich. His works have earned him international recognition as an authority on Tibet and Central Asia. In 1989, he trekked through the Taklamakan, a vast sea of sand in western China. Here he encountered relics of the ancient culture of the Silk Road dating back over a thousand years. In October 2003, he made history by being the first person to cross the sandy heart of the Gobi Desert solo on foot. This one-man expedition marked the ultimate step in his desert quests. In May 2004 he became the first to raft the Sutley Gorge in far western Tibet. Inside this 'Grand Canyon' of the Himalaya he discovered relics of the ancient kingdom Shang Shung, which until then had been regarded as completely legendary.

RAINFOREST

The richest environment on Earth is to be found in the remaining tropical rain-forests. There you may encounter fifty species of ant in a single tree, about the same number as are to be found in the whole of Great Britain; rainforests contain about 50,000 species of tree and 780 have been counted in one 10-ha (25-acre) plot – over twenty times the entire British tree flora. And it is not just a question of diversity. Every plant and animal and insect in the forest has a specific relationship with every other organism with which it comes into contact, whether as host, prey or predator.

The complexity of life can be overwhelming and many explorers have suc-cumbed to the temptation of describing it as a 'Green Hell', where everything is hostile and dangerous. One of the worst offenders was the legendary Colonel Percy Fawcett, whose gory descriptions gripped his readers and whose disappearance in 1925 has left an enduring mystery.

Not so the true discoverer. Charles Darwin wrote in his diary after his first sortie in South America: 'Delight ... is a weak term to express the feelings of a natu-ralist who, for the first time, has wandered by himself in a Brazilian forest.' Some of the best modern explorers have been those who devote their lives to researching the wonders of the rainforest. Scientists who have learnt to survive and study in the heat and humidity, sometimes for years on end, continue to add immeasurably to our understanding of how our world works, and now their reach is being extended into the canopy, where so much is still to be found. And let us not forget the true inhabit-ants of the forest, the people whose very existence is threatened as we destroy it.

The Heart of Borneo rainforest is one of the last surviving areas of primary rainforest, but even this is under threat. In order to help protect it, Martin Holland and his team of scientists are studying the species found here and recording the first scientific data, and communicating the results to a worldwide audience.

GHILLEAN PRANCE
PLANT-HUNTING IN THE AMAZON

IN THE 1970S I CARRIED OUT A SERIES OF BOTANICAL EXPEDITIONS in Brazilian Amazonia for the New York Botanical Garden, in collaboration with the Instituto Nacional de Pesquisas da Amazonia (INPA) in Manaus. Each expedition was planned and organized to visit botanically under-explored areas. One of my four expeditions in 1971 was a walk across part of Roraima Territory (now State), from the missionary airstrip at Serra dos Surucucus to Uaicá, on the Uraricoeira River, a distance of 280 km (174 miles). From Boa Vista, the capital of Roraima, we flew to the tiny airstrip, nestled in a narrow valley. Landing at this strip with little infly and on a considerable slope could only be done by a skilled pilot.

My expedition team consisted of Bill Steward, an undergraduate from Michigan, field assistants, or *mateiros*, Walfir Pinheiro, Osmarino Monteiro and José Ramos, and missionary Fritz Herter, who was stationed at Surucucus and was our Yanomami translator. Shortly after landing at Surucucus we began the important task of recruiting Yanomami as porters. Transporting camping equipment, plant-collecting material, chemicals, trade goods and food required many backs. Fritz enlisted nineteen Yanomami and we divided everything into individual loads. Each of us carried our own rücksacks, with personal goods such as clothes, film and cameras. This was before the days of GPS and we navigated by compass, hiking for half the day and collecting plants for the remainder.

After one night at Surucucus and once the Indians had made fibre panniers for their loads, we set out. We hiked up out of the valley and through forest. The long line of the twenty-five of us then crossed the Surucucus savannah, past a large military airstrip. Following five hours of hiking, with everyone getting used to the routine, we stopped beside a rainforest stream to make our first camp. Since it was still early in the afternoon some of us collected plants; by nightfall we had our first fourteen collections. Rather than lugging heavy plant driers through the forest our method was to place the plants in paraformaldehyde and send them back wrapped in plastic bags for drying in Manaus. The camp had been built hurriedly by the *mateiros* and the Indians and promptly collapsed once we all got into our hammocks, making a quick rebuild necessary. The next morning Bill, José and I were up and out early to collect, while the others broke camp and packed. Once they had caught up with us we walked for three hours until we were near the village of Maiyoobtedi. We collected plants all afternoon and entered the village in the late afternoon, where we were made to feel welcome; instead of pitching camp we were given a hearth, with adequate spaces for our hammocks.

The author collecting a plant specimen for scientific study.

The next day some of us hurried ahead again to collect, and before the others rejoined us we had the first of many rains. We had chosen this time of year for the expedition as it was reputedly the dry season, but this was not evident to us after numerous drenchings. The trail was hilly and, because of the rain, slippery, but we made good progress and collected plants at each rest stop. By evening we arrived at Botamatedi village; this consisted of a completely closed building in which the porters soon strung up our hammocks. In the smoky atmosphere inside our watery eyes made it hard to write and process the plants, but it was shelter from the rain.

The Yanomami use a different formal language when one group meets another. The nineteen from Surucucus were treated like a visiting tribe and so there was chanting in formal talk all night as they exchanged news. They would shout in their hammocks and then a pair, one visitor and one host, would squat on the ground holding each other's shoulders and shout at the top of their voices, much as I had observed previously in one of their rituals involving the use of hallucinogenic snuff.

GAME WAS ABUNDANT BECAUSE WE WERE IN UNDISTURBED FOREST AND FOR MOST OF THE TRIP WE WERE FAR FROM VILLAGES.

As we progressed four hours along the trail the following day, both collecting and hiking were hampered by further heavy rain. We then camped beside a stream where we could bathe and get water. It was amazing how quickly our Yanomami companions erected shelters with a few branches and a palm thatch. For the next four days we stuck to our routine of walking for four or five hours and collecting plants during the rest of the daylight hours. It was now raining hard, making this part of the hike especially difficult as the terrain was undulating and we were constantly scrambling

Fritz Herter watched by Yanomamis and Bill Steward as he experiments with the bow we used to fire a string over a tree branch to haul up our climbing rope.

up or slithering down slopes. We had anticipated it would be impossible to bring enough food with us for twenty-five people for a month and that we would therefore have to depend on hunting for protein. Since the Yanomami live by hunting we were experiencing their normal lifestyle, as they shot monkeys, curassows, coatis, peccaries and a tapir. Game was abundant because we were in undisturbed forest and for most of the trip we were far from villages.

Four days after leaving Botamatedi we felt confident that we were on our planned itinerary as we reached Maitá mountain. From our study of radar photos of the region, we knew that the correct route was over this range. By following a direct line by compass we struggled over hills and waded through flooded forest. In rain we scrambled up and down the steep slopes, but also collected plants on the top. Our clothes were wet almost the entire month. From the signs of people we saw we realized we were nearing the next Yanomami village, so we stopped and spent most of the day collecting. While we were preparing specimens, our Indian porters started painting themselves according to their traditional patterns in order to visit the village.

When we arrived at the Maitá village an elaborate greeting ceremony took place between our group and the hosts. The Maitá were isolated and many of them had never seen a white person; they were curious, but since we were with a large group of Yanomami they were also very welcoming. We were taken to an almost new *maloca*, or longhouse, that had been in use for only a few weeks. The villagers had just deserted a fine looking building nearby and built this new one. This often happens in Yanomami life after some misfortune, such as a death or an evil omen.

Below left This Yanomami youth has just been through his puberty rites and is proud of his tobacco quid placed between his lower lip and teeth.

Below right Our group of Yanomami porters are well painted up to visit another Yanomami village.

The Maitá fed us on roasted coati and bananas. After a hard day we were in our hammocks early and soon fast asleep, in spite of the excited chat around the *maloca* as our porters exchanged news with our hosts. By nine the next morning we were packed and on our way. In an hour we reached a second Maitá village, where we stocked up with food since they had an abundance of bananas, cassava and yams, and then walked another two hours beyond it. This was our first, and only, day without rain on the entire expedition. We camped in the forest and our night was calm and quiet compared with the previous one, the only sounds being the cicadas in the forest. We were thus rested and ready for a long hike the next day.

Although there was little rain, underfoot it was the wettest day of our journey as we were crossing a flat area of swamp with many rivers. At larger rivers we felled a tree and walked along the trunk, often rather slippery. We generally did well except when Bill fell off a log and soaked his backpack. Rain returned with a vengeance the following day, and we spent most of the time walking because it was too wet to collect much, though we did manage to make twenty-one collections of plants and fungi. It was a good day for game, however. Fritz and the Yanomami shot two macaws, two monkeys and a curassow, as well as a large fish with an arrow with the barbed tip they use for fishing. So we were not short of protein that day, and the fire to cook it was also welcome to dry our soaked clothes and the contents of Bill's rucksack.

We intended to have another long hike the next day, but kept losing the trail and twice had to send out search parties to relocate it. It was another meaty day as Fritz shot two pigs and the Yanomami a curassow and two monkeys. We concentrated on making progress and only gathered

A rest stop in the forest on the trek from Surucucus to Uaicá.

Above left and right Two of the Yanomami villages visited on the walk from Surucucus to Uaicá. Many different plants are used in the construction of these *malocas* or huts.

twelve collections, but by now we had a total of 300. We then had a long hike to ensure we would be in time for our rendezvous with our plane. After two days of good progress we were near our final Yanomami village, Paramiteri, on the banks of the Uraricoeira River, so we spent a day collecting. While we were busy with the plants Fritz shot a tapir, which kept us in meat until we reached the village. That evening José prepared a delicious tapir steak for dinner.

We had anticipated we would reach Paramiteri the next day, but lost the trail many times and had to camp for another night. Although we still had plenty of meat, we had used our last rice and farinha and hoped that we would find the next *maloca* soon. We left camp early and continued by compass; around noon we encountered a well-worn path that led us directly to an Indian village, but it was not Paramiteri. We were fed by these people and then walked with them along a trail to the river. From there they took us in canoes to Paramiteri. We needed the Paramiteris to canoe us upriver to the Uaicá airstrip where we had arranged to meet our plane. It turned out we had hit the Uraricoeira River about 5 km (3 miles) upstream – not bad navigation considering the distance and the terrain covered. Paramiteri was a small *maloca* so there was no space for us and we built a camp nearby, which meant the night was more peaceful as we did not have to listen again to the formal talk between visitors and hosts. They fed us well, which was a relief since we had by now run out of all of our food, and were congratulating ourselves on having taken just enough when supplemented by hunting.

THEY FED US WELL, WHICH WAS A RELIEF SINCE WE HAD BY NOW RUN OUT OF ALL OF OUR FOOD, AND WERE CONGRATULATING OURSELVES ON HAVING TAKEN JUST ENOUGH WHEN SUPPLEMENTED BY HUNTING.

A flight to take our porters back to Surucucus was the first time in the air for them, and they were fascinated to circle over one of their villages.

The next morning was spent bargaining with the Paramiteris to take us upriver to the airstrip and to sell us enough food to sustain our large party. Fortunately, we still had enough trade goods. Machetes, axes, cloth and beads were currency with the Yanomami at that time. By noon all was agreed and we embarked in seven canoes with ten Paramiteri Indians to paddle. The canoes were small and with little freeboard, so balancing them was precarious. It took us two days to reach Uaicá because the river was full of rapids and we spent much time dragging the canoes over them. But we arrived at Uaicá airstrip contented that after this long hike through the unknown we had reached it two days before the appointment with our pilot to collect us and take us to our next destination. The next day was spent around the airstrip preparing the ground for the plane. We each did a one-hour shift mowing the overgrown landing strip with a very heavy push mower. We also washed clothes and spent time treating the open sores most of us had on our legs as a result of wearing wet trousers constantly for almost three weeks.

The plane arrived on the agreed day. It made four flights to Surucucus to ferry Fritz and the nineteen Yanomami back home. We were sad to see them leave as they had been both hard workers and good companions. I went along on one flight to survey the terrain that we had crossed. It is useful to get an aerial view to understand the vegetation better. I spotted several places we had visited, particularly the Indian villages and Maitá mountain. The five of us who were not local remained at Uaicá. We had a replenished food supply and planned to stay there collecting plants for five more days. We almost finished our food supply at breakfast on the day we expected the plane to return and began to wait for it to ferry us on to Mucajaí, where we intended to work for another two weeks. By three in the afternoon it was apparent that the plane was not coming, so we set out to gather food rather than botanical collections. We found some trees of the peach palm (*Bactris gasipaes*) in an old Indian field and also some *goiaba da anta* (*Bellucia axinanthera*), a pleasant fleshy fruit. The peach palm formed our supper with our last tin of meat – the fruits are boiled and the flesh around the hard kernel is rather like chestnut in texture. Our isolation at Uaicá continued for another week with little food because our plane crashed on landing, which is another story told elsewhere. No one was hurt, but it delayed our next expedition.

On this single expedition we made 683 collections of plants and fungi from an understudied region, many of which turned out to be first records for those species for Brazil. We also found two new species, *Bunchosia decussiflora* and *Apodanthes roraimae*. The latter is a curious parasitic plant in the same family as *Rafflesia* of the Malaysian rainforests, but unlike the spectacular flowers of *Rafflesia*, *Apodanthes* resembles a series of small knobs emerging from the trunk of a host tree. We also gathered much ethnobotanical information from the Yanomami, and I made notes on hallucinogenic snuffs, fish and arrow poisons, edible mushrooms and much more. We thus felt well satisfied with the results of all our efforts and tribulations on this expedition.

Ghillean Prance (British, b. 1937) is a botanist who has specialized in the flora of the Amazon. He has carried out thirty-nine botanical expeditions in Amazonia and is the author of 542 scientific and general publications on botany and conservation, including twenty-one books and monographs. He worked for twenty-five years for the New York Botanical Garden before becoming the Director of the Royal Botanic Gardens, Kew, London. He is currently the Scientific Director of the Eden Project in Cornwall, England. He is a Fellow of the Royal Society and was knighted in 1995 for his services to conservation.

A dried, pressed herbarium specimen from the expedition filed in the New York Botanical Garden. These specimens are the basis for the classification and identification of plants.

SYDNEY POSSUELO
THE LAST SERTANISTA

BY JOHN HEMMING

THE IMMENSE FORESTS OF AMAZONIA are home to more isolated peoples than anywhere on Earth. Brazil has the most such uncontacted tribes, perhaps thirty-four groups, as well as the largest areas of protected indigenous territories (almost the size of all the countries in the original European Union) and a once fine government service Funai (National Indigenous Foundation). *Sertanistas* ('forest experts') were the elite of Funai – the dozen specialists empowered to make first contact with unknown peoples, in the way that the fictional James Bond was licensed to kill. Almost all the legendary sertanistas are now dead: Sydney Possuelo is the last.

Over fifty years ago, in 1959, a nineteen-year-old Possuelo started working among the Indians of the upper Xingu in central Brazil. His mentors were the magnificent explorers and humanitarians, the brothers Orlando and Cláudio Villas Bôas. Sydney (as everyone calls him) has been in the Amazon forests for most years since that first initiation, apart from some time spent as a very successful president of Funai and also establishing its Department of Isolated Peoples. Sydney is a true explorer. He has penetrated hundreds of kilometres of unexplored forests and rivers, but he did so for the humanitarian purpose of helping indigenous peoples. It never occurred to him to write about his expeditions, to boast about the hardships he endured, or seek headlines for his exploits.

Sydney Possuelo has made first contact with seven isolated groups. One of the earliest such expeditions was in 1978, to try to reach some Awá-Guajá nomads in order to vaccinate them and keep them within protected forests. This was a very difficult task, because the Awá-Guajá are one of only two surviving tribes that live under the canopy but never build huts or villages. They are hunter-gatherers, constantly on the move, the women

Opposite Sydney Possuelo crouches to gain the confidence of newly contacted Marubo mothers and children, western Brazil 1996.

carrying baskets with their few possessions and rubbing sticks to make fires at their bivouacs. Favourite foods are babaçu palm nuts, wild honey, and of course any game that the men can shoot with their bows and arrows.

The women love pets – monkeys, coatimundi 'honey-bears' or baby anteaters – which they breast-feed alongside their own babies and carry draped round their shoulders. The Awá-Guajá roamed in a remnant of dense primeval forest, a rare ecosystem known as pre-Amazonian, in the eloquently named Serra da Desordem (Chaos Hills), not far from Brazil's Atlantic seaboard.

A few Awá-Guajá had been contacted by Funai, and Sydney was assisted by two of these men as guides – no outsider, however experienced,

THEY ARE HUNTER-GATHERERS, CONSTANTLY ON THE MOVE, THE WOMEN CARRYING BASKETS WITH THEIR FEW POSSESSIONS AND RUBBING STICKS TO MAKE FIRES AT THEIR BIVOUACS.

could ever have found the scant traces of the tribe's movements. The expedition started with 390 km (242 miles) of paddling up the Turiaçu River into its rapids-infested headwaters – unexplored streams that were constantly blocked with fallen trees. The team then had to move into the forest, cutting a light trail which eventually covered a further 194 km (120 miles) before they found traces of the people they were seeking.

Although Sydney and his few men were very fit, lean young woodsmen, they still found the going arduous. They could not carry enough food for what proved to be a five-week expedition, and even if there had been time for hunting, the best shots would often have returned empty-handed after a morning's stalking since there are few animals at ground level, shot monkeys are hard to get out of trees without curare poison to prevent them clinging as they die, and most birds are hidden far overhead in the canopy. The only way for non-Indians to move through such forest is by cutting with a machete. Chainsaws or other machines are useless, so trail-cutting is exactly the same now as it was when the first Europeans reached Brazil five centuries ago. Cutting arms grow tired, machetes need constant sharpening, and in the dry season explorers can advance for hours with a raging thirst because they find no water. The ground in the hills they were travelling through was very uneven, necessitating frequent scrambling. Insects were omnipresent, so that they were covered in bites and the glands at the tops of their arms and legs were swollen and painful from filtered secretions.

Sydney's reward was suddenly to encounter a group of eleven men, women and children resting in the forest. His plan was for his Awá-Guajá men to rush into the midst of their compatriots to spare them the

Two canoes of men of Funai, Brazil's National Indigenous Foundation, and their Matis and Korubo Indian scouts on the Ituí River in western Brazil in 2002. Sydney is in a white shirt in the right-hand boat.

frightening sight of Sydney with his heavy black beard (indigenous people have almost no body hair). But, as he recalled:

> at the decisive moment [my Indians] looked at one another and desisted. I tried to push them, but got nowhere. They were scared. In order not to lose this opportunity, I took them by the arms and we advanced into the midst [of the Awá-Guajá] shouting words that I had learned from my brief sojourn with these Indians, like 'Friends', 'We are friends', 'We will do no harm'. This surprise caused some consternation among them. The women fled with their children, but I was surrounded by three Awá-Guajá men.

The tension was finally broken, in the usual way, by presents of machetes and knives. Metal blades are magic to people living in such dense forest vegetation. The small group was taken back to the Funai post, given preventive medicines and the few supplies they wanted, and then returned to their nomadic existence. Sydney and his colleagues succeeded in getting their territory protected against encircling loggers and settlers.

Two years later, Sydney was instructed to attempt a very different contact. The military government of Brazil was forcing a 'penetration road'

THEY WERE APPROACHING THE HOMELAND OF AN ELUSIVE AND MUCH-FEARED PEOPLE KNOWN AS ARARA.

deep into its Amazonian forests – the Transamazonica highway, slashed for thousands of kilometres roughly parallel to the main Amazon River. By 1980 the cutting crews and their earthmovers had reached the forests between the lower Xingu and Tapajós rivers. They were approaching the homeland of an elusive and much-feared people known as Arara (Macaw) – Indians who had almost never been seen but who had

Sydney on one of his many rainforest expeditions, with a Funai operative and a Matis wearing army fatigues and traditional ear discs.

killed some of the few prospectors or jaguar-skin hunters who had ventured into their forests. The two greatest sertanistas, Orlando Villas Bôas and Chico Meirelles, had both tried but failed to find the Arara. Contact with them was critically urgent, since the highway and the colonists who came with it were about to invade Arara lands.

Sydney decided on a waiting game. In a clearing near the route of the highway, he had his men build a couple of thatched huts with slatted palisade sides. Nearby was a watchtower, with the top enclosed against arrows, and in the surrounding forests were *tapiri* shelters: thatch-roofed platforms on which presents were laid out. Sydney left a handful of men in the huts, while he himself led a small expedition to see whether they could find traces of Arara. This team started from the town of Altamira on the lower Xingu and sailed up the Iriri (the river whose headwaters were first explored by an expedition I was on almost twenty years earlier, when our leader, Richard Mason, was killed in an ambush by another then unknown people). At the first major rapids they transferred to aluminium canoes, then ascended 100 km (62 miles) of the Iriri (including more formidable rapids), followed by a first ascent of its Anfrizio tributary, before entering unexplored forest and cutting northwards to the Transamazonica. Sydney and his team were typically Brazilian, wearing minimal clothing, running shoes or flipflops, no socks, and with their loads strapped to boards on their backs instead of fancy backpacks. But they were tough and almost as skilled woodsmen as the Indians they were seeking.

While Sydney was on this expedition, some Arara approached the attraction post. The men in the post lit up their clearing with lights at night and called friendly messages from a loudspeaker – but in what proved to be the wrong language, Aruak instead of Carib. At first light on 12 June 1980, while the Funai men were having breakfast, Arara crept up to the huts and fired their powerful arrows through slits in the palisade wall. The men upturned their table and sheltered behind it, but two were wounded before they could start the generator and turn on the security lights, at which point the Arara vanished. The waiting continued for weeks and months, with more presents (some of which were smashed by the Indians), more loudspeaker calls, music played by the Funai team (they had found Arara flutes – made from bones of dead prospectors), and occasional calls from the forest.

Sydney had meanwhile got the forests south of the highway designated as an Arara reserve. He or one of his bearded men stopped a huge bulldozer by standing in front of it, while hidden Arara were watching,

Sydney won over the elusive Arara people in forests west of the lower Xingu in 1980. The shaven-headed Arara wears only a wooden pin in his nose septum, a nut-bead necklace and a penis sheath. His powerful bow is longer than him, and Sydney holds one of their arrows, barbed for fishing.

impressed by this show of power. The Arara later revealed that this had been a turning point, a moment when they realized that there were 'good' and 'bad' white men. They also began to take the irresistible presents; and in October they responded by leaving two sections of bamboo full of wild honey. They sometimes answered the Funai men's music with their own from the forest. At the same time, Sydney had been conducting a series of minor forays, on one of which he found a massive abandoned hut, on others disused manioc plantations, as well as warning arrows blocking some of his trails.

The breakthrough came in February 1981, when four Arara men and a boy appeared at the post, bringing presents of a jaboti tortoise, roast peccary and more honey. Sydney recalled that 'the atmosphere was festive.... The meeting took place amid many smiles and much talk which, although

incomprehensible, resembled a long conversation among old friends.' Sydney established immediate rapport with the Arara, who had short-cut hair, pale skins and no body paint or adornment of any kind apart from modest necklaces of nuts. One of the Indians at this face-to-face encounter was Chief Tojtxi, the man who had led his people's years of resistance to white invasion. A Carib-speaker translated one of his eloquent speeches: 'My people have been moving for a long time, running, running. Many [foreign] people, on all sides. We have nowhere else to go.'

EVERY ONE OF SYDNEY POSSUELO'S CONTACT EXPEDITIONS OVER THE YEARS HAS BEEN DIFFERENT.

Every one of Sydney Possuelo's contact expeditions over the years has been different. In 1977 he led an encounter with the elusive Mayá in the far west of Brazil, a people who have rarely been seen since; in 1983, after months of deep penetration into forests of Pará, he eventually contacted a group of seventy Parakanã fleeing from the invasion of their territory; he also had a meeting with a tiny band of once feared Avá, not far from Brasília; in 1996 he made contact with the fearsome club-wielding Korubo of the Javari valley, who had previously smashed the skull of one of Sydney's close friends, Sobral Magalhães; and he encountered and later cared for part of the Zo'é people, the last large tribe to be contacted in Brazil.

As the years went by, Sydney became increasingly convinced that peoples in voluntary isolation should be left alone for as long as possible, with the state providing legal protection for their forested territories. This was the ethos of the Department of Isolated Peoples that he created in Funai, and it became the official policy of all the Spanish-speaking Amazonian nations and Paraguay. They confirmed this at a major conference, organized by Sydney in 2005, at which he kindly invited me to give the keynote speech.

Sydney Possuelo (Brazilian, b. 1940) learnt forest skills during five years with the Villas Bôas brothers on the Xingu. He joined Brazil's Indian service, Funai, in 1972 and conducted many expeditions for it, including the seven first contacts mentioned in this chapter. He created and ran Funai's Department of Isolated Peoples for many years until 2006, and in 1992–93 was a very successful President of Funai. During the brief period before he was ousted for political reasons, protected indigenous lands almost doubled. An eloquent champion of indigenous rights, Sydney Possuelo has gained many awards, including the Royal Geographical Society's Gold Medal.

John Hemming fully qualifies as one of the great modern explorers in his own right. Best known as Director of the Royal Geographical Society, London, for 21 years, he helped organize, and visited, eleven major research projects as well as establishing the Expedition Advisory Centre that has helped scores of British expeditions and expeditioners. In addition, he has been on numerous expeditions to every part of Peru and much of Brazil, visiting 45 indigenous tribes, four of them at the time of first contact, in hitherto unexplored country. In 1987/88 he led the Maraca Rainforest Project in northern Brazilian Amazonia. With 150 scientists and a further fifty rainforest technicians, this was the largest research project ever organized in Amazonia by a European country. His many books include *Tree of Rivers: The Story of the Amazon* (2008).

J. MICHAEL FAY

UNCONVENTIONAL EXPLORATIONS OF A CONSERVATIONIST IN THE 21ST CENTURY

MIDNIGHT, 30 JUNE 2011, MAKOUKOU, northern Gabon, central Africa. We gently push the dugout canoe into the glassy black waters that reflect the lights of Makoukou like a pane of glass. Mosquitoes swarm around my head; I sit on a pile of baggage. Guards from the Minkebe National Park mostly sit on sticks balanced on the thin edges of this hollowed out log. With ten people on board, and supplies for two weeks, we only have a couple of inches of wood between us and water. The captain, Moses, a local river rat, guns the 40hp Yamaha, and soon we are beyond the glint of town, bombing forwards into darkness. You could just make out the outline of the tall forest on the banks, plenty to give Moses his landmarks; he knows every log and rock in the Ivindo River.

Cramped and chilled, the engine whine pounds my eardrums – 'This is nuts', I thought. 'An elephant poacher we have in custody, who won't talk, keeps telling us he is a gold prospector. We suspect his gun and his shooters are still in the woods, and we need the gun and witnesses to convict him. We have one of his men, Waka, in the boat with us, hoping he'll talk once we get him alone. So now here we are in the pitch dark, at high speed, on this huge river, sitting in a log, looking for people who might not even exist.' The park warden figured they would slip in under the cover of night, the more chilled I got, the more sceptical I became.

As elsewhere in Africa, elephant poaching was out of control in Minkebe National Park, the largest and most pristine of the parks President El Hadj Omar Bongo Ondimba had created in Gabon in 2002. It had become a killing field. I was now back in Gabon helping getting management going in the parks – and stopping elephant slaughter was a top priority. The poaching was mixed with a gold rush, also fuelled by the resource free-for-all resulting from global demand, particularly from Asia. A gold camp I had left in 2004 containing 200 people had now exploded into a town of over 3,000, mostly Cameroonians and West Africans, many of whom were brought there with debts to be paid off with work. Even here at the terminus of the frontier, in the middle of this last, huge, virgin block of forest, with the elephanticide, the gold rush and the logging of the forest happening at lightning pace, it is a colossal challenge keeping humanity at bay and protecting what nature is left.

A light signalled ahead of us, sending flashes over the water. Boatmen do this when they hear another boat bearing down on them to avoid getting chopped in half. The flashing continued and we pulled alongside. Six men were crouched in a tiny dugout, quiet. The guards scanned the passengers,

THE FLASHING CONTINUED AND WE PULLED ALONGSIDE. SIX MEN WERE CROUCHED IN A TINY DUGOUT, QUIET.

asked two or three questions in Kwele, the local lingo, and said, that is our man. Frickin' miracle, this was the boat driver for the poacher. We invited him into our canoe, said goodbye to the others, and motored off. The guards told him that his boss had confessed and that if he didn't cooperate he was toast. We wanted to know where the gun was and the shooter, who we didn't even know existed for certain.

The park guards check out the passengers of a dugout canoe to see if the man they are after is among them.

After several tries, the boat driver told the guards he'd left the shooter in a village upstream. We pulled up to the village port, a muddy slough, and guided by the driver walked quietly to the house where he said the shooter was sleeping. Jean, one of the guards, rapped on the door. He insisted. The rest surrounded the cabin to make sure no one escaped. Silence. He must have given us the slip or the driver was lying. Jean signalled to us to pretend to walk away and then go still. A minute later there were whispers from inside the mud hut and the gendarmes stormed the place. The shooter was caught, a wiry Baka with a FIFA World Cup shirt on. The village chief and

THE GUARDS KEPT POINTING OUT CLEARINGS ON THE RIVER BANK THAT HAD ONCE TEEMED WITH ELEPHANTS AND BUFFALO BUT WERE NOW ABANDONED.

200 other people now poured out of their huts and the place went into a frenzy. The village chief came over, denied all knowledge of the poacher's activity and scolded the apprehended man for bringing this problem to the village (though nine times out of ten he's in on the deal as well). The shooter was handcuffed to a post in a house with two guards, otherwise he'd just bolt into the forest. The park warden was called via sat phone and he decided to send several of the guards and the boat driver we'd arrested earlier back to town to lighten our load and just take the other two men, both Baka, with us and a few guards. At 2.30 a.m. the show was over and we all hit the sack.

Next morning the village was calm. Jules, the shooter, ate bread and sardines for breakfast, a king's feast for him. Soon we were headed up the Oua River, into the unknown. Jules was still quiet, but now uncuffed. Waka was talking to him in French telling him to collaborate. Jules responded in Baka. Then we got our first breakthrough: Jules told Waka where the boat

A village in the jungle, with small wooden houses, seemingly quiet, and people going about their daily lives.

was stashed. We made our way up the backwater and sure enough there was the boat, its motor hidden away. Continuing up the Oua, which I had passed on my MegaTransect in 2000, the guards kept pointing out clearings on the river bank that had once teemed with elephants and buffalo but were now abandoned. We came to a fishermen's camp. The guards knew these guys, but both sides were subdued and suspicious – nobody is innocent in places like this. We ambled around looking for telltale signs of elephant poaching, but all we found was tiny fish smoking on racks. The guards bought some and we continued.

The river was getting smaller, with snags every hundred feet. The boat drivers have a system – gun the motor before you hit a log and lift the foot of the outboard just as you pass over it at 15 knots. It works – most of the time. We came to an abandoned guard camp. Only women present; they denied that there were any guns in the camp and said the men were back in town selling fish. A quick search netted several 12 gauge shells, one an elephant slug. The contents of the hut were burned and we kept the shells for evidence. The women were told to vacate the camp immediately. These people do everything – fish, hunt pigs, duikers and elephants, and prospect for gold at the same time. They are frontier people, struggling simply to survive. This is the frontline.

Late in the evening we came to an old camp in a spot that was once an enormous elephant clearing, full of animals, but now it was covered in tall grass with just a few lily trotters for wildlife. We built a fire, made smoked fish stew, and started working on Jules. The guards told him that his boss had put all the blame on him and that he would go to jail in Libreville if he didn't take us to the gun, all the while giving him cigarettes, food and a tent

Below left A handful of large shells found in an old guard camp; among them was one capable of killing an elephant.

Below right At a fishermen's camp the guards look around and question people, buying some fish before moving on in the search for evidence of elephant poaching.

We follow the trail gouged out by the huge machinery used to log vast tracts of primary forest at a frightening rate.

to sleep in. He said there was no gun; still no smile, but looks of fear with that image of a cell in a faraway city with no family to bring him food. Waka must have given Jules elderly advice in the night because next morning he was ready to take us to where he'd hidden the gun. We ate breakfast and Jules cracked a half smile. He was starting to be our friend. Off we went on another eight hours of log hopping. At one point our driver dived into the water; before I could wonder why I got zapped in the head by a hornet, then another, then ten. Everyone was in the water. We passed an enormous python, the biggest one I have ever seen, coiled up on a snag in the river like a pile of truck tyres.

Finally Jules signalled us to stop – four hours' walk to the west was where he had hidden the gun. The Malaysian loggers had just bulldozed a road in there. He said that was where lots of elephant poaching was going on right now, because of access and the abundance of nature – but not for long. Next morning we followed Jules through swamps and dense underbrush. He just slipped through the forest without making a sound. The filaria flies were biting my ankles leaving itchy welts, but I was right behind the others. After four hours of pounding I could sense a change: rays of light in the understorey, denser growth, 'a road', I thought. Sure enough, not far ahead was the chasm the Malaysians had just bladed into the forest. D8 Caterpillars are amazing machines and this is the first time one had ever been here. These guys were unbelievably deep, ripping through tens of thousands of acres of primary forest a year, taking every big tree, causing a wave of poaching.

**THESE GUYS WERE UNBELIEVABLY DEEP,
RIPPING THROUGH TENS OF THOUSANDS
OF ACRES OF PRIMARY FOREST A YEAR,
TAKING EVERY BIG TREE,
CAUSING A WAVE OF POACHING.**

Above left The abandoned gold camp at Minkebe. Over 3,000 people had been here just days before, desperately trying to make a living mining gold, often hoping to pay off debts.

Above right Stark evidence that in this part of Africa gun running was also a situation that needed tackling, linked to elephant poaching and illegal gold mining.

We cruised along the road to its end, walked a now abandoned elephant trail, and from under a log Jules pulled out a bit of plastic. Inside was a Slovenian .458 elephant rifle and thirty-eight giant bullets. All I could see was thirty-eight more dead elephants. We filmed his confession. He recounted all the elephants he had killed in the past year for our apprehended poacher, but much more scary was his description of bands of forty-plus Cameroonian hunters he had seen who'd come all the way from the Minkebe gold camp for elephants. He said they were emptying the forest – a complete slaughter, hundreds of elephants being killed, and this was from a man who knew. We knew it too, but his descriptions made the blood rush to my head, I was sick, wondering how could we stop this – over 3,000 people in Minkebe and growing, the price of gold climbing, global demand out of control.

Back in Makoukou I alerted the head of parks who informed the president, Ali Bongo Ondimba. The Minkebe gold camp was an urgent matter of national security. Not only were they slaughtering their way through the last major stronghold of forest elephants on Earth, but West African and Cameroonian poachers and criminals were infiltrating the entire country, smuggling kilograms of gold and ivory north and guns, ammunition and women for hire south.

Two days later a general landed in Makoukou with 100 troops, a Puma helicopter, and all they needed for a long stint in the forest. They were heading for Minkebe gold camp to give the miners 72 hours to leave. I went to the gold camp three days later. Among the shanty town of wooden shacks and the enormous gold pit there were just a few straggling miners, goats, chickens and soldiers milling around. The general said everyone left in a calm, orderly way. For many it was probably good fortune; a lot of the men digging in these gold camps are highly indebted to the people who brought them there. Where hundreds of generators and pumps and boom boxes had drowned out the cacophony of the jungle days before, I could now hear the calls of blue touracos and hornbills. Peace had come to this place, and not a single shot had been fired. The 3,000 miners had walked peacefully over a hundred kilometres back on the same trail they came in on. In the days that followed most of the satellite gold camps scattered in the forest were also evacuated and the elephants of Minkebe were given a reprieve.

ONLY MASSIVE, HISTORIC, DIFFICULT DECISIONS TO PROTECT THOSE RESOURCES THAT STILL REMAIN WILL PUT A STOP TO GLOBAL COLLAPSE.

People have no idea of the resource plunder that is ploughing its way into every last frontier on this planet, bringing the consumptive force of 7 billion humans with it. Only massive, historic, difficult decisions by everyone to protect those resources that still remain will put a stop to global collapse. I live it every day. World leaders dream of saving the planet by trading an invisible gas we call CO_2, and they are even failing at that. We need to get real.

J. Michael Fay (American, b. 1956) volunteered with the Peace Corps before specializing in ecology and conservation. He is best known for his 455-day MegaTransect journey in 1999–2000, when he walked 3,200 km (1,988 miles) across Africa, deliberately avoiding all areas of population. He borrowed the 'transect' concept from biology and used it as a method of evaluating the wildlife levels of the equatorial forests of Africa. In 2004, in MegaFlyover, he and pilot Peter Ragg spent months flying 112,650 km (70,000 miles) in a small plane at low altitude, taking photographs every twenty seconds to produce a photodocumentation of the continent. More recently, in 2006, he became involved in actively seeking out and attempting to halt wildlife destruction in central Africa.

WADE DAVIS
TRAVERSING THE DARIEN GAP

Sebastian Snow (right) leans on my shoulder, in March 1974, shortly after finding the road head in Panama, having walked the Darien Gap in the rainy season.

IN 1974, WHEN I WAS TWENTY, an eccentric geographer attached to the botanical garden in Medellín told me about a British expedition intent on traversing the Darien Gap, a broad expanse of roadless swamp and rainforest that separates Colombia from Panama. The expedition turned out to be one man, Sebastian Snow, an English adventurer who, having just walked from Tierra del Fuego at the tip of South America, intended to continue north as far as Alaska. It was June, the height of the rainy season, and the Darien was said to be impassable.

Our route from Colombia took us on foot from Barranquillita, a ramshackle settlement just off the Medellín–Turbo road, 96 km (60 miles) west across the Tumaradó swamp to Puerto Libre, a row of huts strung out along the bank of the Río Atrato. The Atrato runs 645 km (400 miles) south to north, draining the Chocó, the wettest region of South America, 77,694 sq. km (30,000 sq. miles) of forgotten rainforest cut off from the Amazon millions of years ago by the rise of the Andean Cordillera. Downstream from Puerto Libre is the Gulf of Urabá and the Caribbean. Upstream is more swamp and rainforest, and a land that for Colombians is synonymous with disease and disappointment.

Like so many lowland settlements, Puerto Libre was a place of lassitude, strangely at odds with the intensity of life that surrounded it in the forest. It consisted of ten sun-bleached shacks and three floating outhouses – one to relieve oneself in, one to wash in and one to draw water. The lives of the local women revolved around these riverfront latrines. They were there with the children at dawn, and there they remained for much of the day, washing clothes or idly gossiping. In the evening, when the night air finally offered some relief from the heat, mosquitoes rose

Sebastian Snow (left) and two Emberá companions and porters fording the Río Cacarica.

from the river like a miasma, driving everyone indoors to the isolation of their netted hammocks. Once it was dark, caiman came ashore by the score and for the rest of the night sprawled on the grassy slopes leading up to the shacks, or lay about on the wooden landings where so few hours before children and infants had bathed.

After three miserable days, including a morning when I awoke on the floor to discover that a dog had given birth on my foot, a local skin trader ferried our party upriver to a place called La Loma. There we hired mules to carry our gear beyond the Atrato up a narrow track that crossed the Río Cacarica and rose towards the Darien. Three days later, having abandoned the mules and hired three Emberá Indians as guides, we reached the height of land at Palo des Letras, the border between Colombia and Panama

ONCE BEYOND THE FRONTIER, WE ENTERED A WORLD OF PLANTS, WATER AND SILENCE.

that, as the name suggests, is marked only by a pair of letters carved into the bark of a tree. Once beyond the frontier, we entered a world of plants, water and silence. For the next ten days we moved from one Emberá or Kuna village to the next, soliciting new guides and obtaining provisions as we went along. Nowhere did we stop long enough to understand the lives that we drifted through, but each day became part of a veil that gradually enveloped us as the forest closed in, absorbing our party as the ocean swallows a diver.

It was during those days that I first experienced the overwhelming grandeur of the tropical rainforest. It is a subtle thing. There are no herds of ungulates as on the Serengeti plain, no cascades of orchids – just a thousand shades of green, an infinitude of shape, form and texture that mocks

Sebastian Snow (right) with Don Lubin, standing by an enormous ceiba tree, in the Darien forests of Panama.

the terminology of temperate botany. It is almost as if you have to close your eyes to behold the constant hum of biological activity – evolution, if you will – working in overdrive. From the edge of trails creepers lash out at the base of trees, and heliconias and calatheas give way to broad-leafed aroids that climb into the shadows. Overhead, lianas drape from immense trees, binding the canopy of the forest into a single interwoven fabric of life. There are no flowers, at least few that can be readily seen, and, with the blazing sun hovering motionless at midday, there are few sounds. In the air is a fluid heaviness, a weight of centuries, of years without seasons, of life without rebirth. One can walk for hours yet remain convinced that not a mile has been gained.

Then, towards dusk, everything changes: the air cools, the light becomes amber, and the open sky above the rivers and swamps fills with darting swallows and swifts, kiskadees and flycatchers. The hawks, herons, jacanas and kingfishers of the river margins give way to flights of cackling parrots, sungrebes and nunbirds, and spectacular displays of toucans and scarlet macaws. Squirrel monkeys appear, and from the riverbanks emerge caiman, eyes poking out of the water, tails and bodies as still and dull as driftwood. In the light of dusk one can finally discern shapes in the forest, sloths clinging to the limbs of cecropia trees, vipers entwined in branches, tapirs wallowing in distant sloughs. For a brief moment at twilight the forest seems of a human scale and somehow manageable. But then with the night comes the rain and later the sound of insects running wild through the trees until, with the dawn, once again silence. The air becomes still and steam rises from the cool earth. White fog lies all about like something solid, all consuming.

Sebastian Snow (right) with Don Leo, our muleteer, and Don Lubin, in La Loma, Colombia. Both men accompanied our party as far as the Panamanian frontier at Palo de Letras, where the border was marked by just a pair of letters scratched into the bark of a tree.

After just a fortnight on the trail, our passage began to take on the tone of a dream. In part this was because we rarely slept. With the rain, sleep was not often possible. At the end of long days we simply lay in our hammocks in an unnatural rest, like a state of trance, dulled by exhaustion and insulated from the night by mosquito-netting and the smoke of a smouldering fire. But mostly we became infected by the spirit of the place. The Darien turned out to be less a piece of terrain than a state of mind, a wild frontier utterly divorced from the moral inhibitions of ordinary human society.

In each of the small villages – Paya, Capeti, Yape, El Común – that marked the route from the frontier to the main settlement at Yavisa, there was a recent story of murder or death. On the Río Cacarica five men had fought and wounded one another with machetes. In Capeti a Colombian thief known as Mentiroso Serio, the 'Serious Liar', killed a woman and was himself hunted down, shot and strung up in the forest beyond Paya, just short of the Colombian frontier. Seven Indians were murdered on the Río Chico; a Colombian was killed for his cooking utensils on the trail to Tigre; a man and his wife were fatally tortured near Yavisa. Those investigating these crimes, or at least recording them in their mouldy logbooks, were the Guardia Civil, a clumsy and corrupt paramilitary force then under the command of a young Manuel Noriega.

Midway through our journey, trouble with the Guardia Civil at Yavisa forced us to change our route. Stripped of most of our gear and driven away from the settlement, we followed three Kuna guides up a series of rockfalls and cascades, a serpentine route designed to evade pursuit. In the process the Kuna themselves became disorientated, and for the next week we wandered through the forest lost or, at best, only vaguely aware of where we were. Free of distractions, one became honed by life in the forest – the howler monkeys overhead, the incessant streams of ants, chance encounters with snakes and jaguar, the haunting cries of harpy eagles, iridescent butterflies, teasing with their delicate beauty, and at one's feet bronze and purple frogs, poisonous to the touch. In my journal I noted the simple luxuries of forest life:

WE HESITATED, MOMENTARILY CONFOUNDED BY SO MUCH SPACE.

> the smoke of a fire that chases away the insects, a rainless night,
> a thatch hut found in the woods, a banana almost gone bad found
> lying in a trough, abandoned plantings of manioc, a fresh kill,
> whatever it might be, water deep enough to bathe in, a hint of
> a solid shit, a full night's sleep, a lemon tree found in the forest.

By the time we came upon the roadhead some 32 km (20 miles) east of Santa Fe, the cumulative effect of his two years on the road had physically broken my English companion. In all he had lost 23 kg (50 lb). Leaving him with one of the Kuna, the remainder of our party went ahead to seek help. Several miles on, we came upon the right-of-way of the Pan-American Highway, a cleared and flattened corridor that stretched to the horizon. We hesitated, momentarily confounded by so much space. Then we began to walk past the charred silhouettes of trees and on to a beaten track that meandered through the slash. It was several hours before we heard the sound of machinery – chainsaws at first and then the dull roar of diesel trucks. We walked for another mile or two before coming upon a D9

Sebastian Snow and Don Leo
in the forests of Colombia,
shortly before mules were
abandoned and the expedition
proceeded on foot.

Caterpillar, the largest bulldozer made, buried up to its cab in the mud.
A second bulldozer, snorting and belching smoke, tore into the ground
with its blade, while two others, attached to the trapped machine with thick
cables, attempted to haul it out. None of the workmen noticed us. The
sound was deafening, with the hiss and moan of hydraulics and iron cables
snapping like strings, and the air was full of the smell of grease and oil.

The Kuna had never seen machinery of such a scale. Clinging to their
rifles, struggling through the cloying mud, they walked past the bulldoz-
ers and gravitated towards a small work gang clustered at a bridge site
half a mile beyond. It was dusk and the crew had broken for dinner, served
by Kuna kitchen boys from a mobile canteen. The foreman asked where
we had come from. When I said Colombia, the workers in a single gesture
leaned forward to offer us their plates of food. I looked about, invited my

companions to eat, and then glanced past the foreman to the road ahead, a scene of desolation that ran north as far as one could see. He followed my gaze. 'The civilization of nature', he said, 'is never pretty.'

Four days later, having successfully crossed the Darien, I abandoned Sebastian to his walk, and at Santa Fe I climbed aboard a small plane for the short hop to Panama City. A last-minute addition to the passenger list, I was squeezed into the rear seat, my knees pushed up to my chest, unable to move and scarcely able to breathe. The pilot flew us immediately into a tremendous tropical storm. Visibility dropped to nil. The woman beside me threw up on my lap. Her mother, a corpulent merchant, turned to offer consolation and promptly threw up herself. For a few anxious moments, as the winds buffeted the plane, I feared that having successfully survived the Darien I was about to die ignominiously. When we finally landed at Panama City, I walked off the plane drenched in vomit, with only the clothes on my back and two dollars to my name. As for Sebastian, the last I heard he made it as far as Costa Rica before being admitted to a hospital. In the middle of the night he awoke and left in his pyjamas, starting to walk north. He was arrested and spent a delirious week in jail before being rescued by a staff member at the British Embassy, who bundled him back to England.

Wade Davis (Canadian, b. 1953) has been described as a 'rare combination of scientist, scholar, poet and passionate defender of all of life's diversity'. An ethnographer, writer and photographer, he holds degrees in anthropology and biology and received his Ph.D. in ethnobotany, all from Harvard University. A National Geographic Society Explorer-in-Residence, his work over the last decade has taken him from the Amazon to Tibet, from the Arctic to Africa, from Australia to Mongolia, from Polynesia to New Guinea. He is an Honorary Member of the Explorers Club, a Fellow of the Royal Geographical Society and an Honorary Member and Fellow of the Royal Canadian Geographical Society (RCGS). In 2009 he received the Gold Medal from the RCGS for his contributions to the fields of anthropology and conservation, and in 2011 was the recipient of the Explorers Medal, the highest award of the Explorers Club. In 2012 he received the Fairchild Medal for Plant Exploration. He is the author of many books including *One River* (1996) and *Into the Silence: The Great War, Mallory and the Conquest of Everest* (2011), which won the Samuel Johnson prize.

carefully stowed my insect nets, beating trays, plastic bags, vials, marking pens, notebooks, clippers, aspirators, cameras, water, Oreos, and more. Pre-dawn, the enormous balloon was swollen and glowing in the dark, its primary colours taking on a surreal look. Just prior to launch, Dany Cleyet-Marrel, the balloon's engineer-pilot, detected some trouble with the fuel pump. In the final countdown phase, our mission was aborted. We were sad, but relieved not to experience any breakdowns high above the treetops. This was the first mechanical mishap in 206 flights, an admirable track record when compared to most airborne vehicles.

At 4.30 a.m. the next day we donned our canopy gear again. Liftoff was achieved. Once airborne, it was wonderful to be again high in the canopy. No method is as exhilarating as dangling aloft in the canopy under a hot-air balloon. We sampled nine canopy trees in one hour – a result that would normally require several days using slingshots and ropes. Not only that, but we sampled the uppermost branches of the canopy as well as mid-canopy, making these sled samples more comprehensive than relying on single rope techniques alone. Half way through our transect the sled flew over the larger inflatable raft that is lowered on top of the canopy and rests there as a lofty base camp. Perched on top waving to us was Gilles Ebersoldt, the French engineer who designed the inflatables. He had slept in the canopy the previous night. We hovered over him because Francis had asked me to deliver a small surprise. From my pack emerged a long, crusty loaf of French bread. I shouted 'Patisserie, monsieur' and dropped the bread on his head. To this day, he exclaims about having room service delivered to him in the canopy. Sailing gracefully onwards to new green treetops, my body glistened with sweat, mud, leaf fragments, dew, petals and chips of bark that were stirred up by our fast-moving nets and clippers as we collected flowers, insects and branch material. Soon the centre of our sled became a cornucopia of botanical booty. Fortunately we encountered no ants' nests, one of the biggest dangers of sled-sampling.

NO METHOD IS AS EXHILARATING AS DANGLING ALOFT IN THE CANOPY UNDER A HOT-AIR BALLOON.

When we landed, all the scientists scrambled into the sled like sharks in a feeding frenzy, grabbing bits of botanical specimens that represented their specific interests. Francis wanted collections of woody branches to test his hypothesis about aerial roots. Patrick requested flowering branches for the herbarium in Montpellier, France. I picked out leaf samples from mature branches to measure herbivory levels. And Robin wanted vines, preferably in flower, for identification. On his descent from the raft,

Francis in his delightful broken English asked what I thought of the ride in the new sled. My response, using a word I had picked up from my children, was 'Awesome!' 'Awesome?' Francis mulled over this new word. 'Awesome', he practised several times, and then smiled at me, 'I like that new word.'

Nothing quite describes sleeping in the canopy. For no reason other than my sense of wonder, I sleep in the canopies of every research site. Occasionally I find nocturnal insects worthy of observation, but their discovery does not usually require sleeping at the top. It is simply fun to experience this lofty world by dark. About four of us decided to sleep on the treetop raft one clear, warm night. Without light, our climbing rope looked like a liana that disappeared into a black hole above our heads. We climbed up through the dark understorey, past the cathedral of the mid-canopy, and eventually reached the raft and sprawled out on the mesh, with myriad constellations ablaze overhead. We were silenced by the beauty of this starry galaxy, and by our appreciation of the diversity within the canopy roof beneath us in darkness. Dark clouds rolled in the distance. Soon, thunder clapped directly overhead. We scrambled, desperately trying to hide under one tiny tarp that covered the extra ropes. The heavens let loose. I brought out my field umbrella and for a brief moment felt very smart.

Below left The hot-air balloon hovers over the canopy raft, a third component of inflatables used for canopy exploration.

Below right The tropical forest canopy is hot and dry, a veritable desert, rendering me prostrate with exhaustion on several occasions.

The first canopy walkway in North America was constructed in oak-maple-beech forest at Williams College, Massachusetts.

My joy was short-lived, however. In no time, I was sitting in a pool of water as the rain pelted sideways, soaking every square inch of my body. There was nothing to do but laugh about our wet-canopy-slumber party. We all dozed eventually and awoke to a steamy sunrise, in a soggy, smelly state.

Just think for a minute about the lifestyles of plants – you're restricted to one spot, you cannot move from your enemies and are subject to being clipped or bitten or ripped by mobile creatures throughout your entire existence. How do you survive? It has all the elements of a horror film, with the unsuspecting green plant the victim of every potential marauder that moves in and threatens to devour it. No doubt all plants would have been extinct long ago if it wasn't for their unique mechanisms of defence: chemicals, thorns, stinging hairs and toughness.

Chemicals found in nature have always been a major part of human culture too. Peoples in South America dip their blowpipe darts in toxins obtained from certain plants or frogs (curare), which instantly poison the speared animal. The chemicals in quinine bark provided a cure for malaria. Tannins in oak trees not only prevent herbivores from eating their foliage, but are also used to preserve leather. In the canopy, it is possible to identify plants with the most effective toxins or chemicals to defend their tissues from predators simply because nothing eats them. These chemicals in turn represent the global pharmacy that could be a source of important cures for human diseases.

We might have collected more leaves for chemical analyses had it not been for the weather towards the end of our expedition. The rains began gently. Then, during the final balloon trip, enormous clouds gathered overhead. Down came the balloon and with it the rain. Packing a wet, heavy

Canopy walkways offer continual access to forest canopies to enable observation and discovery, as here in Belize.

balloon was no easy task: waterfalls of rain gushed over the fabric as we folded it. And worse, on its descent the balloon had wafted into the trees and the entire operation nearly got caught in the canopy forever.

That night the heavens really opened. Lying in my hammock, I was thankful that this was my last night for a long time with knees bent backwards in my swaying 'bed', subjected to surround-sound snoring. The wall of rains approached like a tsunami, roaring in the distance. The downpour was magnified on the tin roof, but at least the snoring was drowned out. On the final morning, a few stalwart biologists manned the balloon for its last flight. Francis and I stood by, looking on and discussing our next expedition. Like proud grandparents, we watched that morning's team successfully achieve liftoff. In the heat and humidity after the monsoon-like rains, my entire body was one pool of perspiration. I could barely see through my steamed-up glasses, and clothing stuck to my body like skin. Francis was in the same condition, so we just laughed. Walking back to our last breakfast, after the balloon was safely crated up, we got drenched yet again. Much as I love the challenges of rainforest fieldwork, this trip seemed particularly rough – extreme heat, high humidity and heavy rains. I have never sweated so much, or experienced such a sleep deficit. Nonetheless, the camaraderie of an international group and the thrill of 'sledding' in the treetops formed lifelong memories.

The canopy is a global heritage, and I am honoured to be one of its stewards. If we can educate the public about this important region of the planet, and inspire the next generation of explorers, then the adversity of the expedition is more than justified. And if asked by Francis Hallé to go on another balloon expedition, I know what my answer will be – 'That sounds awesome!'

Meg Lowman (American, b. 1953) pioneered the science of canopy ecology, and uses her research to inspire sustainability of the world's forests. She works tirelessly in Australia, India, South America and Africa (as well as the United States) to promote environmental literacy through citizen science. She facilitates policy solutions using science education as a tool, drawing upon a lifetime of research and conservation. She also built the first canopy walkway in North America. 'Canopymeg' is Director of the Nature Research Center, North Carolina Museum of Natural Science, and Professor at North Carolina State University. Her personal mantra is 'no child left indoors'.

MARTIN HOLLAND

INTERACTIVE IN THE HEART OF BORNEO

I FOLLOWED ASPOR'S EYES to see what he had detected. It was 5 a.m. and the first warmth of the day was making the moist earth and vegetation of the rainforest steam, creating a still mist that hung in the air. Just enough of the cool pre-dawn light was penetrating the forest canopy to give the mist a bluish tinge. Aspor stared, his eyes searching, betraying none of the playfulness he usually displayed as our head guide. This was Aspor the skilled hunter, the Dayak.

I looked for any sign of movement, any shape or colour that seemed out of place. I was staring into a half-lit cacophony of visual noise draped in a shroud of vapour. Huge trees with enormous buttresses vied with lianas, figs, rattan and saplings for sunlight and attention. Not for the first time I looked at Aspor clueless, searching for some guidance. As I turned to face him I caught him wafting the air towards his nostrils for a scent.

Of course I smelled nothing that I could identify, but suddenly Aspor tensed and pointed into the middle distance, motioning for me to listen. I strained to hear, trying to zone out the orchestral drones, buzzes and clicks. Minutes seemed to pass until finally my ears picked up a sound that at first I didn't even really hear. I knew I'd caught something that stood out, and Aspor knew it too. We sat in silence, barely breathing, listening. It came again and now I heard it properly: a deep, rumbling grumble that I thought was thunder. All that fuss for a storm gathering over the mountains. But there it was again, rolling towards us through the forest like a slowly tumbling wave, but it was not thunder – the sound was wrong, and it came from low to the ground. It was guttural and spine tingling. It was animal.

As we tuned into the source, Aspor and I shared glances and listened, enthralled, to this intermittently growling creature moving around in the

The navigable end of the great Joloi River, in the very heart of the island of Borneo.

distant forest, sometimes higher, sometimes lower, until Aspor whispered two words to me: 'macan dahan'– clouded leopard. He said there were two, a mother and a cub; based on my experience with Aspor I was certainly inclined to believe him.

It was January 2011 and we were 5 km (3 miles) from our base camp in the Heart of Borneo rainforest, which in turn was 30 km (19 miles) from the closest village and 140 km (87 miles) from the nearest paved road. Despite the comforts and gadgets we had brought with us, I knew then, in a deep and profound sense, that I was immersed in a world that was oblivious to man.

Aspor and I were out with the canopy access team, Holli and James, preparing for a dawn ascent. We spent the rest of the morning hauling ourselves and our camera gear 24 m (80 ft) up into the canopy to film the wildlife that we hoped would be attracted by a fruiting fig tree. James and I had seen binturong, the so-called bearcat, snoozing in this tree the previous day, but apart from some huge prehistoric-looking hornbills, pumping their wings noisily through the sky, we saw nothing.

DESPITE THE COMFORTS AND GADGETS WE HAD BROUGHT WITH US, I KNEW THEN, IN A DEEP AND PROFOUND SENSE, THAT I WAS IMMERSED IN A WORLD THAT WAS OBLIVIOUS TO MAN.

Back at Camp Foyle, our temporary research station, I cautiously told the story of our encounter to the rest of the team, expecting the usual healthy dose of scientific scepticism. Jan, a German entomologist and specialist in the moths of northern Borneo, quietly slipped away and returned with his camera. He had photographed a print the day before on the Ridgeway Trail, the main path we had cut north from Camp Foyle to

Aspor, a Siang Dayak, true friend and the expedition's head guide.

service our survey transects. We loaded it on to our laptop and scrutinized it. Without doubt it was the print of cat, and since Jan had used his little finger for scale in the picture, we could work out its size, proving that at least one clouded leopard was roaming the area around our base camp. The print was found just 15 minutes' walk along the trail.

This was why we were here: to provide the first scientific data on the species present in an area of primary rainforest that is under imminent threat. We were seven weeks into an eight-week survey, camped close to the River Mohot in the very centre of the island of Borneo, in the Murung Raya district of Central Kalimantan, Indonesia. The densely forested, ravine-ridden Schwaner Mountains rose dramatically out of the forest to the west and the north, while extraction industries and development edged closer and closer to the south and the east. Two villages, Tumbang Naan and Tumbang Tohan were, like us, caught in the middle.

It had taken eighteen months of planning, preparation and fundraising to get the team to Jakarta – and our research area was still so remote that it took a further four weeks of navigating through customs, immigration, market stalls, local negotiations and ever-diminishing rivers to get there. We were completely self-sufficient at this site for two months, meaning we had carried enough food to last one man over three years, as well as 960 litres (210 gallons) of fuel, two generators, three inverters, a bank of car batteries, two solar panels, five laptops, camera and video equipment, and all the research equipment needed for the surveys, including canopy access gear and twenty-five camera traps. In all we estimated our kit and supplies weighed over 3.5 tonnes.

Below left Just before leaving Camp Foyle at the end of the expedition I film a piece to camera with lead scientist Tim van Berkel.

Below right Tim van Berkel using a Toughbook to check camera trap images live from the field, about 4 km (2½ miles) from Camp Foyle.

During an aerial survey as part of a recce of the research area in February 2010 I took the opportunity to film.

Moving from the coastal city of Banjarmasin to our research site in the centre of the island meant loading and unloading all this equipment twelve times on to progressively smaller boats, with one short jeep ride along a logging road. This was a mammoth effort, especially along the last stretch of the Joloi River where we formed a chain gang to pass the bags and boxes up and down muddy banks or along thin, slippery poles leading to half-submerged floating landings, before transferring them into the flotilla of small wooden boats that ferried us between villages.

At Camp Foyle we constructed four huts, covered by enormous tarpaulins, to eat, sleep, work and store supplies in, accommodating around twenty people on average, but sometimes up to twenty-five – plus a rescued sun bear cub called Gumbo and a troop of rowdy chickens. Research went on around the clock: as one team came back after a diurnal survey, another would be preparing to leave for a nocturnal one in search of mammals, reptiles or amphibians. The canopy access team were almost always out, cursing or singing when they returned depending on their luck in the arduous task of using a giant catapult to fire lines 25 m (80 ft) up into the canopy. When not in the field, the scientists on the team would be inspecting specimens for clues to their identification, recording their findings and backing up their results.

WE DID ALL THIS FROM ONE OF THE MOST REMOTE AND DIFFICULT AREAS ON EARTH, USING A SATELLITE TERMINAL THE SIZE OF A LAPTOP.

We were not only a research expedition, however. Technology has reached the stage where it is practical, affordable and simple enough to create what we called an interactive expedition. By making use of the latest satellite hardware and software we could give schools, youth groups and

A logging road snakes through dense rainforest, demonstrating that even the most remote areas of Borneo are under threat.

people all over the world the chance to engage fully with our expedition in real time. We filmed and took photographs every day, turning this multimedia into professionally crafted videos, galleries and blog posts that told the world of our discoveries as they happened, and shared our day-to-day experiences of life in the rainforest.

News of the discovery of clouded leopards reached the world via our website the same day. And when Aspor stumbled upon a reticulated python and king cobra locked in a battle to the death in a stream near our camp, we were able to grab our cameras, rush to the scene and record the first ever footage of such an encounter. We marvelled as the cobra survived forty-five minutes held underwater by the python, before the cobra's venom kicked in and the python succumbed. The resulting five-minute film was sent back for viewing the same evening.

We were even able to take part in the first video link with a live audience in the brand new Attenborough Studio in the Natural History Museum, London. We did two, just for good measure, and also answered questions from live audiences on the *Guardian* newspaper website at the beginning and end of the expedition. We did all this from one of the most remote and difficult areas on Earth, using a satellite terminal the size of a laptop.

But it was worth it. Scientific research into biodiversity levels and species composition is a vital first step in protecting the richest areas of what rainforest is left in Borneo. Without such information, government departments have no way of deciding which areas can be developed and which should be protected.

In the modern world, interactive multimedia allows us to go beyond contributing data to policy makers and advocacy groups, or simply telling exciting stories of new species and writing adventure entertainment articles. Explorers have always had a duty to share their discoveries with the public. Today, that duty extends to pushing the boundaries of the communications technology available in order to share experiences and discoveries as widely and as engagingly as possible. It's not quite taking the world to the rainforest, but it is bringing the rainforest to the world.

And it was fun. Filming them gave each of the scientists a chance to demonstrate the techniques they were using to study the rainforest, and the discoveries they were making. Some of the team were born for the camera, such as our entomologist, Rusty, whose ability to explain the wonders of the insect world in his Bug Diaries made for some of the best videos of the expedition. Others, such as James, our photographer, who set the record for one scene at over sixty takes, took a little longer.

Dale Mortiboys and Tim van Berkel working late into the night in the well-powered Science and Media Tent.

We made adventurous films about exploring above the rapids on the river and also tried to find time to explain topics such as biodiversity and rainforest ecosystems. Dale, the expedition herpetologist, introduced snakes, lizards and amphibians to our audience with his enigmatic wit and prose, bringing the phrase 'doom shot' to the world when he described the bite of a juvenile pit viper. I filmed Lara, our primatologist, simply sitting in the forest at around 5 a.m., barely speaking as she listened to four separate gibbon troops making territorial calls to each other, some as close as just 50 m (165 ft) away. The wonder and excitement on her face as she waited to hear the next great call was mesmerizing. Holli gave an excellent account of her research in the canopy, and Tim, our lead scientist, happily put up with me following him around as he inspected his mammal traps and camera traps.

I was touched by the enthusiasm that each of the scientists had for their subject, and for the films I asked them to make. It seemed to me that the camera offered a release for a frustrated desire to communicate their work, to explain it and share it beyond academic journals.

We ended the expedition with a string of discoveries, including the sighting of a binturong with facial markings not previously recorded in Borneo, and proof that a hybrid gibbon species we were hoping to find was indeed present in the area. As Tim and I filmed the final video of the expedition, being the last team members at Camp Foyle, we were surrounded by gibbons calling in a manner that neither we nor our guides had ever heard before. And as we waited for the last boat to return to collect us, Aspor told us his tales of tigers and nomads stalking the forest-covered mountains above us.

Already, despite the weight loss, subcutaneous worm infestations, skin rashes, cuts, grazes, bites and stings, twisted ankles, bouts of diarrhoea, the monotonous food and constant humidity, the exhaustion, fatigue, and the dreams we all had of cool winds, chilled beer and fresh Caesar salad – despite all that, before we had even left, we were aching to return.

Martin Holland (British, b. 1984) is a young explorer, educator and environmentalist, who attempted his first expedition at eighteen with a solo effort overland from the United Kingdom to Australia. He has worked in over thirty countries around the world, both on expeditions and through his work with charitable organizations. By twenty-one, Martin had established himself as a leader in direct communications and fundraising, building an international reputation, before studying for simultaneous degrees in environmental and multimedia fields. As leader of the Murung Raya Expedition he won the Royal Geographical Society Neville Shulman Challenge Award and ZSL Erasmus Darwin Award, among others, and the expedition was later named Expedition of the Year by *Explorer* magazine. He is a photojournalist and filmmaker, and wrote his first book, *Rodrigues: Paradise Lost?*, in 2009. He is founder and Director of the Heart of Borneo Project.

The Murung Raya Expedition team on the last day of the expedition, after two months living and working in the rainforest. Crossing this felled tree was the only safe route from Camp Foyle to the network of transects used to conduct our research.

MOUNTAIN

The instinct to climb is basic and observable in all children everywhere. In some it remains into adulthood, and is refined by a love of discovery and adventure into the urge to explore unclimbed peaks. Many who start with merely technical ambitions find they develop a love of the mountains themselves, for the views from on high, the incredible sense of majestic, unchanged nature. Man may tame the forest and bridge the river, but mountains remain constant, providing each generation with new challenges and new vistas.

Mountains are cold and windy environments; climbers respond by becoming hardy and creative in the way they deal with this. Depending on the season, a mountain can change profoundly, creating more variations for a climber to explore. And the threat of avalanche or rockfall or crevasse makes climbing one of the most potentially dangerous of exploration activities.

There are many unclimbed peaks on this planet – in the Himalaya and the polar regions especially. Drawn by the promise of blue skies against monstrous pillars of snow and ice, mountain explorers have much to anticipate. Alone, or in small groups, the mountain explorer tastes in great concentration the raw elements of exploration: route finding, discovery, taking risks on an untried path, the final exaltation of victory when they arrive at the summit – and the world laid out, distant and perfect, around them.

The knife-edge ridge of Shivling pierces the sky as Chris Bonington approaches the summit, where no one has stood before.

STEPHEN VENABLES

THE SIACHEN GLACIER: ICE HIGHWAY

NOW THAT THE WHOLE WORLD CAN BE SEEN on our own computers at the click of a mouse, the only real explorers are the people who go underground or beneath the ocean waves; the land surface holds no more secrets. Or so it would seem, until you begin to examine the finer detail, particularly in the steepest places that never quite show up on the satellite pictures. One of the great joys of mountaineering is that – on a microcosmic scale at least – there are still endless nooks and crannies to explore, knowledge gaps to fill. The scope is limitless.

My most memorable climbs have been exploratory ones, journeys into the unknown. In Nepal it was thrilling to leave the well-trodden Everest trail and soon find ourselves in the jungle, kukri knives hacking through dense bamboo, forcing our way up a trackless gorge, to emerge eventually beneath the untouched southwest face of Kusum Kanguru; yet more thrilling, three weeks later, was the discovery that the soaring granite chimney we had eyed through the telescope was indeed a viable route up the final pillar to the summit. Even on that most hackneyed mountain, Everest itself, I felt privileged to join an American-Canadian team forging a new route up the giant Kangshung Face. A couple of years earlier, in Pakistan, I got a similar buzz reaching the summit of the Solu Tower, high above the glacial bowl of Snow Lake, knowing that no human being had stood there before.

There is an undeniable egotistical delight in simply being first. But the real motivation is perhaps subtler – more to do with a sense of curiosity, a desire to see round the next corner, to unlock the secrets of a particular landscape. The less you know in advance about your destination, the greater the sense of anticipation, the bigger the adventure. And that was what made the 1985 Siachen Indo-British Expedition so special.

The tantalizing view from the Siachen Glacier into the Terong Valley. The first Westerner to see into this valley was Dr Tom Longstaff in 1909.

The Siachen Glacier in northern Ladakh is the second longest in Asia, its full extent first identified in 1909 by the great Scottish explorer Dr Tom Longstaff. After Indian Partition in 1947, it became one of the key sticking points in the disputed ceasefire line between India and Pakistan, and for a long time was off limits to foreign mountaineers. Things came to a head in 1984 when Indian troops were flown in to occupy key passes around the glacier. In the following year the Alpine Club was invited to send a climbing team to this now emphatically Indian-controlled glacier.

When the six of us flew from London we were still not sure which mountain we were going to attempt. It was only after we arrived in Bombay (Mumbai) to meet expedition-leader Harish Kapadia that we discovered we had permission to visit the Rimo group at the head of the Terong Valley. As Longstaff had remarked all those years earlier, 'when it is desired to survey this unknown corner, will the party proceed five miles up the [Siachen] glacier and take the first turning on the right'. In 1929 the Dutch explorer Dr Philip Visser, with his wife Jenny Visser 't Hooft and the famous Swiss guide Franz Lochmatter, did just that. However, their account of the Terong basin was sketchy and they published no photos. And in 1985 there were still no detailed satellite photos of the area – at least none available to us. So we were heading for a glacier that was effectively unknown. At the head of that glacier rose some of the highest unclimbed mountains on Earth – the Rimo group – and we had no idea what they looked like.

THE LESS YOU KNOW IN ADVANCE ABOUT YOUR DESTINATION, THE GREATER THE SENSE OF ANTICIPATION, THE BIGGER THE ADVENTURE.

Harish Kapadia is acknowledged as one of the great experts on the Himalaya and Karakoram. Already in 1985 his knowledge was prodigious.

So, too, were his energy, enthusiasm and organizational clout. We British guests had simply to follow instructions as our Indian hosts took us north on the long train journey to Delhi, then Jammu, stopping en route to collect three Kumaoni porters hired for the duration of the expedition. Onward by bus, to Srinagar, then over the Zoji La to Leh. There we had to wait three days while Indian and Pakistani fighter jets skirmished above the Siachen before we could continue over the world's highest road pass to the mighty Shyok River and the subsidiary Nubra, braided silver beneath immense Siachen-carved orange granite cliffs. The present-day glacier snout appeared little more than a dirty heap of rubble, and it was only after climbing up on to it that we got a feel for the huge ice highway heading deep into the greatest mountain range on Earth. But, as Longstaff had instructed, our task was to take the first turning on the right.

That was the great moment. The pitted, rubbly ice of the Siachen spilled sideways into a sandy valley dotted with tamarisk and rose bushes. A mile or two up this valley the Terong River curved around huge granite cliffs. Beyond that we could see nothing, and no one had been there since Philip and Jenny Visser fifty-six years earlier.

On our return journey in July, the river was a lethal torrent, swollen with glacial melt, forcing us into some spectacular evasive rock climbing over the cliffs. However, in early June it was still possible to wade up it and follow the sandy valley bed on its far bank to the snout of the North Terong Glacier. From Snout Camp, our Kumaoni and Ladakhi porters helped ferry loads to Base Camp, or 'Mud Camp' as I preferred to call it. Two of the British climbers, Jim Fotheringham and Victor Saunders, were chosen for the first recce above. They returned wild-eyed, jabbering excitedly about

Most of the Siachen Indo-British Expedition at Advance Base Camp. Left to right: Harsinh Senior, Pratap Sinh, Dhiren Toolsidas, Hamish Kapadia, Arun Samant, Victor Saunders, Muslim Contractor, Dave Wilkinson and Jim Fotheringham.

Our first sight of Rimo I. The Southwest Ridge attempted by me and Victor Saunders descends towards the camera.

beautiful granite pillars soaring into the sky, and soon we all continued, up through avenues of ice pinnacles, to a confluence of the upper glacier branches where we made Advance Base between two little lakes. Here one evening the clouds suddenly lifted and we all had our first sight of Rimo.

In that pink sunset glow it was beautiful; by moonlight it was even more beautiful, the architecture more defined. Four of us on the British team began immediately to explore a possible route up into another side glacier, from where we set off one night, heavily laden, for the crenellated Southwest Ridge of Rimo I, at which point Jim Fotheringham and Dave Wilkinson descended.

For another four days Victor Saunders and I journeyed slowly up the ridge, burrowing through bulbous snow cornices, hooking up walls of shattered crockery, chimneying up granite clefts, weaving and winding, searching for possibilities, enjoying each day's surprises. The immediate tactile detail, the raw geology of the mountain, was absorbing, but so too was the broader context – the steadily expanding vista over the immensity of the Karakoram, stretching all

HERE ONE EVENING, THE CLOUDS SUDDENLY LIFTED AND WE ALL HAD OUR FIRST SIGHT OF RIMO.

the way to the distant pyramid of K2. It was the greatest mountain wilderness in Central Asia, redolent with the names of past explorers – Vigne, Younghusband, Longstaff, Bullock Workman, Abruzzi, Philippi, Dainelli. Now it was rumbling each dawn with the incongruous boom of artillery fire on the Bilafond La.

On the third day we climbed through a cluster of pinnacles, pitching our tent that night right on the crest of an enormous cornice because there was nowhere else to put it. The following day we traversed over and around

more pinnacles. We did wonder how we were going to reverse this intricate terrain on the way down, but by now, approaching 7,000 m (22,966 ft) above sea level, enjoying an extraordinary spell of fine weather, intoxicated by the dazzling scenery all around us, there was an incredible sense of commitment – a growing confidence that the two of us really might reach the top of Rimo I, at 7,387 m (24,235 ft) one of the highest untouched summits in the world.

Unfortunately I ruined it all that evening by losing my rucksack. Dropping tent poles, sleeping bag, spare clothing and food was not necessarily irredeemable, but the loss of the stove was: without the ability to melt snow we could not drink, and at that altitude – with at least another day to the summit, followed by a long, uncertain descent – continuing without water was out of the question.

Victor said afterwards that he was relieved. To this day he still maintains that if we had carried on to the summit – even without the rucksack fiasco – we might never have returned, we were so far out on a limb. I am not so sure, but I know that without the stove there was no choice. After a miserably cold, thirsty bivouac, we set off down at dawn, serenaded by the usual distant artillery fire. Rather than reverse the dauntingly complicated pinnacles, we decided to commit ourselves to abseiling directly off the side

Below left Victor Saunders following one of the key pitches through the Pinnacles on Rimo I.

Below right Our fourth bivouac on Rimo I at about 6,600 m (21,650 ft), with Victor Saunders settling in for the night.

of the ridge. At the bottom of the second abseil, pulling the doubled rope down as we dangled from a single sling draped over a granite spike, we got a horrible fright when it jammed tight far above us. We couldn't climb back up the overhangs above; below us the face dropped over 1,000 m (3,280 ft) to the glacier. We cursed and heaved and tugged and swung our combined weights on the rope and, at last, thank God, a shower of gravel came pouring out of the sky, followed by a snaking line of perlon. We would survive after all.

RATHER THAN REVERSE THE DAUNTINGLY COMPLICATED PINNACLES, WE DECIDED TO COMMIT OURSELVES TO ABSEILING DIRECTLY OFF THE SIDE OF THE RIDGE.

Late that evening, dejected and weary, we arrived back at Advance Base. We had failed on Rimo I, but the six days we had spent up there had given me one of the greatest experiences of my life. To salvage the expedition's honour, Jim and Dave now set off across an unknown pass to the distant Rimo Glacier and returned a week later, having made the first ascent of Rimo III (7,233 m/23,730 ft) – a real tour de force. As for Harish and the other Indian members, they were busily mopping up numerous lower peaks and exploring previously unvisited passes. In the last week of the expedition I set off alone up the Shelkar Chorten Glacier, which had rebuffed Lochmatter and the Vissers in 1929, climbed a new peak at its head, then crossed a pass to the third of the big glaciers in this basin – the South Terong – deviating briefly to make the first ascent of another six-thousander with two fine summits. At Harish's suggestion we gave it a Ladakhi name, *Ngabong Terong* – the double-humped camel of Terong.

Returning to the flooded Terong River, I had a welcome cigarette, after seven solo days of exploration of the Shelkar Chorten and South Terong glaciers.

Stephen Venables (British, b. 1954) has taken part in and led numerous mountaineering expeditions around the world. His Himalayan first ascents include Kishtwar-Shivling, Solu Tower, Panch Chuli V and a new route up the East Face of Everest, when he was the first Briton to reach the summit without supplementary oxygen. He has published twelve books, the first of which, *Painted Mountains*, won the Boardman Tasker Award. He has served as President of the South Georgia Association and the Alpine Club, and has been awarded the King Albert Award for distinction in the mountain world.

CHRIS BONINGTON

SHIVLING: CLIMBING THE UNCLIMBED

I STARTED CLIMBING AS A SCHOOLBOY, SIXTY YEARS AGO. I bought a pair of clinker nail boots, was given a worn hemp rope and was taken on my first climb by a friend of the family on Harrison's Rocks, a little sandstone outcrop to the south of London. I began leading on climbs almost immediately and climbed with a wide variety of partners, some more experienced, from whom I learned, and others who knew as little as I did and with whom I muddled through. It was an exciting adventure of self-discovery that took me from an apprenticeship in the British Isles to the peaks of the Alps and the greater ranges of the world.

Techniques have developed and our game of climbing has evolved in so many different ways unimaginable when I set out, but I believe the basic tenets are universal. For me, it started with the joy of finding a physical activity at which I had talent, much the same satisfaction enjoyed by any athlete. But then there was that extra spice of risk, the rush of adrenalin as I completed a difficult move above a long drop or had a narrow escape. From the very beginning there was also the thrill of exploration, both actual – of finding a new way up a crag – or mental – of stretching to new limits. There was the beauty of the mountains, too, experienced to a more powerful degree because of the level of commitment. There was also the strength of friendship in shared endeavour, where literally one's life is in someone else's hands. And finally there is the drive of competition and ego, something most of us are prone to, to a greater or lesser extent.

These are the feelings that have kept me climbing all these years, and inevitably there are a few climbs that stand out above the rest. The Southwest Face of Everest was undoubtedly the greatest and most complex challenge I have ever encountered. Five expeditions, including one led

Climbing as a schoolboy on Harrison's Rocks, southern England, in 1955.

by myself, had tried and failed before finally we achieved our objective. Planning the expedition, grappling with the complex logistics and leading a large team was both stretching and very satisfying, but it did not sum up for me the full joy of mountain adventure. In this respect, a much smaller expedition to a much smaller peak had it all.

In 1983 I was invited to speak at an international mountaineering conference in Delhi and decided to tack on to it a little expedition. I persuaded the organizers to fly out Jim Fotheringham, a local dentist and my regular climbing partner at the time, and then to include us in one of the post-conference trips to the Gangotri Range of the Indian Himalaya – a little bit of opportunism that I think appeals to every climber. This got us all the way to Tapoban, a lovely Alp at the foot of Shivling beside the Gangotri Glacier.

Our objective was the west face of Kedarnath Dome (6,831 m or 22,411 ft), which we had chosen from a photograph. It is several miles up the side of the Gangotri Glacier and would have been quite a carry for all the equipment, but some of my fellow speakers from the conference had come with us, just for the ride. I persuaded them to act as our Sherpas and help transport our gear for the climb. They were a distinguished bunch – Wanda Rutkiewicz, one of Poland's outstanding mountaineers and well on the way to completing all fourteen of the 8,000-m (26,246-ft) peaks, Laurie Skreslet, who had just become the first Canadian to climb Everest, and John Cleare, a good old friend and outstanding mountain photographer.

With them to help, it was a two-day walk to the foot of the wall, where they left us to set up camp and make our ascent. The next morning we found a good viewpoint and gazed up at this towering mass of compact rock that resembled two El Capitans (the world famous wall of Yosemite)

Our camp below Shivling at Tapoban, with our highly qualified volunteer porters – Laurie Skreslet and Wanda Rutkiewicz have been to the top of Everest and John Cleare, in the middle, is an accomplished mountain photographer.

piled one on top of the other. We spent two days scouting round the foot of the wall, becoming increasingly aware that we didn't have the gear, neck or ability to climb it (some years later it was climbed by a very strong Slovenian team). We discussed what to do instead – perhaps make a classic traverse of Kedarnath Dome, though this would have been a long snow plod, or how about Shivling (6,543 m/21,466 ft)? This mountain is like a gigantic fish tail jutting into the sky, the two 'fins' being the two summits. The main summit, to the northeast, had been climbed in 1974 from the north by an Indian expedition using a large quantity of fixed rope, but the southwest summit remained unclimbed.

So Shivling it was. The route that attracted us was its Southeast Ridge, an airy rock spur that swept up to the summit, but the problem was how to reach it. The mountain was guarded on its southeast flank by a series of huge bastions of crumbling granite split by gullies leading into blind alleys of overhanging rock. We were now running out of time as Jim was due back at his practice and we had just seven days to complete the climb and get back to base camp. That afternoon we walked up the moraine above the glacier to get a better view of the outer defences of the mountain. We spied a broad gully, obviously an avalanche chute, leading up to a chaotic icefall. There seemed, however, to be a rake leading out of sight to the right, which might avoid the icefall. We decided to go for it the following morning.

We set off with a sense of exhilaration and complete unity of purpose, born from the amount of climbing we had done together in the Lake District and Scottish Highlands. We had enough food and fuel for six days,

Below left Jim and I preparing tea at our camp below the East Face of Kedarnath Dome in the Gangotri.

Below right With a pair of binoculars I gaze up at the wall to find a route.

Jim, with a 15-kg (33-lb) rucksack on, rock climbing up the slabs on the lower part of the summit ridge.

a tiny lightweight tent, sleeping bags and our climbing gear. Once packed, our sacks felt heavy and must have weighed around 15 kg (33 lb) each. It was late morning by the time we reached the foot of the gully and it had been in the sun for some hours. We should probably have stopped there, and set out the following dawn when there would have been less risk of stone fall or avalanche, but we were impatient, put on our crampons and set out anyway.

The gully was about 20 m (66 ft) wide and we hugged the right-hand side, getting an illusory sense of cover from the solid rock wall beside us, though increasingly aware of the threat posed by the crumbling icefall looming above us. We were climbing unroped and Jim was pulling ahead when a huge boulder, the size of a car, broke away from high above us. It came bouncing down the gully, ricocheting from wall to wall. There was no cover, and no point in moving because you couldn't tell where it would bounce next. I just stood there and tried to shrink into myself as it hurtled down. It passed about 2 m (6 ft) from my side and then vanished below. Everything was silent once more.

Until this moment I had plodded slowly, regulating my breathing and saving energy, but I now abandoned all economy of effort, kicked fiercely up the slope, lungs aching, sweat pouring off me, to escape the gun barrel as quickly as possible. At last we reached the fork of the gully, could get away from the threat of the icefall and after a hundred metres or so reached the haven of some narrow ledges protected from above by a huge overhang. It was only midday but we decided to stop.

The following morning we were able to find a way past the overhanging rock on to the crest of a ridge, over a minor peak and back to a point just 20 m (66 ft) above where we had spent the previous night. That in turn

led across to the glacier basin above the icefall. We had breached the outer defences and now had the summit arête of our peak sweeping up before us.

Our third day gave us a real rock feast on perfect, easy-angled granite. We climbed, carrying our sacks, running out pitch after pitch under a cloudless sky, until in the late afternoon we reached the crest of a huge boulder. Ahead, the angle steepened: the rock appeared to be more compact and the way less obvious. It was a good place to stop for our third night. We could now gaze across the Gangotri Glacier to the Bhagirathi peaks, and beyond them to an endless vista of shapely, jagged mountains.

The next day we were faced with some serious climbing – the rock was both steeper and more compact, the way never obvious. The rucksack was too heavy an encumbrance for the leader, so whoever was out in front left his behind. We tried hauling the sack, but it kept jamming and was being torn to bits by the sharp rock. We therefore devised a system by which the leader abseiled back down on one rope to pick up his sack while the second jumared up the other rope to get ready to lead the next pitch – but it was slow going.

We climbed through the day, getting increasingly worried about finding a bivouac site that also had some snow or ice that we could melt for drinks – we were already badly dehydrated. At last we found a tiny prow with an ice-filled crack behind it, ran out two more very difficult rope lengths. We left the ropes in place before retreating to our bivvy, which we still had to build up with rocks to make a precarious platform for our tent. As we settled down for the night, huge thunderheads were building up over the mountains around us and we wondered about our prospects if the weather broke that night.

Standing on the summit of Shivling – there was only room for one of us at a time on top.

Fortunately the clouds dissipated during the night. The angle now relented and we made good progress through the day; suddenly we found ourselves on the knife-edged crest of the summit ridge about 100 m (328 ft) below the top, but it was too late to reach it that night. We cut a small platform out of the snow and the following morning went for the top – two spectacular but straightforward pitches on snow-covered ice and we were on a fairy-tale summit that was so pointed that there was only room for one person at a time.

A moment of euphoric exhilaration was quickly banished by concern at how the hell we were going to get back down. Descent by the route we had just climbed was out of the question. We were aware that the Indians had reached the col between the two peaks of Shivling from the north, but we knew nothing of their route. And first we had to reach the col. The crest of the ridge was heavily corniced and the slope was steep, with soft, unconsolidated snow lying on very hard ice. We decided to climb down it unroped, keeping far apart so that if the snow did avalanche, at least one of us might avoid being caught in it. It was the most frightening descent that either of us had ever made. Once on the col, the danger eased, but there was still a long way to go as we descended the north ridge of Shivling by a series of abseils. The rope jammed – fortunately on the very last abseil. It was now getting dark. We continued the descent ropeless and without head torches, since we had both inadvertently dropped them on the way up. Fumbling our way back down in the dark, we got back to Tapoban and our base camp, exhausted but happy, at 10 p.m. on the sixth day of our adventure.

A MOMENT OF EUPHORIC EXHILARATION WAS QUICKLY BANISHED BY CONCERN AT HOW THE HELL WE WERE GOING TO GET BACK DOWN.

To me, that climb has everything that makes a great adventure: spontaneity, exploration, a magnificent objective set in the wildest scenery, superb and varied climbing, the thrill of risk, uncertainty of outcome to the very end and finally the smallness and compatibility of a two-person team.

Chris Bonington (British, b. 1934), mountaineer, writer, photographer and lecturer, started climbing at the age of sixteen in 1951. It has been his passion ever since. He made the first British ascent of the North Wall of the Eiger and led the expedition that made the first ascent of the South Face of Annapurna, the biggest and most difficult climb in the Himalaya at the time. He went on to lead the successful expedition making the first ascent of the Southwest Face of Everest in 1975 and then reached the summit of Everest himself in 1985 with a Norwegian expedition. He is still active in the mountains, climbing with the same enthusiasm as he had at the beginning.

He has written seventeen books, fronted numerous television programmes and has lectured to the public and corporate audiences all over the world. He received a knighthood in 1996 for services to mountaineering, was president of the Council for National Parks for eight years, is non-executive Chairman of Berghaus and Chancellor of Lancaster University.

REBECCA STEPHENS

FIRST BRITISH WOMAN TO CLIMB EVEREST

Harry Taylor, Dr Sandy Scott and myself re-group at Camp 2 at the head of the Western Cwm after Harry's successful ascent of Everest.

IT SEEMS EXTRAORDINARY THAT, as late as the 1990s, no woman born in the British Isles – a place defined by and proud of its pioneering history in the mountains – had even so much as attempted to climb Everest. It is even more extraordinary when one considers that of all the giants of the Himalaya and Karakoram, Everest, the highest of them all, is seen worldwide as a 'British' mountain, because it was first climbed by a British expedition, led by Colonel John Hunt in 1953. How lucky was I, then, to venture to Everest in 1989 as a journalist reporting on an Anglo-American expedition attempting Everest's unclimbed Northeast Ridge, and to fall in love with the mountain – its history, beauty, magnificence – and to have the opportunity to venture to it again in 1993, and for the weather to hold fair and for me to climb it.

I can't claim to have been the first person, of course. That was the privilege of Edmund Hillary and Sherpa Tenzing Norgay. Nor can I claim to be the first woman; that was Junko Tabei of Japan, in 1975. But I can claim to have been high, as high as it's possible to be without sprouting wings, and to have tasted – just tasted – the solitude and rarity of place experienced by the mountaineers of an earlier age.

And it might very easily have been different. I arrived relatively late on the timeline as far as the climbing of Everest is concerned; although commercialization hadn't quite taken hold, Everest was, by the early 1990s, a popular mountain. Had it not been for a decision taken by the leader of our expedition, John Barry, we might have made a bid for the summit with a very large number of climbers from a host of different expeditions from around the world who, en masse, had moved up the hill and established high camp on the South Col together. But we didn't – to my enormous frustration at the time. John's decision was entirely rational, even noble; he reasoned that one of our number – a doctor on our expedition – wasn't well, and that it was windy on the South Col. Still, the Sherpas wanted to climb. So did I. And so, it seemed, did the majority of climbers gathered on the Col that night. It was misery to sit in my sleeping bag, dressed and eager to go, listening through the canvas to the nervous chatter of climbers preparing for their big summit day, to the sound of the scraping of crampons on rock and rucksacks heaved upon shoulders.

But this misery was nothing in comparison to the utter devastation I felt the following day when it emerged that no fewer than thirty-eight people had climbed to the summit of Everest on that day we might have gone but didn't, 10 May. They included our friend Harry Taylor,

THERE WERE NO CROWDS, AS THERE HAD BEEN A WEEK BEFORE.

who reached the summit without the aid of supplementary oxygen but contracted snow blindness and was lucky to escape with his life. Never in the annals of mountaineering had such a massive number of people climbed Everest on a single day. The sky was blue; conditions, as it turned out, perfect. Had we gone, we might have made it forty, or forty-two.

Today, however, the pain of this lost opportunity only makes the prize of our summit bid all the sweeter. For when, a week later, the mountain threw us a second chance – which thankfully it did – there were only three of us kicking steps through newly fallen snow on Everest's Southeast Ridge: two Sherpas, Ang Passang and Kami Tchering, and myself. There were no crowds, as there had been a week before. A part of me feels selfish in even writing this: that others – committed, talented, enthused climbers – were denied the opportunity we were given. But then at the same time I can't deny the extraordinary feeling of privilege, climbing that great mountain as the end of the twentieth century approached, in a small, tightly knit team of three – not another human being in sight.

The Sherpas and I brought nothing back from that trip: no rocks, no fossils thrust to the heavens from beneath the sea, no furthering of scientific knowledge. But we shared an experience at the very edge of where we as human beings can survive, and the depth of that experience leaves its mark.

We were lucky, looking back. The weather wasn't good on the night we were to make a bid for the summit: dark cloud filled the Western Cwm below. This was our second visit to the high camp on the South Col, at just below 8,000 m (26,246 ft); the season was drawing to a close and we were exhausted, though the adrenalin masked this well. Right until the last, we were unsure whether or not we'd climb higher towards the summit. Our leader John wasn't with us at the high camp this time around. We hadn't planned it this way. It was just that he had exerted such extraordinary effort in helping Harry off the hill that he wasn't in a position to be able to climb himself. He was at a lower camp, agonizing over what to advise us to do. Should we go? Or not? For a full hour and a half he deliberated, intermittently talking to us over the radio – valuable time lost. But in the end the balance of his weighing-up just toppled to the affirmative: 'I think you're going to be OK. Over.'

RIGHT UNTIL THE LAST, WE WERE UNSURE WHETHER OR NOT WE'D CLIMB HIGHER TOWARDS THE SUMMIT.

Then of course it was a decision for the Sherpas and me to make for ourselves. I don't believe for a moment we would have climbed had we

Ang Passang at our tents at Camp 4: frail but sufficient shelter in a desolate place.

Several journeys were made up and down through the treacherous Khumbu Icefall. On our final descent, these ladders lay hidden, crushed under a block of ice.

stuck to any sort of rational line of thought, but the magnetism of the summit was irresistible. And, looking out of the tent, we saw three small dots of light in the darkness, moving slowly up the slopes above us on the South Col. If these three climbers thought it possible, so too did we! Into the dark we climbed.

Soon we were catching up with the small procession of three climbers who had set out ahead of us, headlights burning. They were climbing without supplementary oxygen and one of them was struggling with the cold and turned around. That meant lost time for the other two, and we climbed above them, into the illusion of new, untrodden ground. There was now just the mountain and ourselves. Our progress was impossibly slow. Two steps, then just one at a time – kicking big bucket steps in the snow, leaning on our ice axes, gasping. But it was the most touching feeling to know the Sherpas would never leave me on my own; that none of us would leave another alone; that three of us would stand on Everest's summit, or none of us at all. And it was a first ascent of Everest for Ang Passang and Kami Tchering as well as for me: a new, rare, joyous experience, shared ... if short-lived. Hardly had we stood on the summit when our thoughts turned immediately to getting down.

It's tempting to think a climb is over once the summit is reached, but there are challenges on the descent just as there are on the ascent. And for me, there was one short episode on the way down – almost incidental to the climb – that still offers comfort twenty years on. The Sherpas and I were still high on the ridge – above 8,300 m (27,230 ft) at a guess – when the weather closed in around us. We could barely see a thing. We daren't move. We just stood there, waiting. The whole incident couldn't have lasted more than 15 minutes, but of course we couldn't know that then. At the time we worried that if the cloud didn't clear we might be stuck high up there on the ridge until darkness fell, until our oxygen ran out. We had no sleeping bags, no shelter. We knew all too well what might happen if we couldn't descend to our camp on the South Col – we'd seen lives lost in just such circumstances in the last few weeks – and yet surprisingly, comfortingly, felt no fear. Only calm. I have a very simplistic explanation for this, as one who has felt

I HAVE A VERY SIMPLISTIC EXPLANATION FOR THIS, AS ONE WHO HAS FELT KNEE-TREMBLING FEAR ON MANY OCCASIONS.

Tcheri Zhambu and Nawang the cook making momos (Nepalese dumplings). Tcheri Zhambu might have accompanied Ang Passang, Kami Tchering and myself on the summit day but was unlucky enough to contract a hacking cough; he awaited our return on the South Col.

knee-trembling fear on many occasions. My sense is this: stuck up there on the ridge there was no reason for adrenalin to race through our blood, heightening our senses and injecting fear, because there was nothing to fight and nowhere to fly. We were beyond that, in a place of acceptance – and, logical or not, this makes me feel that perhaps when our time comes to face death we each have within us a mechanism to deal with it. The mountains are wonderful like that. Yes, they provide an arena for adventure and thrill, but mostly they allow us to connect deeply with nature and remind us of our very tiny status in the world.

Rebecca Stephens (British, b. 1961) started her career in journalism, which led her to the Himalaya and a love of mountains. She is the first British woman to climb Everest and the Seven Summits. Author of several books, she also delivers keynotes and master classes to schools and businesses around the world. She is an associate of Ashridge Business School and in 2007 established Seven Summits Performance Ltd to deliver professional and leadership development. She leads treks to the Himalaya and is a trustee of The Himalayan Trust UK.

Kami Tchering and myself on top of the world.

HARALDUR SIGURDSSON

STANDING ON THE EDGE OF AN ERUPTION

WE TRAVELLED UP THE MOUNTAIN ALL NIGHT IN A BLINDING SNOW STORM, navigating the all-terrain vehicles most of the time on the basis of GPS alone. This was our second attempt to reach the eruption – the first, on the previous day, had failed because of blizzard conditions and very high winds. The turning point came when the wind picked up two of the snowmobiles and flipped them over like little toys. On our second attempt the wind was a bit calmer, but the conditions were still fierce, cold, stormy and as dark as Iceland can be in March. Finally, we reached the crest of the Fimmvörðuháls mountain pass, just as the weather cleared slightly. Ahead of us was the spectacular sight of the new volcanic fissure, like a fiery gaping red gash in the earth. Surrounding it were rapidly accumulating black cinder cones that were building up around the new craters, with red-hot lava fountains lighting up the night sky and the snowfields around. The surreal visual effect was one of a giant mouth, with beautiful black lips, squirting glowing lava hundreds of metres up into the air. But this was only the first phase of the volcanic eruption of Eyjafjallajökull volcano.

I had been following the developing unrest beneath Eyjafjallajökull for several months before this, in early 2010. From my computer in my laboratory in Rhode Island in the United States I could study the signals from the impressive array of geophysical sensors that the Icelandic Meteorological Office operates on and around the volcano. This is a unique monitoring system that can be examined by anyone with access to the internet, with the geophysical signals displayed in real time. I noted that earthquakes within the lower crust under the volcano, at depths of 10 to 20 km (6–12½ miles), were increasing in frequency and gradually migrating closer to the surface. At the same time, GPS sensors showed that the volcano was swelling

The volcanic eruption of Eyjafjallajökull volcano in Iceland in March and April 2010 culminated in an explosive event that sent clouds of ash all across the North Atlantic ocean. The reaction in Europe was to shut down 313 airports for a week during the height of this crisis.

or bulging up, possibly due to the movement of magma or molten rock towards the surface.

It was time to make a move. I flew to Iceland on 15 March 2010, planning to be on site when the magma reached the surface. An eruption seemed imminent, and on my volcano blog on 18 March I predicted one. Two days later the fissure eruption on Fimmvörðuháls began, but access was initially impossible because of the severe weather conditions. Fortunately, the eruption broke through just beyond the edge of the glacier that caps this volcano, meaning that steam explosions resulting from the interaction of hot magma and ice were not likely – or so we thought.

As we made our observations and collected samples of the new basalt lava, the red-hot magma spread rapidly around the growing fissure. We then suddenly noticed about 1 km (½ mile) to the east a fast-growing cloud of dark grey turning into light grey steam and ash. We rushed to the scene, thinking that a new fissure was opening up. But to our surprise the cloud was generated when a huge volume of the lava at 1,200°C (2,192°F) poured over a high cliff into a narrow, snow-filled canyon below. Here in front of us was probably one of the most spectacular lava falls witnessed by man. The snow and ice in the canyon were suddenly melted and turned to superheated steam beneath the accumulating hot

AN ERUPTION SEEMED IMMINENT, AND ON MY VOLCANO BLOG ON 18 MARCH I PREDICTED ONE.

Dense clouds of ash, steam and volcanic gases were ejected by the volcano high up into the sky.

lava. Confined in the narrow canyon, the steam could not expand and therefore exploded upwards. This in turn shredded the lava to tiny bits, creating multiple explosion clouds in front of us and in the sky above. The largest of the blasts sent me running for safety, but my trusted companion, photographer Ragnar Axelsson, remained cool and calm, waiting for the right moment to capture his unique images.

Two weeks later, the fissure eruption of basaltic magma on the flank of the volcano wound down, but earthquake activity continued at depth. We were all in a state of suspense, wondering what would follow, or if indeed the activity of Eyjafjallajökull had ceased. This volcano had already caused great trouble in Iceland, in 1612 and 1821, with its spectacular explosive eruptions. We did not have to wait long – an explosion began in the summit crater of the volcano, about 10 km (6 miles) from the fissure, on 14

THE CONTINUOUS EXPLOSIONS SENT A CLOUD OF ASH AND GASES OVERHEAD THAT ENGULFED US COMPLETELY IN DARKNESS FROM TIME TO TIME.

April. Conditions at the summit were very different, as the 2-km (1¼-mile) wide crater was filled with at least 250 m (820 ft) of glacial ice. For thirty-nine days the volcano generated a series of violent explosions that sent clouds of ash, steam and volcanic gases up to 8 km (5 miles) above the crater. The ash plume extended to the southeast and south with the prevailing winds, quickly drifting towards Europe, where up to 313 airports were closed as a precautionary measure, bringing passenger air traffic across the North Atlantic to a complete halt for one week.

We were eager to get close to the active crater to see what was going on and to collect samples of the new erupting magma. Was it the same magma that had been erupted in the first phase, or was this something

Above left During the first stage of the eruption, a fissure opened up on the east flank of the Eyjafjallajökull volcano, spewing out firey hot basalt magma (at 12,000°C or 21,632°F) that produced lava flows.

Above right Viewing the first stage of the eruption up close was relatively harmless, and it therefore quickly became a favourite tourist attraction.

new? The eruption was not behaving in the same way, and we suspected that this might indeed be a magma with a different chemistry, causing the explosions. We got closer and closer, with helicopters dropping us off a few kilometres west of the crater, but still too far away to get a good idea of the activity.

Finally, on 16 May we managed to drive up on the glacier from the west, and reach close to the crater rim at Godasteinn: the Rock of the Gods. This is a site of great significance in Icelandic mythology, as it was here that one of the chieftains of Iceland tossed the effigies of his heathen gods into the crater in the year AD 1000, after the people had adopted Christianity and ceased worshipping Odinn and Thor.

The scene now at Godasteinn was not inviting. The continuous explosions sent a cloud of ash and gases overhead that engulfed us completely in darkness from time to time. Ash was steadily falling, and small lumps of lava bounced off our helmets. Breathing was difficult, and we kept coughing up and spitting out ash. The glacier was covered with a uniform layer of fresh ash about 1 m (3 ft) thick; scattered on this surface were pits, 1 m to 2 m (3–6½ ft) deep, created when lava bombs dropped out of the eruption cloud above us. It was not a comfortable situation, but we hurried into the largest of the new craters and excavated parts of the fragmented bomb, which was still warm. We had our fresh sample of the magma and struggled to carry off the 50-kg (110-lb) piece to the waiting truck. It took us just a few minutes to get out of the bomb field, to a safe distance from the roaring crater.

The rocks I collected on Eyjafjallajökull were once red-hot magma deep within the Earth. Such samples have the same significance for the geologist as the samples of blood that the medical doctor draws from the human body for analysis. The analogy is indeed appropriate, since magma is a messenger of the inner condition of the Earth beneath us. Analysis of these samples has already taught us much about the system beneath Eyjafjallajökull volcano. It turns out that this beast has two types of blood. In the second and more explosive eruption, the magma was quite different, of the type known as trachyandesite. For one thing it was slightly cooler, about 1,000ºC (1,832ºF), but the most remarkable difference between the two magmas was the viscosity.

It is a physical property that we normally don't think much about, but viscosity, or the stiffness of a liquid, is a fundamental issue. Compare the viscosity of a few items that you are likely to have in your kitchen. If water has the viscosity unit of 1, then honey is 10,000 times more viscous, ketchup 100,000 and peanut butter 250,000 times more viscous than water. We discovered that the trachyandesite magma that erupted explosively from Eyjafjallajökull in the second eruption was over 100 times more viscous than the relatively thin or fluid alkali olivine basalt magma that erupted in the first episode. This does not account for all the different

features of the two eruptions, but it does go a long way to explaining them, and it also shows us that it is worth taking some personal risks to collect the right samples for a scientific study of a volcanic event. And besides, nothing equals the thrill of standing right next to the crater of an erupting volcano.

Haraldur Sigurdsson (Icelandic, b. 1939) is Director of the Volcano Museum in Stykkishólmur, Iceland. He is also professor emeritus at the Graduate School of Oceanography, University of Rhode Island, USA. He has conducted research on volcanoes worldwide since 1963, both on the ocean floor and on land, including work in Indonesia, Central and South America, the Caribbean, Italy, Iceland and elsewhere, and has written and edited several books on the subject.

Left We enter into the black cloud that engulfs the crater area during the explosive stage of the Eyjafjallajökull eruption. Our mission is to collect fresh samples of the erupting magma for analysis.

Below I emerge from one of the pit craters that are created when lava bombs crash down on to the glacier's surface near the eruption.

KAREN DARKE

DIZZY FINGERS: TO THE SUMMIT OF 'EL CAP'

AT A BREAK IN THE FOREST, WE SLOWED THE CAR AND I SAW IT, almost blinding against the darkness of moss-coated pines and damp boulders: 'El Cap' – El Capitan in Yosemite National Park, California. Later we lay in the meadow for a while, my wheelchair empty in the grass, watching tiny bright specks move over the sheer granite face, more than 900 m (3,000 ft) high. I couldn't imagine it, being up there, climbing.

The next morning, lashed to a rucksack, I held on to Andy Kirkpatrick's neck as he hitched me on to his back and then began to stagger towards the base. I thought of myself thirty years before, only six, standing not far from here on my own feet, looking up with mum and dad and declaring I would climb El Cap one day. That was before I even knew what climbing was, before I'd become a climber, and before the accident that had seemed to put an end to childish dreams of rock. High places had been my world, my freedom, my escape. But I'd long got over any mourning and found new ways of enjoying all that climbing had given me – hand-biking across the Himalaya, kayaking the Inside Passage to Alaska, crossing Greenland in a sit-ski. I hadn't thought about climbing for a long time.

As the sun beat down and we sweated, I gripped on, peering over Andy's shoulder. Either of us could end up hurt by this outrageous piggy-back. Before he put each foot forward, I studied the trail beneath, playing a guessing game. I imagined, if it were my footsteps, where I'd place my soles, searching for steadfast ground. I liked it when Andy's feet went where I imagined I'd place mine.

I hid from the heat among the bags. I'd buried any threads of desire to climb again long ago, with memories of windy Scottish summits, the sound of my crampons scraping on rock, the snapshot smiles of friends,

sunburnt and wasted in Alpine campsites, all sharing adventures and dreaming of more. The idea of climbing El Cap had seemed beyond me then, so how did I think it was possible now, with only my arms and some rusty climbing skills to get me to the top?

The sun had barely crept on to the wall by the time Andy had set off up the Zodiac route's curving-roofed crack. Now he shouts 'Safe'. What a crazy word to use. I could say no, like I should have done fourteen years ago, when I began leading a route in Scotland I knew was too hard for me, moments before the salty cliff slipped from my fingers, and I hit the rocks below. If I'd backed off instead, I'd still be walking now. I'd said yes then, and I said it now. I heard my brother's voice, 'Please don't go, we've nearly lost you once before', as I watched myself, strangely detached, strapping the mountain-bike body-armour on to my skinny legs, readying for the first pull-up. Something in my nature had led to all of this; the part of me that pushes too far had put me in a wheelchair; but the same part of me also wouldn't allow me to be disabled. It pushed me to try to be super-abled.

SOMETHING IN MY NATURE HAD LED TO ALL OF THIS.

By pull-up number ten, I still hadn't left the ground, my jumars sliding up but hauling only rope-stretch. The helmet strap dug into my chin, and the harness shoulder straps into my collarbones. There was so little of my body I could feel, but what was left hurt and I hadn't even started.

By pull-up number fifteen, I felt lift off. 'Wooohooo. Off the ground!'

By pull-up number twenty, I was a spectacular 20 cm (8 in) off the ground. I paused to look up at the first stage: ahead appeared a marathon of pull-ups, though I knew it couldn't be more than 60 m (197 ft).

Hanging from El Cap in 2008 with the ropes tangled by the wind, scared to do what I knew I had to do – unclip the safety rope and spin myself around, again and again, to disentangle myself.

After hundreds more pull-ups, I'd re-graded the route, from its official hardship grade A2 5.7, which didn't mean anything to me, to PU4000+ (over 4,000 pull-ups). I was nearly at the portaledge, sweat trickling into my ears, my collarbones raw. I looked down, and felt a long way up, but when I looked up, I felt a long, long way down.

The rest of the day clenched into a fist of tension and strain: our five ropes were equally knotted, the four of us strung like spiders down the wall. By late afternoon the sun hid behind the Nose, and the stone fell into shadow. We'd be climbing in the dark.

Andy exclaimed how exciting a pitch had been, but it was all the same to me. We were just somewhere, lost on the wall. I noticed other things instead. The swifts that cliff-dived, swooping by my ears, like fast black jets. The lightning white forks of quartz splitting the face. The clean shadow line that crept with the day across the wall. The faint but acrid aroma of old urine that painted dark streaks. The gentle breeze, subtle but enough to set my rope swaying. I wished I felt like a child on a swing, not a foolhardy adult clutching at a rope. How much weight could one of those small metal bolts hold?

I LOOKED DOWN, AND FELT A LONG WAY UP, BUT WHEN I LOOKED UP, I FELT A LONG, LONG WAY DOWN.

Sweaty days and long nights tied to the face. The third sunset: climbing parties were everywhere, their headlamp beams like Christmas lights strung across the wall, as they made their frantic late evening efforts to settle down for the night. I liked knowing we weren't alone. Each day I'd watched the other climbers' progress, happy when we moved at a similar pace, disappointed if we made less ground.

'You see that Korean guy fall off earlier?' Andy asked.

Playing mind games – belaying Andy as he led the next pitch, focusing on the task in hand instead of worrying about the drop below or letting my fear of heights take over.

'Luckily no.' I spooned cold ravioli into his mouth as he lay exhausted on the ledge.

Bats squealed, and a mouse poked its head out from behind a flake. I'd never seen Andy look so wasted, his eyes deadened by effort, his hair gelled with sweat.

'He got up it in the end. He was on the crux. Iron Hawk. It's a hard route.' He swigged his end-of-day treat, a can of Coke. He said the fizz helped him revive. Tomato stains seeped from the corners of his mouth, making red blotches on his drained pale face. I understood that he liked to push himself to this state of exhaustion, to simplify life to this game of staying alive.

So had I.

'Mother-fucking ropes!' I scream into space.

The wind rips my hair. My hair whips my face.

I'm spinning.

Dizzy. Disorientated.

Above, all I can see are twisted ropes, purple, green, blue.

I slide my jumar up but it jams.

I'm dangling in a void beneath a massive overhang. The wind roars up the face. A storm front moves our way.

'Fucking haul bags!' I hear myself shout, my voice weak with anguish. I watch myself lose it, and think it's pointless.

I'm 700 m (2,297 ft) above the ground, way out from the illusory comfort of the face, spinning, stuck, wrapped around the haul bag line.

Below left This was almost the most stomach-lurching moment, leaving the safety of the ledge and swinging out into space to begin hauling up again.

Below right After being stranded with tangled ropes, I reached the others at Peanut Ledge. Andy offered me chocolate to cheer me up!

'Unclip your safety line' Andy shouts from way above.

I hate him for saying it because I know it's what I have to do, but I don't want to do it. It's the first step to untangling the mess. 'Just do it, Karen.' I talk to myself.

I can't do it. I let the tears spill the sweat and dirt down my face, taste them. I feel ashamed to be crying, to be losing it, to be weak. I'm aware the others must be looking down, willing me to get it together.

I unclip my safety line.

I spin to untangle it.

It's quiet above. I know they know just to leave me alone.

Finally my jumar is free to slide upwards again. I focus on it, and at my blistered fingers, torn cuticles, gripping tight on yellow rubber. I notice every movement. Slide, pull, breathe, wipe tears.

The world of El Cap has centrifuged into my dizzy fingers.

The wind died with the sun, the sky salmon and slate, turning to jet as night fell and the cold bit into the tender skin of my fingers. It was silent on our ledge except for us breathing and fidgeting for warmth, waiting for Andy to finish running the last two pitches together. Far, far below the traffic hummed like electric interference in the otherwise quiet night.

A shooting star fell.

'Safe!' echoed through the blackness. This time it was almost true.

My stomach did a sickly lurch as I slipped over the lip of the ledge, and swung into space one last time. I began to pull. The final pitch of PU4000+. It wasn't so scary in the dark. There was no up, no down, no yesterday, no tomorrow. There was just a yellow pull-up bar, with the perlon pattern passing through the jumar. The purple rope ran forever upwards, chasing Andy's voice into the heavens. Grit fell into my eyes. I closed them and kept pulling. My arms were exhausted and bloody, grating against the rock with each pull-up, but not as tired as my mind, fine threads of tension suspended in every synapse, tearing, ready to break. I needed Zodiac to end.

THERE WAS NO UP, NO DOWN, NO YESTERDAY, NO TOMORROW.

At last my rope ran out, but I was still hanging, my body rammed against the final rim, El Capitan unwilling to let go. I was bound in ropes, and whichever way I rolled, my hips or knees were caught beneath the summit lip. I rested my cheek on the cold coarse granite, belly-flopped over the cusp of the prize. I didn't cry. I didn't shout. I didn't even kiss the top. I just hugged the edge, closed my eyes, and waited for Andy to come and remove my shackles.

My first climbing trip to the Alps. Tired but happy, I sat on top of a fairly insignificant summit above the village of Saas-Fee.

It began to snow.

I shivered inside the billow of my sleeping bag, Andy snoring beside me, a damp grey tarp wrapped around us like a shroud, the snow making a deeper and deeper blanket. Tomorrow would be a mammoth piggy-back down to the valley. I wiggled deeper into my bag, the cold seeping through me, and put my hands in my armpits to cuddle myself warm.

Andy must have wanted me to experience what he had on El Cap, eleven times before: that feeling of being free and strong, high on the summit, amid the fanfare of the peaks and towers below. Instead I wanted to run away. Coming climbing again, I felt as though I had stepped back down into the tomb where I'd laid my walking-self to rest. It had stirred buried memories of a life I'd long left behind. I wanted to be back in my wheelchair, to be able to move on my own, in my own direction. As long as I kept moving, I wouldn't have to sit vigil by that tomb.

It had been amazing to climb again, and to visit what had once been, to untie stubborn knots, to dangle my feet about marvellous space, to again live a snapshot of a climber's life. Now I see clearly why I go hand-cycling, for miles and miles, why I can never turn around until I've reached the end of the road, why I push myself past the day's end into the darkness.

Karen Darke (British, b 1971) has touched the lives of many through her spirit for adventure. A keen runner and mountaineer, she was paralysed in a climbing accident on a Scottish sea cliff at twenty-one. Facing a life in a wheelchair, Karen chose to fight preconceived ideas of what was possible for someone who could feel nothing below their chest.

In 1997, four years after her accident, Karen crossed the Tien Shan and Karakoram mountains of Central Asia on a hand bike, raising £12,000 for charity. She then hand-cycled the length of the Japanese archipelago, sea-kayaked a 1,930-km (1,200-mile) length of the Canada–Alaska coastline, crossed the Indian Himalaya by hand-cycle and skied the Vallée Blanche in the Alps. In 2006 Karen made a record-breaking crossing of the Greenland ice cap on a sit-ski. In 2007, she made the bold decision to return to the rock face, climbing to the summit of El Capitan in Yosemite. She won a silver medal at the 2012 Paralympic Games and in 2013 she hopes to become the first person to sit-ski from the edge of the Antarctic ice shelf to the South Pole to raise money for the charity Back Up Trust.

OCEAN

No part of the planet has perhaps attracted more people to test themselves against the elements than the oceans. Our relationship with the sea is ageless, and many seem just as obsessed by it now as in the time when we did not know what lay beyond the horizon. For the early explorers, the lure of a voyage was the promise of unknown lands to be discovered, conquered or tamed. In leaking ships relying on basic navigation, with crews often mutinous and suffering from scurvy, they sought fame and fortune. Recreating those travels has been and continues to be a fascinating exercise.

There are today, however, still challenges presented by marine exploration using sail or manpower. With three-quarters of the surface of the globe covered in water, the sheer scale of the endeavour as a single craft pits itself against the vastness of the sea is daunting. The weather is unpredictable, the timescale often intimidating and loneliness can be demoralizing. Yet people are constantly inspired to test technology and themselves to the limit. The fascination in reading about their achievements often comes as much from what they – and we – learn about themselves as from what they actually did.

Alone on the ocean: Jason Lewis pedalled this small craft solo through the legendary doldrums as part of his larger expedition around the globe using only human power. This journey proved to be as much about self-discovery as discovery.

TIM SEVERIN

SAILING THE ATLANTIC IN A LEATHER BOAT

BY ROBERT TWIGGER

TIM SEVERIN HAS MOUNTED MORE SEA JOURNEYS to prove a historical point than anyone else. In a sense he is the inheritor of the mantle of Thor Heyerdahl, who could be said to have invented the genre with his *Kon-Tiki* voyage of 1946. Severin aims to test the veracity of mythical or prehistoric stories by making epic voyages in craft that have in most cases long fallen out of use.

While still a student at Oxford, Tim Severin had already attempted to ride by motorcycle the complete length of the Silk Road to trace the route of Marco Polo, only to be stopped at the Chinese frontier. He began his career writing books about the history of exploration, and though ostensibly a researcher, he kept up his exploring skills by making journeys in the Mediterranean in a small yacht (which he later had to sell, along with his car, to finance his first real expedition).

Although he has made many voyages – by dhow, bamboo raft and ancient Greek galley – Severin is probably best remembered for his first, and perhaps most audacious, journey. Inspired by an ancient Irish text known as the *Navigatio* of St Brendan, he set out to demonstrate that Irish monks could have visited America in the sixth century, three centuries before the Vikings landed at L'Anse aux Meadows in Newfoundland. The text was curiously accurate about the lands encountered on the way to America, and Severin easily identified the Faroes, Iceland and Greenland. St Brendan and his seventeen monks were said to have used a leather boat for their journey, in effect a larger version of the curragh, a kind of coracle still used for coastal fishing in Ireland, and Severin was able to persuade leather workers and boat builders to help him recreate such a sixth-century Irish leather boat. Forty-nine ox hides were stretched over a frame made of ash and oak, stitched together and lathered in wool grease – the stench was appalling, even after days at sea.

In May 1976 the crew of five set sail in their small boat, called the *Brendan*, from Brandon inlet, also named after the saint, in County Kerry. Having learnt how to sail the unusual craft in the open seas, they arrived in Iceland, where they had wait until the following summer for better weather. On the next stage of the journey to North America they encountered pack ice, whales and horrendous gales. During the worst of these gales, giant waves poured over the stern and broke through the plastic tarpaulin covers that constituted the only shelter in what was effectively an open boat. The waves washed through the length of the ship, swamping it with water and threatening to sink it. With only two small pumps, it fast became clear that the boat was filling as quickly as the crew could empty it. Everything was completely saturated – Severin writes of climbing wet into a wet sleeping bag while his co-adventurer and sailing master George Molony says, 'Christ, I hope your theory is correct that body heat will dry out the wet sleeping bags. I don't fancy being this wet for the rest of the voyage!' As if in answer, an even bigger wave smashed into the stern.

ON THE NEXT STAGE OF THE JOURNEY TO NORTH AMERICA THEY ENCOUNTERED PACK ICE, WHALES AND HORRENDOUS GALES.

The *Brendan* leaving Iceland and setting out into the North Atlantic. The open leather boat seems tiny, dwarfed by the dark cliffs.

The crew of the *Brendan* had to learn quickly how to handle the boat in the rolling waves. Throughout the journey they also needed to come up with solutions to various problems posed by sailing such an unusual craft on the high oceans.

In desperation, Severin suggested turning the boat head to wind and streaming a sea anchor. He knew that the curragh men of Arran (who can be seen rowing through monstrous waves in the film *Men of Arran*) heave to and ride out stormy weather using their salmon nets as sea anchors. But another crew member, the Faroese fisherman and artist, Trondur Pattursson (who went on to accompany Severin on all his later voyages), was doubtful. He pointed out that a large wave hitting the bows would easily smash through the covers. He suggested instead that they needed to fill the gap between the steering gear and the boat to stop rogue waves coming aboard, but the plastic tarpaulin they had to hand split easily and was far too weak for such a job.

As yet another wave hit and threatened to sink the boat, Severin had a brainwave. He was familiar with the Roman *testudo* or tortoise – a tight formation of soldiers sheltering under their overlapping leather shields, which could deflect all kinds of projectile. Even the sea perhaps. Stored in the bilges were several spare ox hides. In a fever of anxiety Severin pulled them out and Trondur, the most physically adept, punched holes in the hides while standing in a perilous position in the stern. He then used leather thongs to lash a kind of apron that fitted around the helmsman as he operated the steering gear. When a new wave hit, it simply cascaded off the apron; the helmsman was submerged in water, but the rest of the ship was protected. In the icy Greenland seas only fifteen minutes of helming could be withstood before a change of crew was needed. But using the ancient rather than modern, Severin had succeeded in defeating the menacing ocean.

The crew of *Brendan* also discovered that sixth-century clothing and food had significant advantages over their modern counterparts. Freeze-

Often traditional methods and technologies proved to be more efficient and effective than modern ones. Trondur Pattursson, a Faroese fisherman and artist, used a harpoon to catch fish to feed the crew.

dried food quickly became soaked and ruined in the open boat. When the voyage continued from Iceland, Severin stocked up on smoked beef and salt pork, oat cereal and cheddar cheese – foodstuffs that were just as good wet or dry and did not deteriorate if saturated by a wave. When they started the journey the crew had worn waterproofs and synthetic fibre clothing, but it soon became clear that wool, which retains its insulating properties even when wet, was a better choice, as it had been for the Irish monks. Woollen underwear from the Faroes, wool mitts, sweaters and woollen caps, even tweed jackets – the kind of garments that are still worn by curragh fisherman off the Irish coast – all proved to be warm and much-appreciated clothing for the voyage.

As *Brendan* approached North America ice floes became more frequent. At one point the little boat was fighting its way through a mass of confused floes and pieces of iceberg. The first collision was 'like hitting a concrete wall', but the boat survived. By raising and lowering the foresail to gain and lose speed the crew managed to work their way through the ice. Only days earlier a reinforced steel icebreaker named the *Carson* had been crushed and sunk in the same conditions. If steel could be vanquished by ice, what hope did they have with leather and wood?

With one crew member looking out and calling out directions Severin made his way slowly through the nightmare maze of ice. At night they used torches to illuminate their course, until eventually their luck ran out. *Brendan* entered a gap between two ice floes which then unexpectedly closed together, trapping the boat. There was a peculiar shudder before *Brendan* broke free. Five minutes later, sea water was swirling around the boards. *Brendan* was holed and sinking.

In the gusting icy darkness the crew manned the pumps. It took two thousand exhausting strokes to empty the boat. And within fifteen minutes water levels were again dangerously high. Rather than attempt to shift their stores at night to find the leak, Severin ordered that they should pump continuously until daybreak. By dawn the crew were exhausted. Both the stern and bow floorboards were taken up but no sign of the leak could be found.

FIVE MINUTES LATER, SEA WATER WAS SWIRLING AROUND THE BOARDS. *BRENDAN* WAS HOLED AND SINKING.

Severin then recalled that he had seen marine phosphorescence both outside and inside the boat the night before – the glowing plankton must have entered through the leak. He recalled this was amidships, and sure enough, when he leant over the side of the boat he located a grapefruit-sized dent. On the inside at the same spot he found a split in the leather, through which water was pouring in. The sheer force of the ice had prised apart the wooden stringers and caused the half-inch thick leather to tear under the extreme pressure.

If *Brendan* had been a plastic or steel boat, repair would have been complicated and difficult, perhaps even impossible. Because she was made of leather the solution was simple: stitch a patch to the outside. But this was still easier said than done. The hole was below the waterline and required one man to bend over the side and reach with his arms into the water. Waves regularly broke against the boat and immersed his upper body in freezing water as he threaded the giant needle back and forth; sometimes it was necessary to help the needle through with a hammer, all the while being soaked by the Arctic waters. Inside the boat, another man punctured the leather with a bradawl before the needle came through with the thread. With admirable understatement George, the man who had weathered the repeated drenchings while hanging over the side, said, 'Well, that's a job I would not like to have to do again.'

THE SMALL BOAT MADE OF LEATHER AND WOOD HAD CONFOUNDED ALL THE CRITICS.

But the patch held and the leak was halted.

Brendan finally arrived at Peckford Island, Newfoundland, fifty days after setting sail from Iceland. The small boat made of leather and wood had confounded all the critics. It had been said that the leather would disintegrate, that the stitching would rot and that the boat would capsize when the first bad weather was encountered. But by methodical experimentation and observation of curraghs before the voyage, and a scrupulous attention to historical detail, Severin and his team had proved them all wrong.

The crew celebrate on arrival at Peckford Island, Newfoundland, fifty days after leaving Iceland and having survived difficult and often dangerous conditions.

As Severin acknowledges, he demonstrated only that such a voyage could have been undertaken by Irish monks, not that it had been – only the discovery of datable Irish relics in America could prove that. These might be hard to find: it is known that Irish hermits lived in Iceland, but no physical traces of them have been found there. Nevertheless, Severin's great achievement lies in showing that documents such as the *Navigatio*, which were once thought to be entirely mythical, contain genuine and useful information, rooted in real experience, albeit encoded in a narrative idiom quite unlike the one we are familiar with today. As a practical archaeologist of the sea, Severin had established this with his *Brendan* voyage, and he then went on to prove it time and again by decoding such other texts of mythical sea voyages as the story of Sindbad or the *Odyssey* – tales that we now know are based far more in historical reality than was previously imagined.

Tim Severin (British, b. 1940) recreated a number of voyages and journeys in order to determine how much of the legends concerning them might be based on factual experience. In 1960, while still an undergraduate student at Oxford, Severin retraced the route of Marco Polo by motorcycle as far as China. To investigate the legend of St Brendan, Severin and his crew set sail from the west coast of Ireland in a boat made of leather and wood to reach North America. He later built a traditional Arab sailing vessel sewn with coconut twine and sailed from Oman to China, a journey described in the book *The Sindbad Voyage*. Subsequently, to test a theory that the Chinese could have been early visitors to continental North America, he built a bamboo raft and almost reached America from China. He has been awarded many honorary degrees as well as the Royal Geographical Society's Gold Medal for exploration.

A water pipit on its migratory flight from North America to Greenland briefly tries to take a rest on Tim Severin's head.

HENK DE VELDE

A NEVER-ENDING OCEAN JOURNEY

IT'S A BOYS DREAM. Wandering along the waterfront, looking at ships, asking the crew where the ship comes from or where it's going to. He feels the mystery of the ship and the journey. And when the boy reaches the age of discretion he chooses to become a captain, and when he advances in the art of the mariner he decides to become a small boat sailor and eventually a single-hander. He roams around the world – one, two, six times – because the world is round and there is nothing more to discover than himself, the reason to live, the reason to sail on forever.

When the only surviving ship of Magellan's expedition returned to Lisbon there was no record-keeping institute to brand it as a first round the world. The ship that came in was almost a wreck, and the men on board were a dying handful of a once proud crew who had sailed away to discover the world. Such discoveries have almost always been made to benefit a

In the Southern Ocean distances are vast and the sea rears up in great waves.

state, a country or some rich families. Most of the men on board must have been of the adventurous type. I say most, but I'm not sure that some of the crew weren't shanghaied, or were only on board to escape the hand of the law. Most of these men did not come back. That's how the world was discovered.

So when did it change? When did a discovery have to be a first? First to climb Mount Everest, first non-stop somewhere, first on the moon. And is it important? Is it important for the discoverer? Or is the discoverer just an adventurous type who cannot or will not fit into the, let's call it, normal world? Amundsen, Scott, Slocum, Moitessier, Knox-Johnston? Between the last two we perhaps begin to see a difference in attitude. Robin Knox-Johnston wanted to be the first, while what Bernard Moitessier discovered during his voyage was that being first is nothing more than returning to where he started from.

The most important rule for an ocean expedition is: one hand on the ship and one hand for yourself. The main objective is to return to tell the tale. You can go for a record, but no one ever achieves a record by not coming back or having a broken mast. Does that mean you must sail defensively? Yes, and it's in your own hands how far you want to push it. Let's look at my case. I choose my boat. Even if you have a sponsor, they can choose the colours but not the boat itself. Choosing your boat means that you trust your boat. Although the boat is not a living thing it becomes a part of yourself. It's the same with the sea. Don't think of the sea either as something that cares about your welfare or as an enemy to fight against. The sea is nothing more than a big piece of cold water. That does not mean you can't enjoy the sea. The colours of the sea are constantly changing as the light changes. Clouds are reflected in the water. Sometimes large creatures come and take a closer look. Once I gazed into the eye of a whale and a warm feeling of mutual understanding came over me. I am the warrior who knows when to stall, when to fight and when to draw back. I am prepared for everything that might happen – hell or high water, and the possibility of facing mechanical as well as personal problems. You are on your own and face the storm.

And then I cast off and don't look back. Of course there are memories, but part of my philosophy is to live in the future, not in the past. Don't look back until the storm hits. Until the sea breaks the deck beneath your feet. Until you look down into bosun's locker thousands of metres deep, the sea beneath you. At that moment the future is no longer important, only

ALTHOUGH THE BOAT IS NOT A LIVING THING IT BECOMES A PART OF YOURSELF.

In Arctic sailing you must be prepared for anything. This photo was taken after the rudders had been damaged by heavy pack ice.

the present. Seas in the Southern Ocean, south of the Roaring Forties, can rear up to enormous heights. The waves can break and when you hear the roaring thunder of the breakers in the night you wish it was daylight, and when it's daylight you long for the darkness of the night so that you can't see the all too real, threatening high seas towering above you.

Sailing round Cape Horn; once it was a boy's dream, now a reality. And after sailing three times round the Horn, once through the Patagonian channels, twice via the Panama Canal, and once north of Russia through the Northeast Passage, or the Northern Sea Route as the Russians call it, then what's left? Look at the map, with all those thin lines showing routes taken – you can see what's left. Is there something still to discover? We are discoverers from the moment we're born. The first question we asked our parents is: why?

Why is also the most difficult question. It's a choice. Following the dream or following your heart is too easy an answer. Why the risks, why the less often taken paths, why the sufferings? Most of what you encounter during an ocean expedition is not written about in a guidebook. Accept anything that can happen. Be prepared. Like I was when I attempted the route north of Russia. Why did I want to take that route? Because it's part of our Dutch history: Willem Barents attempted the route three times and had to overwinter on Nova Zembla island in 1595, never to return. But some of his men did return to tell the story.

I had studied ice conditions for years and was sure it could be done. It was 2001 and as far I knew only the German polar sailor Arved Fuchs had attempted it several times. He sails with a crew; I am single-handed. (In 2002 Eric Brossier with crew on the *Vagabond* and Arved Fuchs with crew on the *Dagmar Aaen* were the first to sail the Northern Sea Route in a single season.) There is one big advantage of being alone – every decision is made by you alone. All responsibility rests on yourself. Three things are most important for a discoverer: self-reliance, personal responsibility and patience.

ELEVEN MONTHS IN A WORLD LIKE ANOTHER PLANET, WHERE WHITE AND A THOUSAND SHADES OF BLUE REIGN.

The Russian authorities refused me permission in 2001. This was in Murmansk, the Atlantic side of the Northern Sea Route. I sailed around the world and entered Russian waters again in 2003, this time from the Bering Sea, the Pacific side of the route. I received the necessary permission and I set out. Don't look back. Go. I had to overwinter the long eleven months of the Siberian winter in Tiksi Buhta. Temperatures -50°C (-58°F); ice 3 m (10 ft) thick. Eleven months in a world like another planet, where white and a thousand shades of blue reign. When I resumed the voyage in 2004 the pack ice damaged the rudders. Five days later I was rescued by the nuclear icebreaker *Vaygatch* and transported by the freighter *Jury Archinevsky* to Murmansk. After repairs I sailed back to the Netherlands.

When I look at the map showing the three voyages of Captain Cook a smile comes on my face. Not a self-satisfied smile, but a proud smile. I've sailed more miles than Captain Cook. In the beginning I used a sextant to navigate. Although I still have a sextant on board I rely on GPS nowadays. Does that matter? Does it take away the romance of seafaring? Not at all. There is no romance in seafaring. There is beauty, there is joy, but no romance. Seafaring is searching for new destinations beyond the horizon, and some of the chosen destinations are hard to get to. Storms, fog, currents, rocks, sandbanks, reefs – all are lying between you and the sun or a white sandy beach.

Two years later, in 2007, I departed again on my Never-Ending Voyage, but this time my intention was not to return. The journey I had in mind was to islands where nobody goes. Some in the tropics, some in higher latitudes. Eventually I found myself anchored in a blue lagoon, sitting with the elders of a native village to discuss the matters of the day. I visited Île St Paul, an active volcano in the ocean with an open crater. I sat with chief navigator Teo Onopey of Puluwat Island and talked about the art of navigating.

Sometimes you are lucky enough to have a calm sea to approach a distant island – here Île St Paul in the southern Indian Ocean.

The entrance into the calm central caldera (crater) of Île St Paul.

You remember my philosophy? Don't look back. But age never stops – I am over sixty now, and this warrior is on his way home. Why do I call myself a warrior? The answer is that I had to fight for all I did or decided to do. So why am I on my way home? Six circumnavigations. Is that enough?

I have learnt to see the world in a grain of sand. Every end of a voyage is the beginning of a new one. Home is where my heart is, and the roof over my nearest kin. It took me quite a while to discover that. Discoveries or expeditions can be part of a lifestyle, but I am not a cruiser. I am a mariner and I am discovering more and more about not being alone. It has nothing to do with loneliness or solitude. The most terrifying and important test for a human being is to be in absolute isolation. Alone, with no witnesses, he begins to discover things about himself. You can easily become an animal: it is not necessary to shave or to wash. Once you have passed the solitude test, you have absolute confidence in yourself, and there is nothing that can break you afterwards. So, it's a strange feeling when you come back to civilization. This transition can be very difficult. But I learnt there is always someone watching over me ... call it my Guardian Angel.

Henk de Velde (Dutch, b. 1949) first went to sea as a deckboy at the age of fifteen. He then studied at the Nautical College in Amsterdam and became a maritime officer. He has now sailed six times around the world in small sailing craft. His son, Stefan, was born in 1981 on Easter Island.

JEFF MACINNIS
THE NORTHWEST PASSAGE BY SAIL

OVER THE SOUND OF THE GRINDING, BOAT-CRUSHING ICE, I shout: 'One, two, three, heave! One, two, three, heave!' Inching our fully provisioned, 318-kg (700-lb) Hobie 18 catamaran forwards requires every ounce of our combined strength. Driven by strong current, the rubble pile of ice is in constant motion. Pausing to rest is impossible – we'd be crushed within minutes. This is truly a 'land that devours ships'.

Mike Beedell and I struggled for two hours to drag *Perception* across 365 m (1,200 ft) of ice. It was a nightmarish conglomeration of pieces of all sizes, shapes and ages, some rising 3 m (10 ft) out of the water, all of it shifting, creaking and grinding away in the current, threatening to pin our legs if we took a false step. At times, the boat's bows would be over our heads as we hauled it along on its runners, hoping it could withstand the stresses and strains it was undergoing.

Waves exploding over our catamaran. Mike Beedell (right) and I brace ourselves as we sail in the Northwest Passage.

Opposite left Pushing relentlessly through ice that is moving fast with the current.

Opposite right We often had to haul our catamaran through many miles of ice. With a fully loaded boat and uneven ice the task was brutally tough.

I can remember the thrill of sailing the Arctic waters of the Northwest Passage in 1986–88 as if it was yesterday. The National Geographic Society in Washington asked for our story and the Royal Geographical Society in London wanted a speech, because we were the first to sail the Northwest Passage. My heroes are the early explorers who pushed bravely into these waters with wooden sailing ships and iron determination.

Across the roof of North America, the Northwest Passage weaves 4,020 km (2,500 miles) through the Arctic archipelago of islands. Early explorers probed it from the mid-1500s, searching for a faster route to the Orient and the riches that lay there. The names of Davis, Hudson, Baffin, Franklin and many others crowd the maps of the Arctic, where these heroic men tried and failed, and often died in their attempts, to sail this labyrinth of ice. Roald Amundsen took three years, between 1903 and 1906, to complete the Passage in his motorized sailing vessel, the *Gjoa*. I hoped we could be the first to sail the Northwest Passage in a solely wind-powered boat, a dream that was now four centuries old.

I HOPED WE COULD BE THE FIRST TO SAIL THE NORTHWEST PASSAGE IN A SOLELY WIND-POWERED BOAT, A DREAM THAT WAS NOW FOUR CENTURIES OLD.

Consumed by this age-old challenge, my team began the fascinating process of devising an expedition to see whether, using today's technology, we could sail the Passage. Our greatest asset was the people who shaped the equipment and tactics for this dangerous endeavour. Without their enormous assistance the journey would never have begun.

Why a Hobie Cat? This was the question asked most frequently. In my mind, the two-man Hobie, with its specially strengthened structure, represents all the outstanding qualities necessary for success in one of the harshest environments on Earth. Fast under sail and with the ability to be hauled over the ice, it allowed us to adapt to the constantly changing conditions. Knowing that the boat was a proven design in more southerly latitudes gave us confidence that it should be able to handle other difficult situations.

Two years of planning, testing and preparation saw our team of advisers grow to more than a hundred people, who all helped solve the multidimensional problems the Passage presented. Borrowing tried and tested equipment and systems from areas as diverse as diving, mountaineering, aeronautics and sailing, we designed our expedition to respond to the conditions in the Arctic, which demands adaptability in order to survive. And by combining today's technology with Inuit ways of working with the environment, it seemed possible that the Passage could be sailed.

One of the most important aspects was choosing the person to sail with on this voyage. Four months before departure I teamed up with Mike Beedell, who has spent years exploring and photographing the Arctic. His experience proved invaluable.

In July 1986, Mike and I set out from Inuvik, which sits on the edge of the silt-brown Mackenzie River. Following the Mackenzie 145 km (90 miles) down to the Beaufort Sea, we headed east through the ice-infested waters. Much to our dismay, we had sailed less than 160 km (100 miles) of open water before a wall of ice blocked the entire route ahead. Slowly we progressed against head winds into the maze of ice.

We settled into the routine we tried to follow throughout our voyage. Rising at 7 a.m., we would eat, break camp and set sail for at least twelve hours. The distance covered each day ranged from a low of ten miles, mostly paddling or hauling the boat along the shore when there was no wind, to a hundred miles of exciting downwind sailing. Generally, the travel was agonizingly slow. Two-thirds of the time was spent tacking into the wind, which nearly doubled the sailing distance.

For safety reasons we always sailed with land in sight. This meant we had to sail deep into and round three large bays in order to cross them. Franklin Bay, the largest, was named for Sir John Franklin in 1826 during his second Arctic expedition. We read some vivid journals of these voyages during our journey, and this heightened our respect for, and wariness of, the Arctic environment.

Where we slept at night depended on the terrain and the availability of fresh water. Cliffs and rocky ground complicated site selection. We also had to haul the boat far enough up on the shore to avoid high tides and big waves. Making camp took time and it was often close to midnight before we hungrily ate our freeze-dried dinner. There is plenty of daylight at this latitude, so between eating and the time when exhaustion sent us to our sleeping bags we explored, took photographs or wrote our journals. Always, though, we kept a wary eye for polar bears.

Snow began to fall in late August, signalling the fast approaching winter. We spent our last night of the first year pinned down by an easterly storm in a place called Starvation Cove. Appropriately, this was where we broke open the last of our food rations. Stuck in the cove, cold and hungry, we could almost understand how the early explorers would occasionally be driven to eat their leather boots.

During that first year we sailed more than 1,600 km (1,000 miles) and left the boat at Cambridge Bay for the winter. The next summer we returned to the bay and surveyed the horizon. There were no trees and no open water, only an endless ocean of ice. It looked hopeless. The ice forecasters appeared to have been right, there would be no sailing this year. It was a problem that plagued us all summer. For the first 16 km (10 miles) we half-sailed, half-dragged our Hobie across the uneven ice. Hauling the boat was so strenuous that sweat dripped from our bodies, despite the sub-zero temperatures. A northwest wind then moved the ice just far enough off Victoria Island to allow a narrow opening. The euphoria of making progress kept us travelling for twenty hours that first day.

Our good fortune ended abruptly when we tried to cross Icebreaker Channel, which took twelve days of fear and frustration. From a deck-level

MAKING CAMP TOOK TIME AND IT WAS OFTEN CLOSE TO MIDNIGHT BEFORE WE HUNGRILY ATE OUR FREEZE-DRIED DINNER.

Right We camped as often as we could on land. It was safer than sleeping out on the Arctic ice on top of our boat, yet never safe from polar bears.

Opposite A moment of celebration out on the ice pack waiting out another storm.

perspective, the ice stretched on to infinity. This maze of ice was constantly in motion, creating a crushing confusion of pack ice. Multi-year ice thrusting skywards over 8 m (25 ft) high in places created an undulating frozen landscape. We picked what looked like a promising lead and sailed into it, only to reach a dead end. Time and time again our efforts proved futile. There was open water ahead but it was rapidly being filled in, and we suddenly realized that the wind and current were conspiring to imprison us in the grinding, moaning ice. With a desperate effort, we dragged the boat across the drifting pans to where the water remained free and sailed down a fast closing lead.

Finally, stranded amid the pack ice, all we could do was to haul our Hobie up on to the ice and wait for conditions to improve. With the ice constantly shifting, our only safe place to sleep was on the netting trampoline between the boat's hulls. The bows of *Perception* were pointed into the wind to present the smallest profile and the tent was securely erected on the tramp. Inside, burrowed deep within our sleeping bags, was the only place of relative comfort. Even as we drifted off to sleep our constant thoughts were of the ice breaking beneath the hulls or of polar bear encounters.

In this way, tethered to the ice and running with an approaching storm, we progressed rapidly due north. Two days later, on 31 August, near the top of Peel Sound winds howled at 105 km (65 miles) per hour, creating waves two storeys high. Mike and I were in the middle of a gale on a piece of ice barely large enough to hold our 5.5-m (18-ft) Hobie. We were riding, it seemed, an endless roller coaster into destruction. Each swell lifted our tiny island of ice up and over the frothy, wind-lashed crest, only to drop us down the other side. Fog obscured our horizon; we were landless on an ocean of boat-crushing ice.

We were prepared for the worst, dressed with every piece of survival equipment: our weatherproof Gore-Tex suits over insulative clothing, our emergency location devices strapped to our bodies, our one-man survival seats tied to our waists, and our stomachs stuffed with as much food as time would allow. Fully equipped, our defences still seemed as nothing in comparison to the white nightmare that engulfed us.

Using all our combined strength, plus two mountaineering ice screws driven into the ice, we rode the storm 16 km (10 miles) across Aston Bay. Finally, we crashed into the main pack of ice. After pushing our boat 3 km (2 miles) over the moving pack we kissed the ground, thrilled to be alive.

For a second year our journey came to a halt. The last day was spent sailing in temperatures of -5°C (23°F) with the lines and deck covered in ice and our bodies numbed by the windchill factor of -20°C (-4°F). That night and for the next day a snowstorm with winds of 72 km (45 miles) per hour lashed the ground where we huddled. To keep the tent from being destroyed, we built a snow wall. Winter conditions forced us to abandon our Hobie on the tundra just 805 km (500 miles) from our goal.

We returned to the Arctic in early summer the following year to repair our Hobie and sail the last distance to the finish. In Cunningham Inlet we were delighted to sail among more than a thousand beluga whales, which accepted us as one of them. Further along the coast we experienced the shock of being woken up by a polar bear. Fortunately, he decided that we weren't what he wanted for break-fast that day. Every moment of almost every day, on the ocean or off, our full focus was demanded in order to survive.

IN CUNNINGHAM INLET WE WERE DELIGHTED TO SAIL AMONG MORE THAN A THOUSAND BELUGA WHALES, WHICH ACCEPTED US AS ONE OF THEM.

Sailing past glacier-capped mountains, we approached the end of our long journey. Memories and experiences flow through our minds. We have been exposed to great hardships and at times terrifying natural forces that made us adapt quickly or perish. From our deck-level perspective we could intimately glimpse a land of incredible beauty and deadly harshness.

At 5:08 a.m. on the morning of our 100th day, speeding into Baffin Bay, the spray from our twin hulls made rainbows in the sun as we completed the first sail-powered voyage through the Northwest Passage. We jour-neyed through these waters on its terms and simply tried to respond to its challenges. We were fortunate to have survived these treacherous waters.

In my journal I wrote:

August 17th, 1988, 6:50 a.m.: I sit here at Button Point snug in the ruins of a Thule Inuit hut that is at least 400 years old: as old, in fact, as the dream of sailing the Northwest Passage. A four-foot high wall of rock and whalebone protects me from the howling wind. The wall next to me is supported by a 100 pound bowhead whale skull, its powder white surface is cracked and crevassed by time. Orange lichen, which takes more than a century to grow, is creeping over its surface.

The now open room is about twelve square feet, and I am sitting on the sleeping platform that runs around the perimeter, writing with bare hands, a luxury not often permitted on this voyage. I've been up for nearly twenty-three hours but I cannot sleep,

Ghosting along in calm water with the cliffs of Prince Leopold Island in the background. The calm and quiet of windless moments gave us an awe-inspiring sense of this incredible wilderness.

the joy and excitement are too great. Our Hobie Cat rests on the rocky beach, the wind whistling in her rigging, her bright yellow hulls radiant in the morning sunlight...

Jeff MacInnis (Canadian, b. 1963) was a member of the Canadian National Ski Team before he achieved a 400-year-old challenge when in 1986–88 he led the first team to sail the Northwest Passage. Amundsen was the first to traverse the passage but he used a motor yacht. MacInnis used a sport catamaran with no power except the wind. The journey covered more than 4,000 km (2,500 miles) over 100 days, surviving one of the harshest environments on the planet, through an ice-choked passage that has claimed more lives than Mount Everest.

JON TURK

KAYAKING THE SOLOMON ISLANDS CHAIN

I WAS PADDLING A SIT-ON-TOP KAYAK IN THE SOLOMON ISLANDS – solo – perched precariously on a speck of yellow plastic in the rolling vastness of the Pacific, seeking the wonder of vulnerability.

When I landed in Honiara airport on Guadalcanal in the autumn of 2009, travel posters displayed seductively paradisiacal images of lovers strolling along palm-lined beaches. This advertising was so ubiquitous and powerful that I was fooled into imagining easy passages, even though I knew that dangerous currents raced between the islands. My goal was to paddle the length of the Solomon Islands chain, alternating long crossings with more tranquil passages along island coastlines. I planned to end my journey at the northeast tip of Choiseul, when I would be in sight of Bougainville Island in Papua New Guinea. On the second day of the expedition, I bumbled across Iron Bottom Sound – and was severely chastened

Weaving, alone, through the ancient mysteries of a flooded mangrove swamp in the Solomon Islands.

by rips and steep breaking waves. Sobered and mildly battered, I pulled to shore on a coral beach, daydreaming now of stern warriors in dugouts rather than Mai Tais at Happy Hour.

For the next week, I paddled in protected waters along the Nggela Islands and then set out in the pre-dawn for a long crossing to Santa Isabel Island. After I blasted through the surf and felt the mature waves of open water, I opened my ditty bag and discovered that someone had stolen my GPS. A strong current ran through the channel. In the darkness and deprived of electronic navigation, I couldn't calculate my course using comfortable, precise, left-brain mathematics. Instead, I had to feel the ocean, to sense the strength of the current from the shape of the waves, to enter, however feebly and imperceptibly, into the ancient arts of Melanesian and Polynesian navigation. And if I didn't learn quickly, I would drift off course and die on the open sea.

I reached land, exhausted, but then paddled peacefully along the shore for ten days. When I reached the northwest tip of Ghaghe Island, last point of land before the next open water, I resolved to camp and study the ocean so my third crossing would be seamless, uncomplicated and technically perfect. I imagined sitting alone on the beach, enjoying the peaceful solitude, carefully timing the tidal movements so that I would cross the deepest part of the channel at slack water. As I approached land, watching for reefs jutting through the gentle surf, I caught a flash of movement in my side vision – not a discernible shape or object, just a blur that triggered the ancestral part of my brain that had evolved to detect the stealthy passage of a lion in tall grass.

AND IF I DIDN'T LEARN QUICKLY, I WOULD DRIFT OFF COURSE AND DIE ON THE OPEN SEA.

In the Solomon Islands, in a photo taken by remote camera. Many kayakers view a sit-on-top as a recreational kayak, but it is seaworthy for long, open ocean expeditions as long as you are willing to embrace the ultimate in vulnerability – the most minimalist of watercraft on the high seas.

JASON LEWIS

PEDAL-POWER ACROSS THE PACIFIC

THE MEANS, THE MAPS, THE GEAR. THEY'VE ALL CHANGED. Under pressure to see and do it all, human exploration undergoes constant metamorphosis; its only unaltered element is gumption. Adventurers survive self-imposed predicaments or die trying. The committed never die quitting.

My ex-college pal Stevie Smith and I crafted a plan to circumnavigate the globe solely by human power, using a variety of means – walking, roller-blading, cycling, kayaking, swimming, rowing, and pedalling a small boat. Our shirts naively, and optimistically, proclaimed: 'The First Man-Powered Round-The-World Expedition. 1994–1996'. On 6 October 2007, thirteen years and 74,840 km (46,505 miles) after we set out, I crossed the Prime Meridian at Greenwich, London, and achieved one of the last great firsts for circumnavigation.

On 4 May 1999, I stood on Hawaii's west coast and the halfway point of Expedition 360 beckoned: a tiny coral atoll named Tarawa. One of thirty-three islets in the archipelago of the Republic of Kiribati, it hovers barely 3 m (10 ft) above sea level and would serve as a replenishing point en route to the Solomon Islands. For the next 3,860 km (2,400) miles across the central Pacific, I would be the human motor for a familiar friend, *Moksha*, an 8-m by 1.2-m (26-ft by 4-ft) pedal-powered boat. The old girl had suc-cessfully carried Stevie and me over 7,240 km (4,500 miles) of Atlantic from Portugal to Miami, and fifty-four days across the Pacific from San Francisco to Hawaii. Our adventuring partnership had come to an end, as Stevie opted to make the Hawaiian leg his last. This time, for the first time, I'd pilot solo, and into a legendary mariner's nightmare – the doldrums.

A few degrees north of the Equator lie 644 km (400 miles) of languid water, sudden storms and windlessness known as the Inter-Tropical

Australia bound: I take a break from pedalling my boat *Moksha* across the Pacific.

Convergence Zone (ITCZ). Sailing authorities had assured me that leg power alone could never punch through its countercurrent, a dastardly region where waters from the southern and northern hemispheres collide. I ignored them, hoping to solve that quandary when it arrived. With faithful certainty that *Moksha's* new propeller unit would endure, I was ill-prepared for what would happen to my spirit.

Exploration lives in the mind. It is born there and festers there if not nurtured. Waving sad see-you-laters to friends in Kona harbour, I imagined that being alone at sea for two months would help me harness again my once-found state of peace and composure. Instead, my thoughts became increasingly unanchored, and mental turmoil took the helm.

The journey actually started out fine. I felt liberated! Land and its trappings had long slipped from sight, and just when I began to doubt my decision and feel vulnerable in the vast blue, a juvenile red-footed booby plopped upon the deck. This was the very first bird to land on *Moksha*, and I welcomed it as a friend and a good omen. Naturally, it defecated on the solar panel.

The familiar atmosphere of the boat's cramped innards felt as much of a home to me as anywhere. The pedal seat became the Office, and the opposite passenger seat beside the denatured alcohol stove served as the Kitchen. The fore and stern decks became my Recreation Room, and my Bedroom remained the beloved Rathole, a glorified broom cupboard beneath the foredeck where I spent a measly six of every twenty-four hours.

Soaring daytime temperatures meant pedal shifts had to be punctuated with hourly dips in the ocean to cool my frying brain. Aided by the northeast trades, charting successive 80-km (50-mile) days was no problem, varying my heading daily between 240 and 180 degrees to ensure one mile south for every two west.

My days were fully engaged. Enslaved by technology, I found little time for meditation. A new electric water pump to bail out freed up more pedalling hours, but I hand-pumped often to reserve enough battery energy from the solar panels and wind generator to power a deck light and radar detector, and keep the laptop, Iridium satellite phone, cameras and GPS charged. To maintain significant forward progress, I had to adhere to the strictest of schedules:

5 a.m.   Wakey wakey. Make tea, sponge out boat,
           take GPS fix to chart the night's drift while sleeping.

Just another day in the Office: pedalling while also keeping a look out for ships.

5:30 – 8:30	First pedal shift.
8:30 – 9:15	Breakfast. Check email, assess latitude and longitude on chart.
9:15 – 12:30	Second pedal shift.
12:30 – 1:30	Lunch and a power nap.
1:30 – 4	Third pedal shift.
4 – 5	Write Expedition 360 website update and transmit via sat phone.
5 – 6:45	Fourth pedal shift.
6:45 – 7:30	Dinner.
7:30 – 10:45	Fifth pedal shift.
11 p.m.	Journey to the land of Nod.

Compared with previous ocean legs, I enjoyed kingly meals. Porridge with dried fruits and jam made for delicious mornings, and lunches became relished dinner leftovers. The heat quickly dilapidated the carrots and broccoli, but the fresh ginger, onions and cabbage held their own for weeks and became dinner menu highlights on top of wild rice with tofu and a sauce of soy, garlic, honey and toasted sesame seed oil. Occasionally, I steamed bread in a pressure cooker, and discovered fleeting gastrointestinal nirvana upon eating my last orange on day 20.

Below left Provisioning a small boat for up to six months at sea can be a challenge, especially when you can't remember where you put the raisins.

Below right Evening meal: with space for only a single-ring stove (burning denatured alcohol), cooking is a circus act of juggling pots, pans, lids, knives and chopping boards.

Ocean visitors were bountiful, and escorted me the entire way. Big, brilliant dorado fish battled gulls for flying fish, and one day a large pod of rambunctious dolphins bolted by. Rinsing my porridge bowl each morning invited a school of fat, zebra-striped pilot fish. Clumsy seabirds kept me busy with a constant rain of faeces. An impressive ecosystem of indefatigable barnacles and crabs had to be regularly scraped off *Moksha*'s hull to prevent drag. Frequent large waves, 5–9-m (15–30 ft) high, crashed enough water over the port beam to keep everything saturated for days, leaving wayward flying fish flopping about the cockpit, gunwales and deck. Luckily for them, my appetite was vegetarian.

By far the most unwelcome guests were the viciously inevitable salt sores. After a month, I was layered in oozing excrescences and ulcerative boils. The chaffing was horrific. My buttocks and underarms were plagued, and pussing abscesses only dried out with regular applications of, bizarrely enough, WD40. I relied on the ocean to cool off, but painfully had to relinquish the current round's victory to the sores.

Breathing became harder as the Office air grew thick with reeking, dead sweat and sopping clothes. My nights were haunted by feverish recurring dreams of being devoured by a menacing Kraken. By day, morose feelings gripped me and my body faltered. I was nauseous and unusually tired. My head hurt and my right fingers were numb. A thousand miles from a hospital, my website updates were becoming jumbled nonsense.

CLUMSY SEABIRDS KEPT ME BUSY WITH A CONSTANT RAIN OF FAECES.

Concerned for my sanity, dedicated expedition partner April Abril emailed and arranged for me to talk with a dermatologist over the sat phone. The good doctor assessed my situation as dire,

A juvenile red-footed booby hitches a ride on the stern deck.

Using a pair of dividers to record the daily mileage on the chart.

and determined that septicaemia had found easy passage from the sea to my blood through the open sores. In forty-eight hours my body would collapse from systemic poisoning, she warned. Frantically, I searched my first-aid kit. A three-year-old bottle of Ciprofloxacin antibiotic had the doc congratulating me on my luck. I popped Cipros for the next three days and kept out of the water. By the fourth morning, I'd regained some of my former health, grateful for, and unquestioning of, the value of proper exploration tech.

The ocean a mirror of eerie calm, *Moksha* slipped into the doldrums on day 45. I could hear my thudding pulse. Squalls loomed on all horizons and palpable electricity crackled. Fearful of lightning bolts blasting the wind-generator pole, I bodged random metal, including a bike lock and a bent fork, to make an ocean grounding rod.

International Date Line: 180 degrees east and west of Greenwich, marking the circumnavigation halfway point.

At 5 degrees north of the Equator, all forward momentum ceased. Three weeks later, the GPS readout confirmed I'd gone nowhere, vindicating the experts. If I didn't pedal, the boat went backwards. Hope grew dimmer with every day, and the voyage began to crush my willpower. My spirit waned and my mind darkened further.

The port side cargo net began cursing at me in a thick German accent. It mocked me, said I was no longer fit to skipper the boat. I looked closer,

**IF I DIDN'T PEDAL,
THE BOAT WENT BACKWARDS.**

and saw that it was not the netting, but a wooden serving spoon we'd picked up in Portugal. His name was Heinz. Then the red-handled stove lighter, Serge, started insulting me in an outrageous French accent. My spatula, an irascible Northern Irishman declared himself as Seamus O'Leary and spat threats of mutiny.

Rigid mental parameters of sanity and reality become blurred after two months of solitary exploring in liquid wilderness. The carrot and stick routine had carried me this far well enough: promising myself guitar time on deck or M&Ms for completing a pedal shift, and a shot of Glenlivet whisky for conquering another longitude line. Now, talking fish and utensils were compatriots I embraced wholeheartedly – fair-weather friends in an emptiness of weary thoughts.

Then, on 3 July, my sixty-first day at sea, the GPS finally displayed 180 and a line of zeros as Expedition 360 crossed the International Date Line and into a new day. Although rescue was now nigh impossible, despair and failure had revealed themselves illusions, and I rebuilt hope around the reality that pedalling and staying in place was better than going backwards, running out of food and starving.

Next day, my fortunes changed. The current shifted and the south-east trades picked up. *Moksha* broke from her static prison; I gripped the steering toggles and pedalled hard. My heart lightened and my imaginary shipmates cheered and jeered me on. Realizing they had served their purpose and could not return to land with me, in a teary moment of near madness I let Heinz, Serge and Seamus drift away to a watery grave.

A mere 64 km (40 miles) from my destination of Tarawa, the last of the three water-makers failed, and pots and pans strapped to the deck collected only a few tablespoons of rain. Overheated, dehydrated and looking forward to ending my isolation, I slogged on for two days without a drink, and on 15 July gleefully found smiling friends awaiting me in Tarawa's Betio harbour with a litre of impossibly cold, life-restoring water.

After seventy-three days and nights in the watery void, my mind had been bent to and fro, nearly breaking my resolve. But I'd adapted in strange ways to survive, and celebrated Expedition 360's fifth anniversary with an assurance my exploring days were far from over. I'd discovered that the ocean is both infinitely interesting and utterly boring, and that the mind can achieve whatever it can be convinced of, even if it meant going a bit doolally. Don't be afraid. Explore.

Jason Lewis (British, b. 1967) is credited with being the first to pedal east–west across the Atlantic Ocean (1995), roller-blade solo across the USA (1996) and pedal across the Pacific Ocean (2000), all part of his circumnavigation of the world by human power (2007), described by The Sunday Times **as 'One of the last great firsts for circumnavigation'. Expedition 360's objectives were to promote environmentally friendly travel, world citizenship between cultures and awareness of climate change among young people. Jason is a Fellow of the Royal Geographical Society and an Honorary Fellow of London University. He divides his time between Colorado and London.**

RIVER

An urge to follow rivers has driven explorers from earliest recorded history. Herodotus tells us of his own expedition up the Nile to reach the first cataract in the fifth century BC, and the obsession with the source of that great river sustained many legendary Victorians in the nineteenth century. A hundred years later, men and women were still being inspired to trace the course of the world's major natural waterways, in some cases to seek the source, in others to find new routes by water across continents.

There is something irresistible about travelling on a river. Even in overcrowded parts of Europe and North America, stretches of river between habitations are often wild and rarely visited, as many canoeists know. In relatively unexplored country, the anticipation of what may lie around each corner can be intense. All kinds of wildlife tends to gather wherever there is water, and there is always the danger of hidden snags or rapids. What creatures live above, below and around this pulsing life force? Who else has passed along this eternal route across the land? And where does that great, seemingly endless volume of water come from?

Such questions have intrigued many explorers, and rivers are the threads they hang their journeys on. As water becomes the new scarce global resource, their experiences may be unrepeatable – rivers change beyond recognition and the flow itself is often interrupted or begins to dry up – but rivers remain the lifeblood of many continents and countries.

One of the three inflatable rubber boats used by Mirella and Lorenzo Ricciardi on their African Rainbow expedition pushes its way through the fast-moving Zaire River. Each evening they had to find a campsite somewhere along the banks.

JOHN BLASHFORD-SNELL

THE CONGO, GIANT OF RIVERS

'David Gestetner', one of the giant inflatables, battling through the rapids on the Zaire River at Kinsuka.

AT SUNSET IN JANUARY 1975, a fleet of unusual inflatable boats emerged from the coastline of Africa and sailed out into the Atlantic. A dozen nations' flags flew from the masts; a British Army chaplain held a brief service and gave thanks for the safe completion of one of the largest river expeditions ever. In 104 days the boats had navigated 4,345 km (2,700 miles) of the Zaire (now Congo) River, a journey which had taken Henry Morton Stanley almost two years a century before. Stanley had been forced to portage his boats around the difficult cataracts, but our expedition had successfully navigated the raging rapids with the exception of two or three with waterfalls.

It had all begun in 1970 when, at the suggestion of historian Richard Snailham, the Scientific Exploration Society (SES) started work on the proposal to navigate the Zaire River. The plan was to use this ferocious waterway as a route through the Congo Basin, so that scientific teams could explore the little-known interior. Then in 1972 reconnaissance teams brought back valuable information on the difficulties we faced.

After intense preparation, the team flew to Zaire (from 1997, the Democratic Republic of the Congo) in President Mobutu's DC 10 in October 1974. We were 165, including 50 scientists. Although the majority came from Britain, there were members from the United States, Canada, New Zealand, Australia, Denmark, France, the Netherlands, Nepal and Fiji, as well as 20 soldiers and scientists from Zaire itself.

From the outset the project had been supported by the Zaire government, and President Mobutu was the patron. We were also backed by the British and US armies, the Explorers Club and over 300 sponsors, including the *Daily Telegraph*, Anglia Television, Gestetner, Avon and many individuals, in particular Walter Annenberg, then American ambassador in London.

THE PLAN WAS TO USE THIS FEROCIOUS WATERWAY AS A ROUTE THROUGH THE CONGO BASIN, SO THAT SCIENTIFIC TEAMS COULD EXPLORE THE LITTLE-KNOWN INTERIOR.

The founders of the SES had pioneered whitewater rafting on the first descent of the Blue Nile in 1968, and Avon boats were developed for this new venture. The giant inflatable boats needed to navigate the enormous rapids were developed on the Colorado River by rafting experts Ron Smith and his brother Marc. Each of these bulbous 11-m (37-ft) long vessels had two Mercury 40hp outboard engines – one mounted amidships giving forward power and one astern for steering. We were also fortunate to have a British Army Air Corps Beaver aircraft for vital air recces and parachute resupply.

Henry Morton Stanley's old house, dating from 1881, at Maniauge near Matadi.

Caroline Oxton working with the specialist team studying river blindness in the region.

Our first task was the navigation of the upper regions of the river from its source near the Zambian frontier to the small town of Bukama. This was a job for our whitewater experts and scientists, who used the smaller Avon inflatables to negotiate the narrow waterway. The wildlife was more of a problem than the rapids, and an angry hippopotamus destroyed one boat.

At Bukama the giant inflatables were launched before a large crowd of Zairois. The first part of our journey was through a wide, treeless morass. Royal Engineers went ahead in small boats to clear blockages formed by weed islands using explosives and mark the best passage. Our first real test came at rapids known as the Gates of Hell. In spite of this forbidding name they proved to be relatively easy. Meanwhile, the scientific teams working on and around the river used the expedition fleet as an umbilical cord. Fearing we might be attacked by anti-government rebels, the Zaire army had issued us with a mass of small arms. Fortunately, however, the people we met were friendly and there was no call to use them. After 322 km (200 miles) of relatively peaceful cruising we reached the Stanley Falls – some seven cataracts in over 80 km (50 miles) of river. Here we received severe punishment and almost lost several of our craft. Nevertheless, by early December we reached Kisangani, second city of Zaire and the halfway mark for our expedition.

While the boat party was our spearhead, many expedition members had the less glamorous but still challenging task of supporting the fleet with fuel, food and supplies at pre-arranged points in the tropical forest. They moved by Land Rover and even a hired train. These support groups also looked after the scientific parties that were studying the botany, biology, entomology, geology and zoology of the region. The botanists

Jeremy Mallinson of the Jersey Zoo encountered this giant mountain gorilla in Eastern Zaire.

were particularly interested in water hyacinth, an attractive little plant that unfortunately blocks up the waterways of Africa. In the centre of this vast country, a nineteen-strong multinational team of eye specialists was studying anomalies in the distribution of river blindness, a disease that affected some 20 million Africans, of whom 2 million had gone blind.

In the tropical rainforest zoologists sought the elusive otter shrew and the scaly pangolin. One group studying primates, led by Jeremy Mallinson of the Jersey Zoo, had a memorable meeting with mountain gorillas. A huge male charged within 2 m (6 ft) of the group, but luckily he was only bluffing. There were also sightings of the rare okapi and a dwarf chimpanzee was discovered by chance under a Zairois lady's dinner table.

THE EXPEDITION WAS NOW SPREAD OUT OVER A VAST AREA AND RADIO COMMUNICATION WAS UNRELIABLE.

From Kisangani the river is easily navigable for almost 1,610 km (1,000 miles) and thus the boats motored along at a steady 80 km (50 miles) a day. The Equator was crossed twice, with traditional ceremony.

As expected there were casualties, especially from a particularly virulent form of malaria, and several of our team became seriously ill. One soldier fell 26 m (85 ft) from a jungle tree while fixing insect traps for the entomologists. Miraculously, he only suffered a minor brain haemorrhage. Roger Chapman was struck down with a liver abscess and his life was saved by our medics; we then commandeered a freight plane to evacuate him for further intensive care.

We had Christmas where we regrouped, in the capital, Kinshasa. The expedition was now spread out over a vast area and radio communication was unreliable. Political difficulties were my constant worry; our

Beaver had spotted jungle camps of foreign soldiers and we often picked up Chinese radio transmissions. However, after generous entertainment by the British Embassy and expats, we returned to the boats for the final stretch, the Livingstone Falls, which run for 322 km (200 miles) to the sea.

An enormous crowd turned out on New Year's Day to see us tackle the first of these cataracts and watched as the big inflatable 'David Gestetner' struck a rock and had its engine thrown upwards. The propeller slashed through the fabric and the stern collapsed; the huge boat plunged into large waves and for a moment it seemed it would be swamped and destroyed. Luckily, by now, the expedition had been joined by two 5.5-m (18-ft) New Zealand Hamilton jet boats, which were able to motor against the current. As one jet went in to pick up a line from the stricken craft, it reared up on a wave and crashed on top of us. I saw the midships propeller racing above my head before we broke free and managed to haul the hull to a nearby beach for repair.

THE UPTURNED BOAT WITH ITS CREW OF THREE CLINGING TO IT WAS SWEPT TOWARDS THE YAWNING WHIRLPOOL.

On reaching Isangila Rapids, which had finally forced Stanley to abandon his boats and leave the river, I decided to portage the giant rafts a short distance and avoid a suicidal stretch. While they moved over land, the smaller boats could continue down the calmer edge of the river. In the final rapid, 'La Vision', our flagship, was momentarily trapped in a whirlpool, like a cork in a wash tub, and was bent downwards and spun round and round with motors screaming. Before I could prevent him following, Alun Davies's Avon was capsized by a wave. The upturned boat with its crew of three clinging to it was swept towards the yawning whirlpool. The jets at

Below left The Inga cataract was navigated by small inflatables creeping down one edge, while the giant inflatables had to be portaged past the worst rapid.

Below right Avon Professional rafts navigated the rapids of the upper reaches of the river.

this point had returned to Kinshasa, and by now downriver I couldn't see what had happened. However, Royal Marine Neil Rickards, skipper of the boat behind, saw the accident and took his craft through the mountains of tossing water, right into the whirlpool and circled around inside it, like a motor-cyclist on a wall of death at a fairground.

In the centre of this swirling mass he could see Alun's capsized Avon with its crew still clinging frantically to the lifeline. Eventually, by going the same way that the water was revolving, Neil got alongside the stricken boat and pulled the crew to safety. He then circled up in the same direction that the water was turning and out of the whirlpool. Emerging, they looked back to see the upturned craft disappear into the vortex. Downriver, I was surprised a few moments later when the abandoned boat bobbed up beside me. The engine was smashed and the floorboards wrecked; there appeared to be no survivors. But the men had all been saved thanks to Neil's courage and skill, for which he was later awarded the Queen's Gallantry Medal.

From here it was plain sailing to the ocean. Back in Kinshasa we were received by President Mobutu, and HM The Queen sent her congratulations. The medical work of the expedition greatly aided the treatment of river blindness and the scientific research was a clear success. These results were achieved by a combination of careful planning, good equipment and teamwork. On a large-scale scientific expedition such as this, it is not a question of getting one man on top of a mountain – the whole team must get through. And I count myself privileged to have led such a team.

In these dark days of world tension, this expedition showed that people of many nations, inspired by a sense of adventure and with a healthy contempt for difficulties and dangers, can come together to perform a worthwhile task.

Training in the UK in preparation: John Blashford-Snell with Pamela Baker (left) and Valerie Jones on rough tidal water in the Menai Strait.

Colonel John Blashford-Snell (British, b. 1936), one of the world's most seasoned explorers, is known for his work in the desert and tropical regions, as well as his support for disadvantaged young people. In 1978 he established Operation Drake, which became Operation Raleigh, a youth development charity. As a Royal Engineer he developed innovative means of crossing obstacles and exploring rivers. He is President of the Scientific Exploration Society and the water charity Just a Drop.

ROBIN HANBURY-TENISON

SOUTH AMERICA NORTH TO SOUTH

IN THE SUMMER OF 1964 SEBASTIAN SNOW INVITED ME to accompany him on an attempt to bisect the South American continent from north to south by river for the first time. Sebastian was famous for having been the first person to travel down the Amazon from source to mouth, and he had persuaded the *Telegraph* to sponsor us for this journey. This was a logical sequel to the expedition I had made six years previously with Richard Mason, when we had achieved the first east–west crossing of the continent at its widest point, manhandling a jeep 10,000 km (6,214 miles) from Recife to Lima, more than half the distance being across country where no vehicle had been before. Tragically, Richard had been killed in 1961 by a group of uncontacted Indians while on another expedition with John Hemming.

This time our purpose was to demonstrate that there was an inland river route from the Caribbean to the South Atlantic, by travelling, as far as

The Avon Redcat inflatable rubber dinghy, in which I travelled some 10,000 km (6,000 miles) from the mouth of the Orinoco to the River Plate. The two large containers for fuel took up most of the space on board, but when dismantled everything could be carried around rapids and over the watershed.

possible by water, from the mouth of the Orinoco to the River Plate. Since there would be impassable rapids and a couple of watersheds to cross, we would need a boat that could be transported overland with relative ease and yet could travel reasonably fast on the water. We settled on a 4-m (13-ft) Avon Redcat inflatable rubber dinghy with two 18hp outboard motors. In this we could carry two large, rubber 164-litre (36-gallon) fuel containers and precious little else.

As we set off into the choppy waters of the Orinoco from Puerto Ordaz in Venezuela on Sunday 15 November 1964 in our grossly overloaded little craft, it seemed very unlikely we would make it all the way to Buenos Aires. Sebastian, who for all his charm was always a bit unstable, admitted after a few days that he was not feeling at all well and he was later diagnosed as suffering from Ménière's disease, a disorder of the inner ear which affects balance. As a result he kept dropping vital bits of kit overboard and after three weeks he had to fly home, leaving me to continue on my own.

AS WE SET OFF INTO THE CHOPPY WATERS OF THE ORINOCO … IN OUR GROSSLY OVERLOADED LITTLE CRAFT, IT SEEMED VERY UNLIKELY WE WOULD MAKE IT ALL THE WAY TO BUENOS AIRES.

By then we had already covered some 2,500 km (1,553 miles), about a quarter of the journey, and had successfully reached Manaus in Brazil. Maipures Atures rapids on the Orinoco. However, thanks to the extraordinary geographical phenomenon of the Casiquiare 'canal', the only major river in the world to run over a watershed, we had not needed to make a portage between the basins of the Orinoco and the Amazon.

Now I was to be alone for the next two months, forging up the Madeira, Marmore and Guapore rivers to the tiny headwaters near Villa Bella do Mato Grosso. Here I spent Christmas in a place beyond the law,

I slept each night in a lightweight army jungle hammock. Once I was zipped inside the mosquito net, no insects could get in and I could use a torch to read and write. But the night sounds of the surrounding forest were often terrifying.

where escaped prisoners ran to hide and where there were daily gun battles in the street, but everyone was kind to the mad Englishman with his funny little boat. On the rivers I slept each night in my hammock, slung high above the water level in case there was a flood in the night. The only people I met were occasional rubber tappers, *seringueiros*, who advised me to make my camp on an island whenever possible, as they said the still uncontacted Indians on the upper reaches of the rivers were likely to attack me.

The fear I experienced on those long lonely nights surrounded by the din of the forest was exquisite, as I was far beyond any possible help, but it was matched by a deep contentment from feeling totally self-sufficient. This is a pleasure it is hard for travellers to experience today, when it is irresponsible not to take a GPS and beacon system on dangerous journeys and so be able to summon help in an emergency. I feel fortunate to have been able to do my early exploring at a time when it was still possible to disappear without setting off alarms.

By the time my boat and motors had been carried the hundred or so kilometres over the watershed between the Amazon and Paraguay river basins and relaunched on the little Jauru River, it was leaking badly. From now on, as I progressed down the ever-widening Paraguay and Parana rivers, I was kept at work behaving like a frenetic one-man band. I had a foot pump for air to keep the three compartments inflated, which was constantly in use, and I operated a hand pump both to transfer fuel regularly from the large rubber tanks to the outboard motors' metal tanks and to remove the water leaking into the bilges. Each of the motors had its own handle to control speed and direction, and there was a compass to keep an eye on as well as the extraordinarily detailed US Air Force maps to consult

Sebastian Snow lowering our inflatable boat down a small rapid on the Casiquiare 'Canal', an extraordinary river which runs over the watershed between the Orinoco and Amazon river basins.

Some of the rivers were small and virtually unexplored. Others were major highways, where large ships might be met around the next corner.

from time to time. Meanwhile, the river banks flashed past with glimpses of caiman slipping into the water and occasional capybara and deer scrambling up the sides to disappear into the continuous forest. Only in the evening was there some peace, when I could hear the howler monkeys in the distance and watch the macaws as they flew to roost. I lived on porridge and fish, mainly piranha, which are very easy to catch, and I always carried a large bunch of bananas, obtained at the last settlement.

On the downstream stretch towards the River Plate, the danger came more from man than from nature. As I passed through the edge of the great Pantanal swamp and approached the Brazilian border with Paraguay, a popular area for smugglers of drugs and much else in those days, I was strongly advised to steer clear of all in authority, as it was illegal for a foreigner to travel by boat and I had no papers. I slipped past the customs posts at Corumba and Puerto Esperanza late one Saturday night, briefly dazzled by bright lights and tempted by loud music and laughter, but was caught the next evening camped on an island just before the border. I had planned to drift silently across at midnight, pretending to be a floating island of water hyacinth, but a patrol boat of heavily armed guards spotted my orange rubber craft where I had hidden it and I was escorted to Forte Coimbra. There, the officers were so impressed that anyone should even consider travelling and camping alone that they omitted to ask me for my non-existent papers, put me up in their Mess, fed me, gave me some fuel and sent me on my way into Paraguay.

MEANWHILE, THE RIVER BANKS FLASHED PAST WITH GLIMPSES OF CAIMAN SLIPPING INTO THE WATER AND OCCASIONAL CAPYBARA AND DEER SCRAMBLING UP THE SIDES TO DISAPPEAR INTO THE CONTINUOUS FOREST.

A few weeks later, on 6 February 1965, I limped into the canals of Tigre, the smart suburb of Buenos Aires, where the rich had holiday homes. As it was a Saturday afternoon, as it almost always seems to be when one emerges from the bush into civilization, many families were sitting in their gardens enjoying themselves. They were not impressed by the ragged, blackened character in a dirty little boat with a Union Jack on the front and were not interested that I had just come 10,000 km (6,214 miles) from Venezuela. In desperation I followed a smart rowing eight and found myself at the Buenos Aires Rowing Club, where the Secretary, a retired English major, took pity on me. Soon after, I was fetched by the Embassy Rolls Royce and was later fêted by the Buenos Aires media as 'El Intrepido'.

Although my two long journeys bisecting South America proved little of value to science or to the greater understanding of the planet, they did provide me with an opportunity to see the interior of that continent before the massive devastation of its forests and its indigenous people began to accelerate. As a result, much of my life has been devoted to campaigning against the destruction of rainforests and for the protection of indigenous societies. I believe that exploration, to deserve the name, must have a purpose which is of value to mankind and that pure physical achievements, if they have no wider objective or follow-through, can in some way

In 1968 we took an SRN6 hovercraft from Manaus to Trinidad, retracing part of my route from four years earlier. On the upper Orinoco, while the scientists on board did their research, an extraordinary encounter took place between some only recently contacted Yanomami Indians and the latest example of modern technology.

be regarded as no more than stunts. Those of us lucky enough to have been able to travel through wild and unexplored country and to have received unstinting hospitality from those who live there owe it to them and to ourselves to play our part in the future of both.

Some months after my return from South America, I was invited to lunch at Buckingham Palace. Prince Philip, in his usual forthright manner, turned to me and said, 'So what was the economic significance of this journey you have just completed? Would that river route be valuable for commerce?' Struggling to find something intelligent to say, I replied, 'Well, sir, much of the time the water was very shallow with rocks and sandbanks and so normal ships could not get through. But I believe there is a new vessel called a hovercraft, which could be ideal for the job.' I genuinely did not know that the man sitting on his other side was Sir Christopher Cockerell, inventor of the hovercraft. He was not best pleased to be told by the Prince that he should give me one of his vessels, but that conversation did result in the first hovercraft expedition, when we took an SRN6 to retrace the first part of my route. We went from Manaus to Trinidad via the Casiquiare and the Orinoco, becoming on the way the first vessel of any sort to pass through the dreaded Maipures Atures rapids. Unfortunately, hovercraft never caught on in South America. If they had, I believe it would have been possible to have allowed economic development of the interior via the rivers without the massive destruction of the rainforest caused by the huge network of roads that now criss-cross Amazonia.

AS A RESULT, MUCH OF MY LIFE HAS BEEN DEVOTED TO CAMPAIGNING AGAINST THE DESTRUCTION OF RAINFORESTS AND FOR THE PROTECTION OF INDIGENOUS SOCIETIES.

Robin Hanbury-Tenison (British, b. 1936) has been described by the *Spectator* as the doyen of British explorers. As a founder and now President of Survival International, he has campaigned for more than forty years for the rights of threatened indigenous peoples. Since leading the Royal Geographical Society's largest expedition to the interior of Borneo in 1977/78, for which he received the Patron's Gold Medal, he has played a leading role in making the world aware of the value of rainforests.

MIRELLA AND LORENZO RICCIARDI
AFRICA EAST TO WEST BY BOAT

I BELONG TO A FAMILY OF 'ADVENTURERS' and adventure leads to exploration – there are many types of exploration, ours was of the geographical kind, for as Henry Morton Stanley wrote in his autobiography:

> Another enduring pleasure is that which is derived from exploration of new, unvisited, and undescribed regions.... Each eminence is eagerly climbed in the hope of viewing new prospects, each forest is traversed with a strong idea prevailing that at the other end some grand feature of nature may be revealed....
> If he is a true lover of wild Nature, where can he view her under so many aspects as in the centre of Africa? Where is she so shy, so retired, mysterious, fantastic, and savage as in Africa? Where are her charms so strong, her moods so strange, as in Africa?'

Mirella and Lorenzo Ricciardi travelled widely and well together for many years.

When I was twenty-five, I married Lorenzo, who, it turned out, was a kindred spirit of the adventurous kind, and because of that, for better or for worse, we somehow made it through forty-five years of turbulent matrimony and came out at the other end bruised and scarred, but hugely enriched, to find ourselves apart in our old age. Unbeknown to us, Stanley's words epitomized the driving force that propelled us through our life together, side by side. The first line of Lorenzo's entry in the preface to our book *African Rainbow* was 'I was born in jail'. He explains that 'the clinic of the San Vittore prison in Milan was the nearest place my mother could be rushed to when the birth-pains started'. And as he recalls elsewhere:

I was raised a Catholic from the waist up; at the age of eight I was told that I had 'a touch of the devil' in me, as often during Mass I would blow my sailor's whistle to kill the boredom, I sang merry tunes at funerals and I cried at weddings. Once after shooting a soldier in the buttocks with an air rifle, I was exorcised with a boring ritual in which I was sprayed with holy water and left for hours kneeling with my hands under my knees on the cold stone floor of the Sanctuary of Divine Love near Genoa where I lived. I was a shy and clumsy boy. One day while eating dinner in the beautiful house of my friend Roberto Gancia, I spilled a glass of red wine on the white linen tablecloth. There was a deathly silence as everyone around the table watched the stain spread across the table. That day I made a decision that I would one day hitchhike around the world, climb Everest, sail across the Pacific, swim in the Ganges. I would listen to the surf pounding on the reefs and fall in love with a Vahine. Then perhaps I could spill a glass of wine without wanting to shrivel up and die ... that day my 'adventurer's' seed fell on to fertile ground and I emerged and grew into what I am today; I joined the elite club of the 'romantic' travellers and have lived my life accordingly, no one ever told me how or what I should do with it – 'I am what I am, take it or leave it' was the parameter by which I lived ... with no regrets.

For better or for worse it brought Mirella into my life – I quickly recognized we shared the same intrepid nature and thirst for travel, in many ways I found in her a sort of soul-mate who was able to adapt to my unorthodox character, so I asked her to marry me three days after meeting her and for nearly four decades she never let go of my hand ...

Our eighteen-month African Rainbow expedition in 1985, which crossed Africa from east to west on the rivers and lakes of the Equator, was our last epic journey together and was the jewel in our crown of adventures, a fitting exit into the vastly more complicated and hazardous journey into dreaded old age that no one escapes and few, if any, are ever prepared for. All that's left for us now is to write about and share it with the next generation.

An initial journey down the Zaire River from Kisangani to Kinshasa inspired by V. S. Naipaul's *A Bend in the River*, fulfilled the words of a dinner partner in London who, on hearing of my plans said 'take 100 rolls of film with you … it is an intoxicating journey for a photographer'. When I returned a month later and recounted the experience to Lorenzo, I told him of my frustration at being confined to public transport, however unusual and exotic it was, for I was unable to leave the 'floating village' with its thousand 'temporary' inhabitants that was the *Colonel Ebea*, the 'grand pouceur' that ploughs the muddy waters of this mammoth river for its ten-day descent and fifteen-day ascent between the two sprawling African towns.

With a large map of the region and my sheets of photographs spread out around us on the floor of our home in Kilifi on the Kenyan coast, I watched Lorenzo's intense scrutiny of every detail without speaking – I could only imagine the ticking of his adventure-brain-cells going wild.

Next day he said to me: 'I will organize an expedition down the same route that will allow you to stop and get out whenever you wish so you can take all the photographs you want.' And that is just what he did.

One year later we found ourselves on the banks of the Rufigi River in Tanzania with three 3.65-m (12-ft) Italian army inflatable rubber boats, each kitted out with two 25hp Yamaha engines, two jet boats, fifteen

The African Rainbow expedition kicks off down the Kilifi Creek from our home on the Indian Ocean with three Italian army inflatables, two Castoldi Jet boats and the team members.

expedition members, three Fiat Panda vehicles and a 5-ton Bedford truck for ground support along the river, ready to kick off our epic journey. Fired by his single-minded determination, a gruelling one-year self-inflicted confinement in Milan had borne fruit – he had raised 1 million dollars on which to float across the African continent. That was Lorenzo, the man I had married and stuck with for all those years.

Africa received us with open arms, she was warm and gentle and extraordinarily beautiful. Our fears of finding ourselves in muddy swamps surrounded by clouds of mosquitoes that would devour us and drive us beneath our nets from dawn to dusk proved mercifully unfounded. Instead, the further upriver we travelled the more welcoming our surroundings appeared. Each evening a campsite revealed itself as a source of celebration. We rejoiced in Nature's undisturbed vitality, in the 'frozen

EACH EVENING A CAMPSITE REVEALED ITSELF AS A SOURCE OF CELEBRATION.

echo of the silent voice of God' – tiny leaves and blossoms bursting into life after a rain shower and dead by nightfall, butterflies hovering on decaying trees, the smell of damp moss in the undergrowth, beetles rolling dung balls along tiny paths, crickets announcing nightfall, the haunting call of the rainbird – this was our Africa.

Every day a few hours after daybreak until a few hours before nightfall we travelled, sometimes in tandem, sometimes in convoy, sliding effortlessly over our liquid highway. River navigation, even in fully developed countries, is in itself quite an adventure. Rivers often deviate, zigzagging in fluvial freedom, linked to the geographic and geological lie of the land. In Africa this freedom runs wild. At noon when the sun reached its zenith, the heat clung to us like hot blankets, slowly silencing us. As the midday

Below right We were sometimes forced to abandon the river and portage all our equipment and boats overland to circumvent obstructions on our route – it was a tough and exhausting exercise.

lethargy set in we would slip into a soporific trance and watch the moving scenery through half-closed eyes, lulled by the smooth mechanical hum of our outboard engines in perfect tune. The hours between noon and four were always the most difficult; we would stop for lunch and a stretch in the shade of an overhanging tree or rock, with a dip in the water to refresh our sunburnt skins.

When we reached the Shuguli Falls we undertook our first portage across some flat, exposed rocks that stretched from one bank to the other, a natural barrier that forced us to disembark and carry all our equipment on our backs. The inflatable boats were pulled over the smooth stone by means of equally inflatable rubber rollers created for just such inconveniences. Once deflated they could be folded away and stored, as with the rubber fuel bladders, which greatly facilitated carrying large quantities of fuel.

WE WOULD SLIP INTO A SOPORIFIC TRANCE AND WATCH THE MOVING SCENERY THROUGH HALF-CLOSED EYES, LULLED BY THE SMOOTH MECHANICAL HUM OF OUR OUTBOARD ENGINES.

From dawn to dusk our days were bathed in expectancy and our travelling punctuated with visions and sounds that belong only to the world of the river. We met people rarely, but we travelled in the knowledge that we were not alone. Life on this river is harsh and demanding, man does not compete with Nature but has instead learned to live with it. When we stopped for the night in a clearing cut by local people on the banks, they would silently appear from among the reeds, poling a canoe, to throw us a rope of twisted fibre in a gentle gesture, no greeting could have been more appropriate.

A herd of buffalo stood for an instant and stared transfixed at us before crashing away through the rushes; a delicate biscuit-coloured antelope

To allow Lorenzo to use his much loved HD Sony movie camera his daughter Amina would sometimes take over the boat's steering wheel.

peered through the long grass and then leapt like a ballet dancer through the water. On rivers one can travel for miles and hours without encountering any sign of life; one moves through a silent world of colours and shapes where one's awareness is stretched to its limits, so that a sudden movement or appearance jolts one from reveries.

Some voyages are remembered by colour, forms or objects, but the scenery of the Zaire River leaves one with a memory of silence and solitude, of immobility and emptiness – our journey at times seemed to go on and on, endlessly, sometimes in repetitious monotony, but it was perhaps this very monotony that was its fascination. The Zaire River is a moving lagoon, a running marsh, a bog that is never still. But in this aqueous expanse we never felt lost because the river gave direction to everything, we just had to let ourselves flow with the current and we were bound to arrive somewhere; it felt like travelling into eternity on a rolling carpet. As we approached the vast spreading delta and prepared to meet the Atlantic Ocean the banks were ever more scattered with the ruins of abandoned Belgian buildings, constant reminders of the European colonization of Africa, ultimate monuments to the barbaric invasion and hypocrisy of our society so succinctly set out in Joseph Conrad's *Heart of Darkness*.

Eighteen months after we had first cast off into the Rufigi River south of Dar es Salaam in Tanzania we entered the delta in a labyrinth of magnificent mangroves, whose huge roots bleached white by the sun and bird droppings resembled carcasses of giant prehistoric crabs in an endless liquid grave of black mud. We were heading towards Banana, our final destination on the Atlantic coast. The Zaire River stretches from a width of 732 m (2,400 ft) to 16 km (10 miles). 'I sensed the Atlantic Ocean before

Below left We were often greeted by people on the river banks when we stopped for the night.

Below right Lorenzo ventures forwards slowly from thick papyrus groves into a shallow marsh covered by a carpet of dark green vegetation; it was very hot and still in there.

When we reached the Atlantic at Banana, Lorenzo was hurled overboard by our crew, a custom reserved for the expedition leader.

I saw it,' Lorenzo later wrote in his diary and added tellingly, 'at the end of a journey such as this, which had been our life for so long, a feeling of melancholy begins to creep in, giving rise to an unbearable apprehension of returning to mundane life where the unexpected does not exist'.

A slim sliver of land jutted out into the ocean ahead of us, barely visible; a row of scraggy, wind-torn, salt-encrusted palm trees, silhouetted against the bright light that ricocheted from the ocean waves, stood out starkly against the limpid sky. This was the Atlantic Ocean, the end of our 6,035-km (3,750-mile) journey. We had arrived. 'I felt a sense of loss, like when a close friend goes away for a long time or when I get to the last page of a good book,' Lorenzo confided to me later that night.

Before turning into Banana Bay, where we would abandon our boats, we sped at full throttle into the waves and a mile into the ocean. 'I was glad to be with Mirella, together we had seen Africa as few people have done', he scribbled in his notebook. He put his arm round my shoulders and said nothing. His silence spoke louder than words; he reached for the water gourd he had filled in the Indian Ocean and solemnly emptied it into the Atlantic Ocean, intoning 'Indian Ocean, Atlantic Ocean' with just a touch of emotion in his voice. He then turned to shake each one of us by the hand and said 'we made it, thank you'. Before he could say any more Brian and Mario, two of our crew members, seized him and hurled him overboard to the resounding cheers from the rest of the crew who threw the Italian and Zairian flags after him, so I could take my last photo of the expedition.

So why do journeys of this kind matter to us? Because they open up frontiers to many people who are not as fortunate as us to experience them personally, because they further a deeper understanding of Africa and its people, the way my book *Vanishing Africa* had done before. And exploration can bring unexpected rewards, as W. H. Murray wrote in connection with an expedition to the Himalaya in 1951:

> Until one is committed there is hesitancy, the chance to draw back, always ineffectiveness. Concerning all acts of initiative (and creation) there is one elementary truth, the ignorance of which kills countless ideas and splendid plans: that the moment one definitely commits oneself, then Providence moves too. A whole stream of events issues from the decision, raising in one's favour all manner of unforeseen incidents and meetings and material assistance, which no man would have dreamt would have come his way.

It proves the Latin proverb that Lorenzo learned at school '*audaces fortuna iuvat*' ('fortune favours the brave').

Mirella Ricciardi (b. 1931) was born in Kenya of an Italian father and French mother. She began her photographic career in Paris before attending the New York School of Photography. She returned to Africa, where she worked as a photographer and acted as technical advisor, cameraman, guide and hunter on more than fifteen safaris. She has advised on and appeared in films and documentaries and has published several internationally bestselling books of her photographs and travels with Lorenzo Ricciardi, including *Vanishing Africa*, *Voyage of the Mir-El-Lah*, *Vanishing Amazon* and *African Visions*. She remains dedicated to photography and also works with African charities such as the African Rainforest Trust.

Lorenzo Ricciardi (Italian, b. 1930), also known as 'Il Magnifico', began travelling at an early age. He was head of the Rome office of the advertising agency J. Walter Thompson and then moved to New York. He was later assistant to Federico Fellini and began to make films himself. When filming in Africa he met his wife Mirella. They made many voyages together, including to the Far East, the Persian Gulf and the Seychelles, as well as the African Rainbow expedition across Africa, which he also filmed. He is a fellow of the Royal Geographical Society.

WONG HOW MAN

THE TRUE SOURCE OF THE YELLOW RIVER

IN THEIR POEMS, THE FAMOUS EIGHTH-CENTURY TANG DYNASTY writers Li Bai (Li Po) and Wang Zhi Huan both praised the Yellow River. Li said, 'The Yellow River water comes from the sky [heaven]'; and Wang described it in a similar way: 'Yellow River far and high among the white clouds'. But for me, in 2008, high on the ridge that forms the watershed between the two great rivers of China, the Yellow and the Yangtze, the Yellow River came from right below my feet – I was standing above its source. Furthermore, the water of the Yellow River at its source is not yellow. It is pure and clear.

This discovery came after almost three weeks on the road, with a two-day hike at high elevation and at times riding on a yak. Our team of eighteen finally reached a new, true source of the Yellow River on 29 June 2008, but both knowledge and legend surrounding the source of this great river had been growing for many centuries. The ancient book of 'Yu Gong' from the Spring and Autumn Period, around 2200 BC, described the upper Yellow River as issuing from the Jishi mountains, an area between today's Lanzhou and Xining. By the Yuan Dynasty of the thirteenth century AD, the imperial court began sending teams to explore the river's headwaters. During the Qing Dynasty of the seventeenth century, many more expeditions were dispatched, expanding our knowledge of the source region. Some expeditions made offerings to the river gods at what they considered its source to assuage the flooding and turmoil the Yellow River created downstream.

In modern times, especially after the founding of the People's Republic of China, only two scientific expeditions were launched to try to improve our understanding of the source of the Yellow River, in 1952 and 1978. Both came back with differing and inconclusive results. In the 1990s more theories were proposed, but it was only at the beginning of the twenty-first century, with the advent of new ways of handling satellite data that made it possible to locate places notoriously difficult to pinpoint, that the question of the real source could finally be settled.

Our team included Martin Ruzek, former NASA scientist at the Jet Propulsion Laboratory, and for many years a friend of mine. By comparing satellite data from various sources, Martin had studied the length of four probable sources of the Yellow River, arriving at a tentative figure that the southern branch is at least 15 km (9⅓ miles) longer than the official source, though both are tributaries of the Ka-ri Qu. It was the source of this longer tributary, called Jarong Qahu in Tibetan, that we were attempting to reach.

Two tremors in China in 2008, one severe, slowed down our pace. Because of the 8.0 magnitude earthquake at the eastern section of the Tibetan plateau, further complicated by political turmoil in the region, security measures were extremely tight en route from Yunnan to Qinghai. We had to make a huge detour to skirt round the main part of the plateau and make our approach from the west of the Xining–Lhasa railroad. This untraditional approach did at least allow us the opportunity to enjoy the vast scenic beauty of the plateau, as well as to encounter the wildlife of the region. With the new awareness of conservation, animals such as Tibetan gazelles and wild asses have multiplied very quickly; even foxes frequently crossed our path.

Today, nomads generally herd their yaks with motorcycles rather than from horseback as in the past.

Sitting in the lead car, I soon tired of calling out sightings to Bill Bleisch, our chief biologist, though at one point I shouted over the radio, 'nine o'clock, a horse'. Horses have indeed become a rare sighting, as practically all the nomads have switched to motorcycles within the last

Trekking over snow and ice sheets dotted with water-filled potholes was not easy going.

decade, and we frequently saw Tibetan nomads herding their yak or sheep from these machines. Black yak-hair tents have likewise been replaced by green or white canvas army tents. Practically every element of the social fabric of the plateau is undergoing change.

At the final village closest to our destination I discovered the joke was on me. There were no horses to be procured for our final approach to the source. 'If you need twenty horses, it may take twenty days to round them up', quipped Tashi Jianduo, the party secretary. In years past, horses were the main method of transportation for both the nomads and government officials when they needed to get around, but helpful as he was, there was no way he could find so many horses these days.

We followed the Ja Cao Qu, one of the tributaries of the Tong Tian He (upper Yangtze), and set up base camp. From here, we had a two-day hike over the watershed to our destination at the Yellow River source, 18 km (11 miles) away measured in a straight line with our GPS. Two local Tibetans were recruited as caravan helpers, bringing with them twelve yaks to carry our load. Luckily, three of the animals could be ridden, which spared me the agony of a long hike at high elevation. Later on, however, I discovered that the agony in my legs was simply relocated as a pain in my butt as my yak came with no saddle. By now, no guides could help us as we were seeking a little-known creek with no Tibetan name on the map, just a spot with longitude and latitude.

After the first day's hike we set up our advance camp. In order to reduce weight, we cut the number of tents from ten to seven for our party of eighteen. The weather had been rather unpleasant, with rain, hail and snow, but one benevolent gift from heaven was that it was concentrated mainly at night, sparing us the worst during our daytime hike. On the morning of 29 June I woke to discover our tents were enveloped in snow. To my utmost amazement, our two caravan helpers, with no tent for cover, were sleeping under heavy yak blankets, using two umbrellas as their shelter. From then on, we joked that we had seven and a half tents.

With fresh snow on the ground, at 9 a.m. we began our hike to the source some 6 km (almost 4 miles) upwards from our camp. What appeared on the map as a few contour lines materialized as an exhausting and slow advance over several ridges. Fog enshrouded us, so Martin gave us only a general direction of approach. In some places we dragged ourselves forwards over soft ground as the wet mud sticking to our boots got heavier and heavier. We could barely walk in a straight line. At this high elevation a particular plant produces cushions, hugging the ground and forming innumerable humps and potholes filled with water. Such terrain creates havoc for any hiker who does not pay full attention to every step.

TO MY UTMOST AMAZEMENT, OUR TWO CARAVAN HELPERS, WITH NO TENT FOR COVER, WERE SLEEPING UNDER HEAVY YAK BLANKETS, USING TWO UMBRELLAS AS THEIR SHELTER.

As we marched on, the fog cleared and we could see two mountains with snow patches; our final goal was a creek between these two peaks. By 11.30, we cleared one ridge, catching a mother shelduck and her ducklings by surprise with our large entourage. Below us a creek flowed

Advance camp one day from the source, with the half tent of the caravan helpers under snow.

north towards the plain far beneath and Martin confirmed that this was the source river of the Yellow River. If we followed it upstream, we should soon reach the true source, as we hit the ridge that formed the watershed between the Yangtze and the Yellow rivers.

Despite the fact that everyone was tired, we all scrambled eagerly uphill. The gradient was by now more gradual, and some younger members of our group marched ahead. I called out for everyone to stay together – one of my few orders as expedition leader was that I wanted all of us to arrive at the source as a group, and that no one should forge ahead to stake a claim on this important moment. I strongly believe expedition success depends on group effort, not solo adventure.

Martin guided us to a particular point as we followed the stream towards the top. This spot, he told us, was the theoretical site of the source. But in front of us the stream clearly continued further upwards towards the ridge. It was narrowing quite quickly and I asked that the Olympic torch for the Beijing games that I had carried with me be taken out of the backpack.

Everyone had a turn with the torch as we set our sight on the ridge in front of us. My intention was to make our final steps to the source as significant as, if not more so than, the torch relay for the Olympics. After all, we were well above 4,800 m (15,748 ft) and aside from the official relay to the top of Everest at 8,848 m (29,029 ft), this was the highest point the torch would reach.

I take a drink from the source stream of the Yellow River at an elevation of 4,878 m (16,000 ft) on 29 June 2008.

The moment had arrived.

34° 29′ 31.1″N, 96° 20′ 24.6″E. Elevation 4,878 m. Time 12:15, 29 June 2008.

This one line seems short and simple, but it was arrived at after a lot of anxiety and hard work. The map of China, and indeed that of the world, has changed since that moment.

Eighteen of us, including members from different countries and several minority nationalities, including four Tibetans, two Bai and someone from Taiwan, had arrived at a newly defined source of the Yellow River, which was at least 15 km (9 miles) longer than previously thought. The China Exploration & Research Society, which had been behind the expedition, had reached new triumphs in its exploration achievements. We had redefined the Yangtze in 2005, the Mekong in 2007 and now the Yellow River.

We set up a long string of Tibetan prayer flags to mark the spot. Paper wind horses, called *Longda* in Tibetan, were released to the wind to honour the mountain deity. Kneeling respectfully, with one knee on each bank of the Yellow River, I cherished my special moment as I drank from its source. I collected water samples to take home for tests, just as we did at the Yangtze and Mekong, and also a few small rock specimens as my mementos. Finally, we opened our Moët et Chandon champagne and shared it around. But it could never taste as delicious as a sip of freezing water from the source.

The team taking it in turns to hold the Olympic torch at the source.

I release sacred *Longda* (wind horses) at the source of the Mekong.

Wong How Man (Chinese, b. 1949) is an explorer and photojournalist, and founder and president of the China Exploration & Research Society (CERS), a pre-eminent nonprofit organization specializing in exploration, research, conservation and education in remote China. Between 1974, when he began exploring China as a journalist, and 1986, when he founded CERS, Wong led six major expeditions for the *National Geographic* magazine. His writing for the *National Geographic* was nominated for the Overseas Press Club Award of America. In his 1985 *National Geographic* expedition, Wong led a team that found a new source of the Yangtze River that is internationally recognized as the true geographic source of the river, which he documented in his 1989 book, *Exploring the Yangtze: China's Longest River*. Twenty years later, he led a team to discover a new source, 6.5 km (4 miles) west of the source that he had previously discovered. Subsequently, Wong led CERS expeditions that pinpointed the true source of the Mekong in 2007 and discovered a new source for the Yellow River in 2008.

MICHEL PEISSEL

WHERE THE MEKONG RISES

WITH ADDITIONAL TEXT BY SEBASTIAN GUINNESS

I HARDLY CONSIDER MYSELF A MODERN EXPLORER. On the contrary, I fear I am an old-fashioned explorer, trying to fill in the gaps left by traditional nineteenth-century explorers. Such was the case in 1994 when I decided to try to settle a long-standing controversy regarding the exact location of the source of the Mekong River, the third longest river in Asia.

Exploration is, by definition, research in remote, inaccessible regions. Why the source of the Mekong was still a mystery at the end of the twentieth century can be explained by politics – that Tibet was closed to foreigners for centuries – and by the fact that its isolated, landlocked regions were unreachable. Knowing this, and aware that uncertainty clouded the claims concerning the exact location of the source, I was quick to avail myself of the opportunity offered to me by the Chinese agriculture ministry to travel in the long restricted region where the source of the Mekong lies.

The mountainous landscape and high grass plains of Tibet were long closed to foreign explorers in search of the source of the Mekong.

Sebastian Guinness, Michel Peissel and Dr Jacques Falck standing next to the young Mekong in the Rupsa Pass.

I owed this opportunity to my interest in Tibetan horses, which had obtained for me from the department of animal husbandry the right to seek out these animals almost anywhere in Tibet. Having overcome the political obstacles, I now had to set up my expedition.

Today many so-called explorers seek sponsors. 'Can you be sure you will discover the source when fifteen previous expeditions over 120 years have failed?' The answer being 'No', I was obliged to finance the project myself with the help of friends. Thus it was an old-fashioned expedition, with just three members: Sebastian Guinness, my companion on a previous expedition, whose energy and youth compensated for my old age, and Dr Jacques Falck, who as both a gifted medic and cameraman had accompanied me on four previous journeys. Our small team was soon to be increased by the presence of a Chinese 'moderator', two chauffeurs and later on several muleteers.

As usual I tried to keep equipment to a minimum: one large 'mess' tent to eat in and shelter our men and baggage, as well as three small individual tents. More problematic was the matter of maps and securing a reliable GPS. The librarians of the Royal Geographical Society in London, along with the geographer in charge of the map room, were a great help in establishing our route. I should mention here in view of future controversy that at the time I was unable to consult the classified Russian satellite maps of the regions. These were later to reveal that what was known as the 'White Mekong' was possibly longer than the 'Black Mekong', the branch considered for over a century and a half by map-makers, explorers and geographers alike as the principal affluent of the upper Mekong. I therefore chose to seek out the source of the latter, the historical branch

A Nangchen nomad – the horses of Nangchen, though small, are renowned for their strength and stamina.

of the Mekong's headwaters, which previous expeditions had attempted to reach. Permits in hand, we at last set out in the autumn of 1994.

In 1866, 128 years prior to our departure, the first committee for the discovery of the source of the Mekong had been set up in Paris. The initial expedition was a dismal failure, its leader dying on the way, while the rest of the team, blocked by rapids, retreated across China. Then in 1894 Dutreuil de Rhins claimed to have located the source, but was promptly shot by Tibetans, while his companion Fernand Grenard returned to France and made a rather weak case for their joint discovery.

THE HEADWATERS ARE NOT FAR FROM THE TERRITORY OF THE MUCH FEARED NOMADIC GOLOK TRIBES, THE 'PLAGUE' OF TIBET.

In all there had been fifteen failures. Would we have better luck? One thing that should be noted is that the headwaters are not far from the territory of the much feared Nomadic Golok tribes, the 'plague' of Tibet.

Our journey took us first by air to Beijing then, still flying, to Xining, the capital of the Chinese province of Qinghai, once an integral part of Tibet. From there we were to drive 1,200 km (746 miles) to Moyum, an abandoned Chinese military garrison from which we would set out by car and on horseback in search of the elusive source. We were under some pressure because of the presence in the region of a small Japanese expedition of agriculturalists. We heard that they were interested in the water reserves of the upper Mekong. Fortunately, they were either ignorant of the fact that the source of the Mekong had never been located in the field or they were just not interested in the subject, as their subsequent testimonials seemed to demonstrate.

Locating the exact source of a great river is no easy task. Many a rivulet may vie for being the point furthest from the sea. As we progressed up the

Black Mekong we came upon the lateral affluent claimed by the assassinated Frenchman Dutreuil de Rhins as leading to the source – quite evidently he had been mistaken.

Thanks to my knowledge of colloquial Tibetan I was able to discuss the matter with the various nomads en route. They directed us to a rivulet that came down from a pass known as the Rupsa Pass. Here was the watershed between the Mekong river basin and that of the Yangtze River.

....

Sebastian Guinness
Unfortunately Michel Peissel died before finishing this article, I was asked to step in to add this brief account.

Michel Peissel, Dr Jacques Falck, our cameraman and doctor, Mr Ling, our official interpreter, or 'moderator', a few Chinese drivers and myself spent, all in all, six weeks on this expedition. Five weeks were in Tibet and Qinghai, never descending below 3,810 m (12,500 ft) and often camping at 4,267 m (14,000 ft) plus. Beyond Yushu, the provincial capital of this particular region, we were joined by various local guides, approved of by the Chinese, yet Tibetan.

A votive mound of prayer stones rises in front of the Gar monastery, in Nangchen, the region through which the Mekong flows.

On the ascent and descent we were bivouacked under Chinese orders in their old garrisons. These were built as forts for the Chinese army before the car became all-pervasive and are now largely abandoned. The conditions within were indescribably grim. Nightly we begged to be allowed to camp outside, but due to the supposed threat of bandits this was always denied. I am surprised we weren't done in by the carbon monoxide from the stove in the middle of the dormitory, though there was little enough glass in the windows.

Peissel, Falck and I spent every evening wandering up and down the breeze-block high street that had grown up next to these garrisons – Peissel talking to the children, Dr Falck filming and, as the light faded, holding impromptu clinics. Me? I was to be found looking for a Tibetan- or Muslim-run restaurant and beer to avoid the processed gloop found within the walls.

It was here that Michel would come into his own, asking the children in his fluent Tibetan endless questions about the area. After a while the parents, watching on protectively, would join in, shyly at first, but increasingly vocal, either with directions to monasteries or defrocked abbots or asking for photographs of the exiled lamas.

IT WAS HERE THAT MICHEL WOULD COME INTO HIS OWN, ASKING THE CHILDREN IN HIS FLUENT TIBETAN ENDLESS QUESTIONS ABOUT THE AREA.

Up until Yushu, the main tribe would have been the Golok, famous for their ferociousness both against the French and the Chinese, but now reduced to drinking and smoking, kicking cans down the path for entertainment. Yushu and beyond is predominantly Khampa, great warriors who put up fierce resistance to Chinese forces in 1959.

The roads between the outposts we stayed in varied from metalled to the dried-up beds of rivers. I will never forget the disbelief before, and the relief after, a particularly bad stretch as the Toyota Landcruiser made it through. They are truly extraordinary vehicles.

At one lunch stop I looked up at a cliff above to see an eagle owl and two chicks calmly watching the human interlopers fish for guppy in the creek. The Chinese were much amused by this, yet the Tibetans were strangely quiet. Peissel explained that, of all animals, it is thought the greatest crime is to kill the fish, as one of the great Buddhist gurus had remarked that it would be a terrible thing to kill a being without the capacity to shed a tear.

I will miss these Peissel-ianly unattributable asides.

As we wended our way up towards the source, it became apparent that the permissions we needed were not nearly as clear as we had been led to believe and we were often held up for days. This drove us mad with boredom on the one hand and paranoia on the other. The paranoia arose from the fact that Michel had hired a new assistant the September before and, during a final, exquisitely timed argument she had left, swearing that she would beat us to the source of the Mekong with her photographer lover. We had it on good authority that they were but days behind. Every jeep that passed was scrutinized in case they were stealing a march. This added to the feeling that we were in a race, something that became increasingly important to us as time marched on and we became more and more isolated from the world.

We were delayed for five days at the last proper village as Ling waited for our official passes. Wild with anxiety, at first I failed to take in the beauty of the valley where we had been forced to pause. It was a Shang-ri-la, with weeping willows over the Mekong turning golden in the autumn light. Even the food was better, as by now it was fresh and Tibetan. Aged yak, dried yak, yak sausage, yak yogurt and yak cheese supplemented with handfuls of chillies, scallions, almonds and apples. The only horror was the inevitable visit to the loo, a communal affair, which, quite literally, drew crowds of spectators whenever one of us approached.

We were beginning to fear the worst when the permissions came through by short-wave radio from Yushu.

We could carry on.

Once away from the 'main road', the expedition camp came as a great relief. The cold, not as bitter as the following year on our quest to find the link between the Przewalski and the modern horse, was, all the same, harsh. I spent many nights in my tent, unable to sleep, frozen and with a thumping altitude headache, the BBC World Service on the radio clasped

A Tibetan herdsman and his horse, richly dressed. Horses are still of great importance in Tibet, though the way of life is changing rapidly.

to my ear, longing for first light. However, this was what exploring was meant to be about, wasn't it?

The altiplano approaching the source of the Mekong is a mix of sweeping pasture, dotted as far as the eye can see with yak herds punctuated by the tents of the nomadic herdsmen, and mountain ridges with high passes. Dramatic in the extreme, it is a scene from prehistory. Wild ass, or kiang, and chiru, the Tibetan antelope, wander between the herds. This though, is a fraction of the wildlife that once roamed these planes. The Red Army arrived in 1950 in a land where the wild animals had no fear of man; the massive herds of tame ass were machine-gunned for army provisions. The chiru have faced the same sort of decimation more recently thanks to the insatiable Western appetite for fine shahtoosh shawls. This primordial view in front of us was broken only by the odd Landcruiser throwing up a cloud of dust going from here to there.

We took to horseback only in the last few days of the trip, since there was a road to the 'village' 48 km (30 miles) from the source. We arrived at this settlement early enough to set off the same day. Not having spent a night on this highest of plains we had not the slightest idea of what was about to hit us. At 4 p.m., while setting up camp, the sky turned black and we were blasted by a withering wind followed by marble-sized hailstones. Two hours later it was over. To celebrate I broke out one of the bottles of wine hidden in my bags to accompany the dinner of day-glo pink sausage and cabbage stir-fry. Conversation was of legendary hailstones that hit with the force to kill a fully grown yak.

The wine was to prove a dreadful mistake.

At this point Peissel hadn't had a glass of wine for weeks. By 1 p.m. on the following day he was complaining of a backache. As we made camp three hours later, he was on all fours, vomiting with pain.

The mess tent was just set up as what we now realized was a daily storm arrived with astonishing ferocity. To protect the flimsy tent, designed for a camping site on the Costa Brava, we piled up all the equipment on the windward side. Hailstones pinging off the metal casings drowned out Peissel's dry heaving groans. He was now running a fever of 39°C (102°F) and Jacques was increasingly worried. It was a kidney stone brought on by the wine and the riding. We were five days from the nearest village clinic.

This time the storm did not let up but instead gathered in strength as the whole team protected Peissel with our backs to the tent wall, buffets of wind threatening to knock us off our feet. In all it lasted until an hour after dark when, as suddenly as the day before, it gave up, just like that.

During the storm a wolf had taken the foal from one of our horses and the four Tibetans disappeared into the evening in a fury. I wondered if they would come back. Over the course of the evening, Jacques and I discussed options as Michel's condition deteriorated. At about 10 p.m. we decided that the next morning we'd rush for the road in an attempt to reach a hospital. Sleep was difficult, especially as the night air was rent at about 4 a.m. by an almighty scream. There seemed little more to be done but pack up and go home.

Well before breakfast, Jacques and I approached the mess tent, where Michel had spent the night, to break the news to him that we had to call off the trip, only to find him tucking into eggs and day-glo pink-sausage.

The scream had been caused by the stone ripping its way through his tubes. However, he was now restored, pooh-poohing any suggestion that we call anything off. Michel was old-school.

The Tibetans returned in the early morning with what remained of the foal, leading two other horses. These local beasts are the cavalry horse of the old Mongol hordes. Historically, they were the backbone of Sino-Tibetan trade. Yearly, five thousand horses were sent to Peking in return for women, treasure and slaves. From a distance they are easily mistaken for a pregnant thoroughbred. At just 122 cm (48 in) at the withers, they are well proportioned with an 'Arab' head, flared nostrils and eyes that you could knock off with a cricket bat. They appear to be pregnant due to their massive lung capacity. These machines move at a rolling trot for six hours a day, without seeming to draw breath. That being said, there is an old Tibetan saw, 'a horse is not a horse that cannot carry a man to the top of a pass, but a man is not a man who does not walk down'.

FED FROM THIS GENTLE HILL, THE RIVER BEGINS AT THE BOTTOM OF THE FINAL ASCENT AND IS IMMEDIATELY IMPRESSIVE – ONE CAN ONLY JUST STAND WITH LEGS STRETCHED WIDE OVER THE STREAM AS IT STARTS ITS LONG JOURNEY SOUTH.

As we made the final approach to where we believed the Mekong rises we could see a large area of springs framed by two peaks. Fed from this gentle hill, the river begins at the bottom of the final ascent and is immediately impressive – one can only just stand with legs stretched wide over the stream as it starts its long journey south.

We arrived late in the afternoon, too late to stay for more than rudimentary readings, in truth. Did we discover the source of the Mekong? In Victorian terms, most certainly. (Though satellite technology later showed that the White Mekong branch is longer.) In modern terms? Well, that is debatable, since there was a family of nomads camped at the side of the highest point of the river. Their encampment consisted of two black yak-hair tents, with a white tent, belonging to the brother, who had become a monk, at their side. Their washing and ablutions were all done in the nascent river, a cheerful thought for the hundreds of millions of people who take their water from this extraordinary river.

Michel Peissel (1937–2011) was a French explorer and ethnologist who undertook numerous major expeditions to the Himalaya and Greater Tibet, including the small and isolated kingdoms of Mustang, Bhutan, Ladakh and Zanskar. He also travelled up the Kali Gandaki River in Nepal, in part by hovercraft. Elsewhere, he journeyed along the eastern coast of the Yucatan peninsula, discovering Maya sites, and also sailed a replica Viking longboat from the Baltic to the Black Sea. He was the author of over twenty books, including *The Lost World of Quintana Roo*, *The Last Barbarians* and *Tibet: The Secret Continent*, and a filmmaker. He was a Fellow of the Royal Geographical Society and a member of the Explorers Club.

Sebastian Guinness accompanied Michel Peissel on several of his expeditions, including the one in search of the source of the Mekong. He has an art gallery in Dublin.

Michel Peissel stands with one foot on either side of the infant Mekong, which rises behind him in the Rupsa Pass.

UNDER SEA, UNDER LAND

Deep underground there are an almost infinite number of caves and tunnels waiting to be explored. Using more and better equipment, people have descended cavern systems of hundreds of kilometres, revealing spectacular caves and formations, often where no human has reached before.

It is often said that the depths of the sea are more remote and strange than outer space. In a way this is true – the sheer pressure that increases with depth makes it a difficult and dangerous environment to explore. But the rewards are great, as the special conditions preserve much that is lost on land.

Since we know only a fraction of what is there, we can assume there is much still waiting to be discovered in the oceans and underground. These are the last great terrestrial frontiers of our planet to be investigated. Much future exploration will undoubtedly take place in such places.

A member of Jean-François Pernette's team lowers equipment into a sinkhole in the limestone rock of Madre de Dios, one of the islands of Patagonia. Pernette has discovered spectacular new caves in this prehistoric-looking landscape.

GEORGE BASS

DIVING INTO THE PAST

FOR NEARLY FIFTY SUMMERS I'VE LIVED IN REMOTE CAMPS, excavating remains of pre-Classical, Classical Greek and Roman, and Byzantine shipwrecks. I've located dozens more from our two-person submersible, *Carolyn*, cruising 46 m (150 ft) deep for hours at a time beneath the Turkish Aegean. I've even explored remains of *Titanic* from a Russian MIR submersible. But my most rewarding underwater exploration began in 1984 at Uluburun, Turkey, and continues still, now as an exploration of the distant past.

My first glimpse of the shipwreck off Uluburun, Turkish for 'the Great Cape', held no surprises. Rows of four-handled copper ingots, two-handled Canaanite jars, a stone anchor and a scatter of larger jars, like those in the tale of Ali Baba – all had been carefully sketched a year earlier by my brilliant student assistant, Cemal Pulak, and a small team from our Institute of Nautical Archaeology (INA), based at Texas A&M University. But I could not guess that beneath the sediment lay remnants of a royal shipment from the century of King Tutankhamun, a shipment so rich it has been compared to that pharaoh's spectacular tomb as one of the world's greatest archaeological discoveries.

At the time, I was thinking only of how to excavate the site safely. Common wisdom dictates that ordinary scuba divers go no deeper than 40 m (130 ft). This wreck's remains lay on a slope 44–60 m (145 to 200 ft) deep – deeper than any of us had worked in more than two decades of underwater excavations. Of greater concern was the fact that some of our archaeology students had only just learned to dive. The diving had to be routine – no more adventurous than driving a jeep to a land site.

Before the excavation was over, ten summers later, we'd overcome the challenge. We'd completed more than 22,500 dives to the wreck, making

Buoyed by an air-filled lift bag, a basketful of copper ingots and ingot fragments is walked carefully from a depth of 50 m (160 ft) up the sloping seabed to water-filled holding tanks in the expedition camp ashore.

it the deepest large-scale project of any kind undertaken with compressed-air diving. Safety was always uppermost in our minds. We dived in pairs. All of us first acclimatized ourselves by diving just a bit deeper ever day, starting with dives to only 18 m (60 ft). Eventually we descended and ascended a shot line hand over hand while facing one another. We attached the bottom of the nylon line to our 'telephone booth', a Plexiglas hemi-sphere 1 m (3 ft) in diameter, which was filled with fresh air by a hose to a surface compressor and chained to tons of steel plates to keep it from float-ing away. In an emergency a diver could grab one of the full scuba tanks we scattered around the site, swim to the booth and stand, dry from the chest up. Without swimming back up to the surface, he or she could change equipment and talk either to the surface or to a partner. We added a second booth as we worked slowly deeper down the slope.

Below left This gold pectoral is the largest piece of Canaanite jewelry from the wreck.

Below right The granulated depiction of a falcon holding hooded cobras in its talons can be recognized because clearer examples of the same motif appear on a pair of earrings, probably from the Levantine coast, purchased in 1828 by Leiden's Rijksmuseum van Oudheden.

The problem was nitrogen. As we dived, the increasing weight, or pressure, of the water around us would quickly have crushed our sinuses, ears and lungs had not the regulators on our tanks provided air that increased in pressure as we descended. Unfortunately, however, 80 per cent of the air we breathe is nitrogen, which becomes narcotic under pressure. We were facing dangerous levels of nitrogen narcosis, Jacques-Yves Cousteau's 'rapture of the depths'. Divers speak of the 'martini rule' – every 9 m (30 ft) deeper one dives is like drinking another gin martini. Even at the shallower end of the wreck, it was as if we had five martinis under our belts. Experience showed that we could partly defeat narcosis by constantly rehearsing in our minds what we were to do once on the sea floor; we knew we would not be able to make sensible decisions at that depth.

Breathing mixed gases without nitrogen would have solved some problems, while creating others by adding complexity to the operation.

EVEN AT THE SHALLOWER END OF THE WRECK, IT WAS AS IF WE HAD FIVE MARTINIS UNDER OUR BELTS.

Nitrogen caused another problem, too. The deeper we dived, the greater our chances of suffering decompression sickness, or the bends. If we rose to the surface too quickly, the air would come out of solution in our blood, forming bubbles like those in an uncorked bottle of champagne, resulting in pain, paralysis or even death. To wash the nitrogen from our bodies more rapidly, we switched to breathing pure oxygen from regulators dangling 6 m (20 ft) below the surface at the end of each dive; no deeper, because oxygen can cause convulsions under pressure.

We made twenty-minute dives twice a day, or fifteen-minute dives at the deepest part of the site, where only the most experienced divers worked. Surface support was critical. We took turns as time-keepers, sending electronic signals to warn the divers two minutes before sending the 'come up'

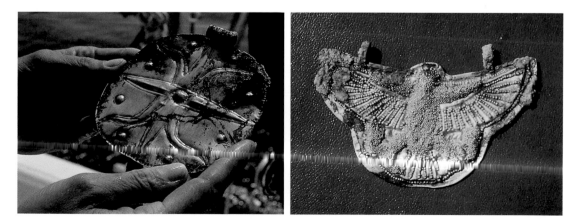

signal. *Virazon*, INA's small diving vessel, held a double-lock, multi-person recompression chamber for treatment of possible cases of the bends, with a physician on duty.

Once we had moored *Virazon* and constructed a camp or 'village' on the cliff face that continued down under the water as the slope on which the wreck lay, we began actual excavation. We removed loose sediment by sweeping the sand by hand towards the lower ends of air lifts, or suction pipes, which spewed it out to be dispersed by the current 18 m (60 ft) above our heads. A crust of hard seabed concretion, however, often demanded hammers and chisels.

Ultimately we brought to light enough ancient treasure to fill a newly constructed building in the Bodrum Museum, the most visited archaeological museum in Turkey. The finds included a golden chalice; the largest single collection of Canaanite gold and silver jewelry ever found; Egyptian scarabs; tools, weapons and musical instruments; full sets of merchants' weights; the world's oldest book; thousands of beads of various materials; duck-shaped ivory cosmetics boxes; faience drinking-cups shaped as rams' heads; merchants' seals; more tin vessels than previously found in all the lands of the eastern Mediterranean combined; terracotta jugs, jars, cups and lamps; and twenty-two trapezoidal anchors made of sandstone, many identified by petrographic analysis as coming from near the Bronze Age port of Tell Abu Hawam in northern Israel.

The main cargo was less spectacular, but archaeologically as important as gold or jewels. This took the form of 10 tons of copper ingots, a ton of tin, ebony logs, elephant and hippopotamus ivory, scrap gold and silver, ostrich eggshells, Baltic amber, terebinth resin, and foodstuffs – 15 tons of raw materials on a vessel of apparently Near Eastern origin.

The ingots were like those I'd excavated in 1960 at Cape Gelidonya, just to the east. They're known as 'oxhide', because of their characteristic shape with four ears or handles, which resembles the flattened hide of an animal. That excavation rewrote the history of Bronze Age trade in the eastern Mediterranean, at least in the minds of the scholars who agreed with controversial conclusions I published in my 1964 doctoral dissertation. Prior to my excavation of the Cape Gelidonya ship, which sank just before 1200 BC, towards the end of the Bronze Age, most ancient historians believed that Bronze Age Greeks, or Mycenaeans, held a monopoly on maritime trade. Vast amounts of Mycenaean pottery had been discovered in Egypt, on Cyprus and along the Levantine coast. Because corresponding quantities of Near Eastern artifacts were not found in Greece, scholars

An exquisite gold chalice was less archaeologically valuable than the terracotta vessels on the wreck because its age and place of origin remain uncertain.

assumed that Semites did not play a seafaring role prior to the Phoenicians of the later Iron Age. Personal possessions on the Cape Gelidonya ship, however, pointed to a Near Eastern crew. That discovery drew my attention to Bronze Age Syrian seafarers represented in Egyptian art and mentioned in contemporary cuneiform tablets – both overlooked or ignored by generations of scholars.

I proposed that Near Eastern seafaring merchants had not been recognized simply because their cargoes left few traces. And what would leave fewer remains than raw materials? On reaching port they would have been quickly transformed into objects representative of the culture that imported them. From their outward appearance, what archaeologist could tell who had traded the copper and tin which were mixed to form the bronze of a Mycenaean sword, an Egyptian bowl or an Italian pin?

But we were not excavating simply to vindicate a single idea. We wanted to extract as much detailed data from the Uluburun wreck as possible. No matter how precisely positioned on our plans, no matter how delicately raised, cleaned and conserved, our finds were only old and often beautiful objects, like the gold pendant with a depiction in repoussé of a Canaanite goddess holding gazelles, or another with a falcon clutching hooded cobras in its talons, or the partly gold-clad bronze statuette of a goddess, perhaps the ship's protective deity. To give meaning to objects we spend two years in laboratories and libraries for every month we dive. Where had the ship's final voyage originated and where was it heading? Following clues is the real adventure, an intellectual endeavour every bit as thrilling as working deep in the sea.

FOLLOWING CLUES IS THE REAL ADVENTURE, AN INTELLECTUAL ENDEAVOUR EVERY BIT AS THRILLING AS WORKING DEEP IN THE SEA.

Around seventy-five Canaanite jars in the cargo contained a hardened resin, which laboratory analysis identified as terebinth resin from a relative of the pistachio tree. Ours was the first archaeological discovery of the substance and we had half a ton. What was its purpose and source? The French Egyptologist Victor Loret wrote an entire book, published posthumously in Cairo in 1949, with the sole aim of identifying Egyptian *sntr* as terebinth resin; if he was correct, inscriptions revealed that tons of it were imported by the pharaohs of Egypt from the Levantine coast to burn as incense in religious rituals. In an Egyptian tomb-painting of a royal storeroom, the word *sntr* is even written on a Canaanite jar depicted with a row of four-handled copper ingots. The resin left few traces because it was all burnt. Terebinth trees are common around the eastern Mediterranean, but

Part of the highly accurate site plan, drawn by Cemal Pulak with the aid of multiple photo mosaics taken on the seabed, depicts rows of copper ingots, a large jar, and two of the many stone anchors from the wreck.

Cemal Pulak determined that two of the varieties of snails trapped in the Uluburun resin are found together only in one place – a small area near the Dead Sea, not far from Tell Abu Hawam.

Cemal, as much a naturalist as an archaeologist, noticed that murex opercula, little button-like doors, were the only parts of murex shells on the site and thus had to be cargo. What were they for? Years later he handed me a tiny bag of powdered murex opercula from Oman, where today they are an ingredient of incense. Were our opercula an additive for the terebinth resin?

Much later, Cemal learnt that the jars holding the resin were made in northern Israel. At the time of their discovery I assumed that fourteen hippopotamus teeth were from Nile-dwelling animals. Later, however, in a library I discovered that hippopotamus skeletons had been unearthed from Iron Age and later strata near Tel Aviv. If hippopotamuses lived on the Levantine coast at that time, surely they were also there in the Bronze Age. The partial elephant tusk we found could have come from the same region; Pharaoh Tuthmosis III hunted elephants for ivory in north Syria in the fifteenth century bc. Years after our excavation, a picture of our ancient ship's final voyage was taking shape.

Another unexpected raw material was a disk of cobalt-blue glass, about 15 cm (6 in) in diameter, the earliest intact glass ingot known. Cast as an inexpensive imitation of the rare stone, lapis lazuli, it is physical proof of the 'lapis lazuli from the kiln', as opposed to mined 'lapis lazuli from the mountain' mentioned on cuneiform tablets. It was, however, only the first of nearly two hundred ingots, some cobalt blue and others cast in colours imitative of precious turquoise and amber.

Analyses showed that our cobalt-blue ingots were chemically identical to glass in both Egyptian bottles and Mycenaean beads. Clearly, glass ingots were widely distributed and again were transformed into other objects, leaving little trace unless shipwrecked. I assumed that they were another raw material from the Levantine coast, a source of glass throughout antiquity – clay tablets mention shipments from there of mekku and ehlipakku, which had earlier been suggested as meaning raw glass. Years later, Cemal discovered a clue that proved my assumption in this case wrong. After artifacts had slowly dried out in our conservation laboratory, he realized that a piece of terracotta which split from an ingot to which it adhered was part of the mould in which the ingot was cast. Laboratory analysis identified it not as Levantine, but Egyptian clay. So had our ship also visited Egypt?

Archaeologists and students work together to construct a multi-storey camp – their home for eleven summers – on the barren cliff that continues the steep slope of the seabed above the wreck.

Another initially misleading clue was a scarab. Although I'd studied ancient Egyptian, I could not read the name on it until I returned to my books. We'd found the first gold scarab of famed Queen Nefertiti. The form of her name suggests that she was co-regent with her husband Akhenaten, the monotheistic pharaoh who tried to change the religion of Egypt. However interesting this was in itself, it told us little about the ancient voyage. A radiocarbon date showed that olive stones, twigs and leaves on the ship are from 1335–1305 BC, after the downfall in disgrace of the royal couple. By then the scarab, perhaps dangerous for an Egyptian even to own, held no value other than the weight of its gold, and was part of a small cargo of scrap gold and silver.

Cemal painstakingly pieced together from dozens of fragments a two-leaved boxwood 'book', or diptych, with ivory hinges. Its recessed wax

The author sweeps the accumulated contents of an open-mouth jar into his air lift, the suction pipe that carries sediment into the current far above the site for disposal. Most of the sediment, however, was kept for sieving and flotation ashore in a search for organic remains.

writing surfaces had disappeared, but because the diptych was discovered in a large jar that carried whole pomegranates, it probably was inscribed with an inventory of the jar's contents, a Near Eastern practice.

Before leaving port, perhaps Tell Abu Hawam, on its final, fatal voyage, clues suggest that our ship took on its cargo of copper, which lead isotope analyses show had been mined in northern Cyprus, and tin, a metal which cuneiform tablets state was brought overland by caravan from some source further east, perhaps Afghanistan. At the same entrepôt, quantities of unused Cypriot pottery – jugs, jars, bowls and lamps – were packed in large Cypriot jars. The ship hugged first the Syro-Palestinian coast and then the southern Anatolian coast, where it sank from unknown causes. In addition to the vast majority of Near Eastern possessions on board, two seals, two swords, two glass necklaces, all Mycenaean, and a small amount of Mycenaean terracotta dining wares suggest the presence of two Mycenaeans of high status, perhaps envoys to accompany the precious cargo from a Near Eastern ruler to a Mycenaean king.

The adventure continues, with the ongoing study of 15,000 catalogued artifacts by Cemal Pulak, now a professor at Texas A&M University. He has replicated part of the wooden hull to test its strength, and had one of his students create a computer model to test the stability of the ship with its cargo in its original position.

Archaeologists explore mountain ranges, jungles, caves and the sea floor in their quest for knowledge of our past. I'm frequently asked what has been my most exciting discovery. My answer is always the same: something I learnt in the library about an artifact, which gave it meaning.

George F. Bass (American, b. 1932) is Chairman Emeritus of the Institute of Nautical Archaeology, which he founded, and Distinguished Professor Emeritus at Texas A&M University, with which INA is affiliated. Since 1960 he has excavated Bronze Age, Archaic Greek, Classical Greek, Late Roman and Byzantine shipwrecks off the Turkish coast. He is the author or editor of numerous books, including *Beneath the Seven Seas* (2005). He holds the highest awards of the Archaeological Institute of America, the Explorers Club and the National Geographic Society, as well as the National Medal of Science.

ANDY EAVIS

MULU: DEEP UNDER BORNEO

WHAT ON EARTH AM I DOING SITTING ON THE TOP OF THIS TREE? I am sixty-three years old and I am sitting on the very top of a 20-m (66-ft) high tree in the tropical rainforest of Borneo. What the hell am I doing here?

The explanation goes back almost exactly thirty years earlier, when two years after a record-breaking expedition with Robin Hanbury-Tenison and the Royal Geographical Society I jointly led a caving expedition back to the Mulu National Park, Sarawak, in 1980. One of our expedition scientists, Hans Fredrick, had found an entrance that by Mulu standards was small, at only 10 m (33 ft) wide and 30 m (98 ft) high, but there was a huge draught of air blowing out, which usually indicates a large cave passage beyond.

As leader of the southern group, I tried to recruit a team to join Hans and explore this new-found entrance, but initially not many were prepared to break off from the monumental discoveries they were finding in other

Cooking at a camp in Granada Chamber in 1984, in a photograph taken by Jerry Wooldridge. Note the helmet-mounted carbide light.

caves. I can remember making a radio call advertising the trip and saying we were going to find the largest cave in the world. Tony White and Dave Checkley joined me. Tony pointed out that the chances of finding the largest cave in the world were very remote and almost chastised me for being over-pushy with my salesmanship.

The four of us, plus a local guy called Danny Lawi, made the first trip into the entrance, having set up a forest camp nearby. Unbeknown to us the cave was in flood. A kilometre swim was the only way of making progress. At the end of the swim we climbed out into rapids. The cave looked fabulous, although not getting much larger; but it was an enjoyable passage. Unfortunately, at this point Hans had to leave to do science elsewhere. The TV crew, plus Dave, Tony and myself, went in to film the initial cave exploration, which had very rarely been done before. At the end of the entrance canal we climbed up through the rapids as Sid Perou filmed. Soon (although I have to say thirty years ago it seemed much further), we came to a spectacular whirlpool.

Sid decided that his non-waterproof camera was not suitable for filming further, so the crew retreated to the surface. Beyond the plunge pool we were initially fighting through the stream and then traversing above it on ledges. Eventually the roof rose and we were able to scramble over sizeable blocks well out of the water. We clambered on from boulder to boulder, surveying our way in 30-m (98-ft) legs using tape, compass and clinometers. The going got steep and we found ourselves ascending among boulders as large as houses.

Our small carbide lights at that time were not a patch on the remarkable Scurrion LED lights we use today, and all we could see was a small patch of floor. No walls, and no ceiling. Surveying like this seemed pointless, so we turned to find a wall, which we reached after 100 m (328 ft) and then followed it. Initially it went up very steeply, dangerously steeply. Huge boulders were perched precariously and we were in grave danger of dislodging them on to one another. The wall climbed at the same angle for a further vertical distance of 200 m (656 ft).

Eventually, the pure exhilaration of cave exploration began to be overtaken by fatigue and discomfort. Caving in the tropics, particularly in 1980, was not always a comfortable affair – a wetsuit in these warm, gritty bacteria-ridden conditions produced extraordinarily painful skin conditions, from which we were all suffering. After we had gone up, around and down a long way, the idea that we were in a chamber was first suggested by

Tony. The other two of us were sceptical, but we wanted to exit as quickly as possible. We had after all been underground for seventeen hours.

Tony suggested that if it was a chamber, a compass bearing worked out from our survey notes would take us straight back to the cairn we had built at the top of the entrance slope. Tony calculated this angle and we marched off on fairly easy going. Bizarrely, we passed the skeleton of a cave bear, one of a very few known to exist deep inside caves in Mulu. Sure enough, after over half a kilometre of nothingness we arrived back at our entrance cairn. We then retraced our steps to the surface and got back to camp as dawn was breaking after a twenty-hour trip.

SURE ENOUGH, AFTER OVER HALF A KILOMETRE OF NOTHINGNESS WE ARRIVED BACK AT OUR ENTRANCE CAIRN.

Christmas was upon us so we returned to base camp and a couple of days later I flew back to England. I announced to the world that our survey showed that we had discovered what we believed to be the largest cave chamber in the world, later named Sarawak Chamber.

Lots of caving expeditions went to Mulu after this. The rich cave pickings meant that other big passages took priority, and Sarawak Chamber was thought to be fully explored. However, on studying the survey closely it was obvious that there was a huge passage coming into the chamber from Hidden Valley, but the only known exit from the chamber was small and immature. Somewhere there was a gigantic passage missing.

Some thirty years later, in 2011, Kevin Dixon, Meg Stark and I arrived in Mulu, flying into the international airport that had been built especially to bring tourists to the show caves. Leaving the other two to start testing the latest laser-scanning equipment in Deer Cave, I did a reconnaissance

A panoramic photograph by Robbie Shone of the bottom half of Sarawak Chamber showing an inlet passage some 700 m (2,300 ft) from the camera.

The classic photo by Jerry Wooldridge of Deer Cave, taken in 1980 before any show cave walkways were added. This is still one of the largest and most impressive cave passages in the world.

to the Sarawak Chamber entrance, called Nasib Bagus, Malay for 'Good Luck cave'. The water level was incredibly low: the passage I had swum several times before was ankle deep in water so, leaving my local guide Chris Victor behind, I ran through the first three-quarters of a kilometre and climbed up the first few cascades, getting almost to the plunge pool. In low water it was wonderfully easy. I returned and joined the others. The technology had worked brilliantly, putting 20 million measurements into the computer to enable us to produce a 3-D model of what is possibly the largest known cave passage in the world.

Meg, Kevin and I then went into Sarawak Chamber with the scanner nicknamed 'The Beast', owing to its weight and size. We camped for four days while we carefully moved the machine from place to place, each set-up taking up to four hours and producing over two million points. While the scanner was working, we were either sleeping or searching for the elusive, missing passage. Although our big lights now gave us a remarkable view of the roof and walls of the chamber, we could not see any place where the big passage might continue.

Once the scanning was complete we decided to change tack and look for an entrance from the outside in the cliffs above the known passage, working in from the surface rather than trying to trace it out from underground. Mark Brown, Mark Richardson and I decided to go back to the Nasib Bagus entrance and climb up to an obvious black hole we had spotted earlier. So the three of us started up the cliff, traversing to where the going was easy, to try to find a line that would take us close to the cave entrance. Mark Richardson led and I rather stupidly followed him. Mark Brown more sensibly took up the rear. After a particularly difficult section we decided it was time for somebody to go down and start directing by radio. As Mark Brown was at the back and the saplings we had been climbing on had been dropping off behind us, it seemed he had to be the one to descend and direct. We left a fixed rope across a difficult section and traversed on with a ridiculously short rope, Mark again leading and me seconding. The climb was from sapling to sapling, with the biggest acting as fixed belays.

Once Mark had got down into position on the ground, he was able to tell us that we were a long way to the right and 20 m (66 ft) below the black hole that was our objective. We climbed and traversed. On one section Mark went particularly quiet; when I joined him I realized why – all the holds had dropped off as he climbed over them leaving nothing but overhanging rock and a big, big drop. He tensioned me across, we both then wondered, but never discussed, how the hell we were going to reverse it to get back down. Again the radio directed us onwards and upwards. Without direction, we would have had absolutely no chance of finding the entrance.

Eventually we were told we were below our objective. Mark climbed vertically up. After what seemed a very long time I heard echoing cries of exclamation – he had made it. I followed to find a beautiful cave entrance, dropping steeply down into the cliff face. Could this be the missing passage? I had seen a number of other cliff entrances just like this, practically all of them opened out into enormous cave passages. Unfortunately this one didn't. After 10 m (130 ft) it closed up altogether.

It then got dark and started to rain. We decided the most sensible way to return to the ground was to abseil straight down the cliff face, but we were now at least 200 m (656 ft) above the valley floor and we had only a

Kevin Dixon using the laser scanner in Sarawak Chamber to produce a very accurate 3-D model, in a photograph by Robbie Shone.

Scientist Gina Moseley takes a break from her work to pose for the photo by Robbie Shone beside a water spout with a backdrop of beautiful rock architecture.

40-m (130-ft) rope. We would have to abseil down on a double rope and tie off to the most substantial thing we could find, then pull the rope down behind us. The biggest danger in doing this is the rope getting stuck. If it sticks you are stuck.

The first four or five drops went well. But with the short rope, we couldn't drop more than 20 m (66 ft) at a time, so if we came to a completely blank piece of rock we had a problem, and that is exactly what happened. Mark had to pendulum to find his sapling and then belay on, he shouted up that I wasn't going to like it, and when I abseiled down and joined him he was right. It was a 'tree', 3 cm (little more than 1 in) across, with no other vegetation on the plain rock face, and both of us were tied to it.

Mark then abseiled down the next pitch. As I waited for him, I realized the tree I was tied to was gently moving and could easily have been coming out of the rock. If it did, with both of us fixed to it, we would have dropped 100 m (328 ft) below. Mark shouted up, saying again that I wasn't going to like it ... and that is how I came to be sitting on the top of a tree.

When I got there I discovered lightning or a boulder had chopped the crown off the tree and Mark was sitting right on the very top of it. I joined him. The cliff disappeared underneath us – it was completely overhanging. We abseiled down the tree, followed by another five pitches down the cliff before we reached Mark Brown in the valley below – seventeen vertical drops in the dark and rain, but we survived.

Cave exploring is a varied occupation, never or rarely dull, full of improvisation, and it can be made relatively safe. The one piece of utter stupidity was the belaying to the sapling: there was no way to make that safe, and two people hanging off a twig is definitely not to be recommended.

Andy Eavis (British, b. 1948) began discovering new caves in Britain in the late 1960s and since then has led expeditions all over the world, locating over 500 km (310 miles) of new cave passage, including some of the largest enclosed spaces on the planet. As an engineer he has also always been involved in the science and technology of cave exploration, pioneering new caving techniques and assisting in their scientific aspects, particularly climatic history. His caving career culminated in becoming the chairman of the British Caving Association and President of the World Caving Association.

JEAN-FRANÇOIS PERNETTE

CAVING IN THE ISLANDS OF PATAGONIA

IN MARCH 1995, ONE YEAR AFTER EXPLORING THE GIANT SHAFT of the Great Papuan Plateau, four of us were pacing up and down a windy Puerto Natales wharf in Chile. Our aim was to check the geological possibility of karst features and caves in two remote, uninhabited islands – Diego de Almagro and Madre de Dios, in Patagonia – and we were trying to find a lift to the first. We eventually met Edgardo and his son, skippers of the *Katita*, a 14-m (46-ft) long fishing boat, who agreed to take us. After three days and nights of navigation, including a risky U-turn in the middle of the furious Union Canal, we finally reached Diego de Almagro.

Captain Edgardo stared unbelievingly at us and asked three times: 'Do you really want to disembark?' Sure we did, and after crawling our way through the thick austral jungle, we eventually reached the limestone we were so eager to set foot on. As I was climbing the steep terraces, carved by heavy rain into an icy-looking luminescent marble cliff, I could feel once again the spirit of exploration accelerating my steps upwards. Of course this discovery was not that important, but my emotion was intense. In unexplored territory, the true cave explorer fully opens his wings. It was the same when I was prospecting in the Spanish Pyrenees in search of unknown underground rivers, in the 1970s, or exploring the giant potholes of Papua New Guinea in the 1980s. For me, speleology is essentially exploring. It combines a love of adventure, the attraction of the unknown and an appetite for understanding – and even better if the explorer adds a grain of sand to our knowledge of the world.

AS I WAS CLIMBING THE STEEP TERRACES, CARVED BY HEAVY RAIN INTO AN ICY-LOOKING LUMINESCENT MARBLE CLIFF, I COULD FEEL ONCE AGAIN THE SPIRIT OF EXPLORATION ACCELERATING MY STEPS UPWARDS.

Sadly, this time we spent only a few hours on solid ground – or to be more exact, clambering over dense vegetation – and ended on a stunning barren plateau with numerous crevices and shaft entrances, all obviously unexplored. We had no gear and no time, and were lucky to have two hours of sun (the only time for a week), just enough for a short video and a few pictures of the extraordinary 'Marble Glaciers' we had discovered. These images were decisive in planning a new expedition and for obtaining later a National Geographic Society grant, and led to my Rolex Award for Enterprise in Exploration and Discovery.

1997: It took two years to prepare a full-scale expedition with ten members. Without financial support, the cost of renting a larger boat, the *Explorador*, was divided among the ten of us for just twenty days of service. The day after flying into Punta Arenas, the wind was blowing 130 km (80 miles) per hour. Welcome to Patagonia! Three days' sailing were taken up to return to our previously discovered plateau. Four members disembarked to set up camp, while the boat dropped the other six of us on the opposite side of the plateau. After a two-hour climb, we were in trouble: the almost sunny morning calm was replaced by a hailstorm with winds of 100 km (62 miles) per hour. The boat retreated to a safer place 20 km (12 miles) away, but fortunately was able to come back for a marine-type rescue before nightfall to pick the six of us up. The four campers had to spend a memorable night

Below left On these Patagonian islands precipitations erode and carve the limestone to form typical runnels, which have their own beauty.

Below right All the water disappears into narrow crevices that often lead to large underground cave systems.

Exploring vertical caves with waterfalls like the Perte de l'Avenir is very technical, and can be dangerous when flash floods occur after sudden heavy rain.

FLOODING IS CRUCIALLY IMPORTANT IN CAVING, BECAUSE A FLASH FLOOD MIGHT EQUAL DEATH TO A CAVER.

before we could reach them. It was a good lesson: from then on, we would use the boat as our base in a more secure mooring in Abraham Fjord.

Karst is visible from the fjord, but it turned out to be a two-hour climb up through the magellanic vegetation. We didn't know it at the time, but the expedition's most important discovery, the Perte de l'Avenir cavern, would be found right above those cliffs. Its entrance is impressive: the copious overflow of two glacier lakes falls into a 50 m (164 ft) deep shaft. We descended on the opposite side to the waterfall, but the last 10 m (33 ft) were still quite wet. At the bottom the underground stream runs calmly in a high, wide gallery to a sump. A dry passageway continues above the sump and after a 17-m (56-ft) deep pit, we

Strange mushroom-shaped rock formations are unique to Madre de Dios island. Such shapes occur because erratic rocks protect the limestone underneath from erosion.

were back in the stream. The tunnel here is 4 m (13 ft) wide and the wind was strong enough to tear a sheet off our mapping note book. Deep pools required us to use long wall rigging and the exploration was very technical. Perte de l'Avenir cavern was the first we discovered, and therefore very historic in Patagonian cave exploration.

Nowhere did we see traces of flooding. How could we determine the significance and speed of floods in Patagonian caves? Flooding is crucially important in caving, because a flash flood might equal death to a caver.

2000: On this expedition we decided to look for a mooring closer to our objectives and we based ourselves in the Eleutorio Fjord on Madre de Dios. After serious mechanical problems on the ship we were forced to stay

made of whale bones used as a burial site. Dating of the bones yielded an age of about 900 BC.

The giant Whale Cave revealed a new surprise, with the discovery of whale bones on a ledge at 37 m (120 ft) above sea level and dating to 2600 BC. There is no evidence for a post-glacial marine level at this height, so this deposit is probably the result of a tsunami.

2010: This Ultima Patagonia expedition was strongly oriented towards more scientific and archaeological research, with the installation of a 'laboratory cave' equipped with satellite data transmission. We also made detailed studies of reference sites, the archaeological caves, clear-water fauna, Whale Cave, and much more.

More than one hundred new caves were discovered, explored and mapped. I was lucky enough to locate a new shelter: Cueva de las Lapas, which contained mysterious shells as well as the remains of fires. It is hard to believe that for some reason humans used this cave, hidden in the middle of nowhere, for shelter.

The islands of Patagonia may not reveal caves of world-record depths, but they are among the most challenging karst regions for surface and underground investigation. After our explorations, Chile gave Madre de Dios official protection, and the process is underway for the island to become a UNESCO World Heritage Site.

Other expeditions are planned both on and beneath this magical island, with its continuous spectacle of exuberant rainbows and fantastical light-shows. Picture in your mind a prehistoric landscape and an almost supernatural ambiance that it is impossible for anyone to experience and remain unmoved by. It is this that stirs the explorer that lies dormant in all of us.

Jean-François Pernette (French, b. 1954) was nineteen when he made his first major discoveries in the Spanish Pyrenees, and twenty-six when he led the first French national expedition to Papua New Guinea in 1980. Since then, he has also explored major caves in Patagonia, Siberia, Mongolia, Borneo and China. He is former Director of the expeditions committee of the French Federation of Speleology, Honorary President of the Centre Terre Caving Association, and author of five books and many articles. He received a Rolex Award for Enterprise in Exploration and Discovery in 1998 and a grant from the National Geographic Society in 2000.

Looking out from the interior of Whale Cave: the giant entrance is 70 m (230 ft) high and 50 m (164 ft) wide. Whale bones were found on the ledge on the left of the photograph, 37 m (120 ft) above sea level.

LOST WORLDS

Lost ages of the Earth, lost cities and lost civilizations are some of the most intriguing areas of exploration. They combine the thrill of being first with discovering hidden treasure, of a sort. *The Lost World* of Conan Doyle's imagination was a *tepui* in South America: a vast, flat-topped mountain with a different ecosystem on its lid, a thousand metres above the rainforest below. It is this promise of somewhere cut off, remote, inaccessible for centuries that is one attraction of the lost world.

There are still surprises to be found out there, places where humans once lived or toiled and died and that have given way to the encroaching jungle or are located in completely unexpected terrain. The search for lost species, for fossil remains of dinosaurs or extinct mammals, leads the explorer directly into a lost world of the past, connecting with the richness of life on Earth long before humans arrived.

Will we run out of lost worlds to discover? As our methods of unravelling the mysteries of the world develop, so too will the scope for the adventure that accompanies all such exploration – and the knowledge that comes with it. So much has happened on Earth since the human race appeared and during the unimaginable aeons that went before. Our curiosity will ensure that we will go on unearthing exciting secrets from the past.

After centuries submerged beneath the sea off the coast of Egypt, two colossal granite statues, over 5 m (16 ft) high, are laid out to view after they have been raised from the waters of Aboukir Bay and freed from concretions and seaweed. On the left is a Ptolemaic queen dressed as Isis and on the right is a god of fertility, probably Hapi.

MARK NORELL

DINOSAUR-HUNTING IN MONGOLIA

WHEN I WAS A CHILD, MONGOLIA WAS THE ULTIMATE PLACE in the pantheon of obscure, poorly known geographies. Even today it is an exotic destination, though now more traveller friendly. It is also a mecca for palaeontologists. My involvement began when I was hired at the American Museum of Natural History in 1989. AMNH has a long history of association with Mongolia; in the 1920s the museum's scientists had made impressive discoveries and collections there, not the least of which were dinosaur eggs.

As a result of political realignment at the end of the 1980s, the Russians, who had made important palaeontological discoveries in Mongolia after the Second World war, were out, and the museum was invited in. In the spring of 1990, I set off with colleagues Michael Novacek and Malcolm McKenna to forge an agreement with the Mongolian government. Leaving Beijing in the morning and heading northwards on the trans-Siberian

Unpacking expedition supplies from our truck at Khulsan. On the left is Perle, on the right Lowell Dingus.

railway bound for Ulaanbaatar (Ulan Bator), I got my first taste of the Gobi, a desert that would define so much of my life for the next two decades.

Mongolia was a tough place at this time. The economy was in shambles as the locals tried to navigate a path from communism towards democracy and a market economy. Russian infrastructure was flowing out on every railroad car north. We were successful, however, in that we were able both to sign an agreement with the Mongolian Academy of Sciences and undertake a quick traverse of the Middle Gobi – including a pilgrimage to the Flaming Cliffs, where our predecessors at AMNH had made some of their greatest discoveries.

Returning to New York, we prepared for the following summer, and in June 1991 I was back in Ulaanbaatar. Having flown in, our first task was to break out our three shipping containers that were being held at the rail yards on the eastern outposts of the city. These had been carefully packed by Michael Novacek and myself three months earlier in Los Angeles. Even at this nascent point in my career, I had already had experience on expeditions in deserts ranging from the Mojave to Baja, Patagonia and the Atacama and Sahara, and I felt I knew what to pack. Our previous year's short reconnoitre of the terrain had also given us hints of what to expect.

In the early 1990s Americans were a curiosity. But even more curious than ourselves was what came out of our containers. As suspicious and humourless customs inspectors (the same the world over) inspected our documents and manifests, a crowd gathered. After hours of waiting, out rolled three new Mitsubishi SUVs. In a country whose rolling stock consisted of rusting Ladas and ailing Russian ex-military vehicles deemed not healthy enough to return to the motherland, these shiny marvels with their bright magnesium rims, powered winches and electric windows – not to mention then state-of-the-art cassette players – were terrestrial space capsules. Every tyre was kicked, every piece of chrome rubbed like a religious icon and every detail carefully scrutinized. Others who saw Mongolia's capitalist future more presciently were making attempts to buy our meagre food supplies to stock the barren shelves of their new, privately owned stores.

In early July our expedition departed, travelling south in parallel with the railway laid on the old Beijing-Urga caravan route. Climatic conditions in the Gobi Desert are difficult year round – in August 2010 we encountered 46°C (115°F) while only three months before at the Flaming Cliffs it was -26°C (-15°F). Food was in short supply. Midway through the trip, we audited what remained. If we stayed in the desert for the required

Above left Malcolm McKenna and Michael Novacek plan our route, while I cook dinner. Navigating through the desert on old caravan tracks was not easy.

Above right Ensuring our fuel supply for the expedition was also often a problem, and involved transferring gasoline into smaller containers.

number of days, lunch would consist of four crackers and 1⅞th sardines per person, breakfasts would be weak tea and sugar cubes, while for dinner we would enjoy a single helping of freeze-dried rations and whatever else we could scrounge.

Our traverse of the southern Gobi was tough. GPS was in its infancy, and anyway it is not useful without accurate maps. Google Maps hadn't been invented and the only maps in our possession were inaccurate international air charts and very deceptive, so-called classified Mongolian military maps. Because this area borders with China, precise maps were Soviet state secrets. We got lost a lot as we drove down old caravan tracks knowing that they must go somewhere.

Finding fuel was our biggest challenge. Only at a few outposts was it available and even then unreliably. Sometimes you had to wait for days. One of the towns, Sainshand, although much changed now, was a not so-delightful place in 1991. It was remarked a couple of years later (1993) in a Lonely Planet Guide that 'there are so many [drunk] men staggering around the streets it seems the city might have been hit by a germ warfare

Taking a bath in a camel well in the southern Gobi.

attack'. While waiting for the gas station to be resupplied, we chatted to a Russian army officer charged with shutting down the local base. Bored, this highly cultured man invited us to go to his base and 'shoot some missiles', as his orders were to destroy everything before he left. Sadly, science called and we demurred. Years later, such bases are now scavenged hulks of destroyed concrete buildings and toxic waste dumps.

The first part of our 1991 trip was in the eastern Gobi, collecting at localities to which we would not return for over a decade. Topographically this is about as low as one can travel in Mongolia, and is notorious in the spring for big windstorms. At this time of the year sandstorms from the Gobi and adjacent Central Asian deserts reach such proportions that they close airports in Beijing and Seoul, foul the air in Japan and colour sunsets in Vancouver, Seattle and Los Angeles. Geologists have shown that most of the dust landing on the Greenland icecap originates in the Central Asian sand fields. It is this dust that makes the northern lights so much brighter than their southern equivalents. On our first evening, John Noble Wilford, Pulitzer Prize-winning *New York Times* journalist who was covering our work, retired to his tent, which shortly blew away with him in it. Over the course of several nights we endured serious sand and wind, punctuated by rain.

During one of these storms we were initiated into the curious practice of sand bathing by our Mongolian colleague, Perle. Basically this consists of removing as many clothes as you are comfortable with, shutting your eyes and letting the sand pelt you for as long as you can take it. Perle claimed it generates static electricity, rejuvenating the body, but it just feels like a painful sandblasting, or perhaps a cheap dermabrasion session.

After a quick traverse of the middle Gobi we passed through the Flaming Cliffs. Then, leaving our media contingent behind, we passed over the Gurvain Saikhan mountain range into harsher environs – eventually to Khulsan and the Nemegt Basin. There we laid the groundwork for discoveries in subsequent years that would add significantly to the legacy of the American Museum in Mongolia. In this area we collected thousands of specimens that have changed how we understand animal evolution. But with the science there is the hardship. I am not going to overdramatize it. It is not like being part of SEAL Team 6 or anything, but it is still hard. Weeks without baths, insufficient food supplemented with greasy, maggot-ridden mutton, backbreaking excavation work, sleeping on hard ground, and very hot temperatures. But funny stuff happens. Midway through the season in 1991, we had just met our Mongolian colleague, Dashzeveig, at the spring of Naran Bulag – a crossroads where a stream of ice cold water percolates up in the midst of a harsh desert. Such an anomaly attracts all sorts, from palaeontologists, to semi-feral camels, to those whose business you don't really want to know about. It was here that we came to meet

IN THIS AREA WE COLLECTED THOUSANDS OF SPECIMENS THAT HAVE CHANGED HOW WE UNDERSTAND ANIMAL EVOLUTION.

Dashzeveig and to refill our nearly empty water reserves. Just after brain freeze set in, a thirsty camel came nudging in. After a few sips it brayed loudly and then, right in front of us, promptly died. We all glanced furtively around, as each one of us checked our pulses, wondering if we would be going back in a tarp on top of the truck.

At the end of the 1991 season we limped back into Ulaanbaatar, exhausted but satisfied. Weeks later when I met my girlfriend in Beijing, she barely recognized me – I was now brown, with shoulder-length hair and I had lost nearly 9 kg (20 lb).

Since then, we have had other memorable desert experiences. Trucks wallowing in the mud for days, problems with food and water, scorching hot days and ones filled with sleet and snow, mechanical breakdown, difficulties with drivers, etc. But the work has resulted in a complete revision of much of what we know about dinosaurs and their contemporaries. Lots of new dinosaurs have been named, thousands of mammal and lizard specimens have been found, and the cache has yielded important information for my research interests focusing on the evolution of 'typical dinosaurs' into birds. Discoveries have included embryonic dinosaurs and even adults sitting on their nests brooding their clutches, just like modern-day birds.

Malcolm McKenna using a very primitive GPS while I lie on the ground to examine a specimen.

Mongolia is now a much better place and Ulaanbaatar bustles with commerce. These days, I enjoy my ice-cold Tiger beer (brewed in Mongolia and cooled by our solar refrigerator) after another filthy day in the desert, while nibbling on the appetizers of Greek olives and prosciutto (all available in Ulaanbaatar), waiting for the plat du jour, be it Thai, Mexican, Chinese or Italian (actually, it's all just fusion). Even if it is still baking outside, we live in comparative luxury and it is fun to recount the stories, especially that summer of '91.

Mark A. Norell (American, b. 1957) received his Ph.D. in 1988 at Yale University. He works at the American Museum of Natural History in New York, where he is a Curator and Chair of the Division of Palaeontology. His current research focuses on the relationships of small carnivorous dinosaurs to modern birds, as well as naming new dinosaurs, deciphering growth patterns in dinosaurs and attempting to develop new ways of looking at fossils using CT scans and imaging computers. He has taken part in over fifty international scientific expeditions worldwide, including in Patagonia, Cuba, the Chilean Andes, the Sahara, Laos, Thailand, China, West Africa and Mongolia. He has published over 150 scientific articles and his award-winning books include *Discovering Dinosaurs* (2nd ed. 2000), *A Nest of Dinosaurs* (1999) and *Traveling the Silk Road* (2011).

TAHIR SHAH
IN SEARCH OF KING SOLOMON'S MINES

A GREAT MANY EXPLORERS LIKE TO BELIEVE THAT EXPLORATION is a field best left to the experts. I'm not sure why that is – perhaps it's a vestige left over from the grand old days of Victorian adventure. In my own experience you don't need specialist knowledge, big budgets or a well-groomed entourage to embark on a really great quest.

All you need is determination.

Over the last twenty years, I've mounted dozens of expeditions on a shoestring. They all started with a burning desire to get to the bottom of a mystery. Who are the birdmen of the Amazon? Where is the fabulous lost treasure of Ahmed Shah? Or does Paititi – the secret refuge of the Incas – really exist?

In my personal view, forget high-tech gear or corporate sponsorship. Instead, go on eBay and get yourself some third-hand army kit. It lasts forever and can be cannibalized as you go along. Better still, save your funds until you reach the target zone. Any basic hardware store – whether it be in the Upper Amazon or in war-torn Afghanistan – is sure to be packed with all the gear you'll ever need. This shoestring technique was what I relied on during the months I scoured Ethiopia for King Solomon's Mines.

Since childhood, I had been obsessed with Rider Haggard's novel of that name, and by the notion that the fabled mines might really exist. For two years I studied the historical archives, and the Septuagint, the oldest known version of the Old Testament. This religious text describes the magnificent temple that Solomon constructed in Jerusalem, near to where the Dome of the Rock now stands. The building's interior was overlaid with the purest gold, and that gold was supposedly brought from the mysterious land of Ophir.

Opposite above Dozens of men, women and children mine the alluvial deposits at an illegal gold mine near Shakiso in southern Ethiopia.

Opposite below A young gold miner in western Ethiopia hands a panning tray down to his father in one of the mine tunnels that form a labyrinth far below.

The ancient Greek geographer Ptolemy said that Ophir lay near the Straits of Malacca (off the Malay peninsula); Christopher Columbus was certain he had found it in modern-day Haiti; while Sir Walter Raleigh thought it was hidden in the jungles of Surinam. Others have located it in India or Madagascar, China or even Peru. I was sure they were all wrong – they should have been searching in Ethiopia.

There's plenty of evidence. According to the biblical account, the Israelites gained their knowledge of mining and working gold from the Egyptians during their slavery under the pharaohs. We know, too, that the Egyptians mined gold in Nubia, near Ethiopia's western border (*nub* meant gold in ancient Egyptian). The imperial family of Ethiopia claims descent from the child born to King Solomon and the Queen of Sheba. And of course, Ethiopia has an abundance of pure gold which – unlike in other parts of Africa – is close to the surface and can easily be mined.

BUT ONCE ON THE GROUND THE TASK AT HAND WAS DAUNTING. AFTER ALL, A FOREIGNER TRAVELLING IN ETHIOPIA IN SEARCH OF GOLD IS LIKELY TO BE REGARDED AS A SPY.

So I packed a Bible, a pair of third-hand hiking boots and a couple of kit bags filled with old army gear. Then I bought a cut-price ticket to Addis Ababa. Sitting comfortably at home in London, it was easy to talk about searching for King Solomon's mines. But once on the ground the task at hand was daunting. After all, a foreigner travelling in Ethiopia in search of gold is likely to be regarded as a spy.

Then, out of the blue, I met a young taxi driver called Samson. As it turned out, he had worked as a miner in the illegal gold mines of southern Ethiopia and had secretly studied the country's ancient history during the oppressive Derg regime. I hired him on the spot. Samson said that an important manuscript was preserved at a monastery in the extreme north of the country. He told me that the text – known as the Kebra Nagast (meaning 'The Glory of Kings') – contained clues to the whereabouts of the mines. So we travelled northwards, through the highlands and over the Semien Mountains, to a cliff face called Debra Damo.

The monastery, which is perched at the top of a precipice, is home to three hundred priests. No women or female creatures of any kind are permitted to ascend. At the base of the cliff, we deliberated how we could scale it. The rock face was completely sheer, with almost no footholds. But as we stood there, gazing up, a plaited leather rope was gently lowered down. Wrapping it around my waist, I tied it in a reef knot and, as if by magic, I was pulled slowly upwards.

An elderly monk led us through dark cloisters, thick with the scent of incense. Sweeping a scarlet cloth from a lectern, he revealed a very large book: the Kebra Nagast. Handwritten in Ge'ez, the ancient language of Ethiopia, it recounts in detail the story of Solomon and Sheba. The monk translated some of the text in a whisper. I asked him if it gave the exact location of Solomon's gold mines. Narrowing his eyes, he barked something ferociously in Amharic.

'What's he saying?'

Samson replied: 'He says that the book does have the answers, but we're not to reveal them to foreigners like you, or else you'll steal all the gold for yourself!'

I tried to press the monk with more questions about the gold, but Samson was growing nervous. He nudged me, insisting that we leave immediately. It was maddening, especially as I thought I was on to something with this ancient manuscript. Samson later told me that the monks at Debra Damo had a direct line to God. As far as he was concerned their wishes had to be respected. Negotiating the cliff face once again, we beat a hasty retreat.

Samson suggested we head to the south, where he had mined gold for eight years. The journey lasted many days, taking us through some of the most dramatic landscape on the African continent. There were great expanses of farmland, endless forests and rivers seething from heavy winter rain. But while there may be vegetation, throughout much of the country poverty is endemic. For the destitute, there's almost no hope of ever breaking this cycle. The only real chance of escape is found in the illegal gold mines of the south, like the one at Shakiso.

Nothing could have prepared me for the mines.

They were like a scene from a Hollywood epic set in Old Testament times: hundreds of men, women and children, drenched in mud, were digging the ground, many with their bare hands. They had excavated a crater the size of a football pitch. At the bottom of the pit was alluvial silt, which Samson told me contained the gold dust. The silt was scooped into rounded wooden pans and hurled to the surface in a relay.

The mine is one of many that have sprouted up in southern Ethiopia over the past fifty years. The alluvial seam probably wasn't worked in ancient times; if it had been, it would have been depleted long ago. But

THE ROCK FACE WAS COMPLETELY SHEER, WITH ALMOST NO FOOTHOLDS. BUT AS WE STOOD THERE, GAZING UP, A PLAITED LEATHER ROPE WAS GENTLY LOWERED DOWN.

A pilgrim is hauled up the sheer rock face at Debra Damo, in northern Ethiopia, where a secluded monastic complex guards the heritage of the ancient Ethiopian scriptures.

what was so interesting was that the mining techniques were almost identical to those that could have been used millennia before by the Egyptians. King Solomon's slave labour must have mined tons of gold in the same way – using wooden trays, sluices and panning pools. The big difference was that the people I saw mining near Shakiso were not slaves. They were working for themselves.

Life was cheap there, especially for the fraternity of young miners, many of whom worked in tunnels, digging down to the seam. In the rainy season, when the ground is soft, fatalities are common. The tunnels collapse, burying brave men alive. Such risks may explain the miners' way of life. In the makeshift village adjacent to the pit they spent their money as fast as they earnt it. All kinds of illicit services were available in the dark, grass-roofed shacks – including gut-rot *araki*, gambling and prostitution.

Although I'd hoped at first that these mines could be those once worked by Solomon, I realized there was little real chance of that. Yet, as we left the mines and continued westwards following another lead, I was buoyed up by having seen such ancient methods in action.

In the 1920s an eccentric Englishman called Frank Hayter claimed to have found a cave on a remote mountain near the border with Sudan. There, he said, he came upon a cache of gold and precious stones. He thought the find was somehow connected to King Solomon's mines.

In western Ethiopia we hired mules. They were savage, resented having to work and bit anyone who got near them. Having been bitten and bucked, we made the long trek to the mountain, through forests and stretches of deep mud, in search of Hayter's cave. It rained non-stop for a week. We searched the mountain for days, but the only cave we came to ended after a few feet in a natural stone wall. If the cave was indeed there it

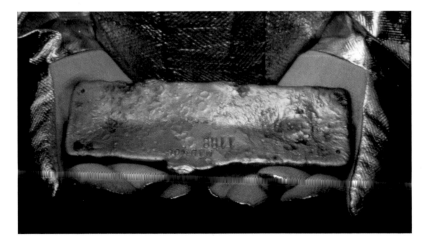

Right and opposite Holding a newly made gold bar, hot from the furnace at Ethiopia's only legal gold mine.

eluded us, yet I felt certain that we were close to where Solomon mined the gold for his temple.

I decided to retreat, and by the time we finally reached the main road, morale was very low, made worse by mule bites and the constant downpour. Samson and I hitch-hiked towards the capital. We stopped for the night in the small town of Nejo and put up at the only hotel that wasn't a brothel. Its Ethiopian owner, Berehane, overheard us talking of gold and Solomon's mines. It turned out that his grandfather was an Italian prospector called Antillo Zappa. I knew from my research that Zappa had been a friend of Frank Hayter, and had mined gold nearby.

Next morning Berehane led us out of the town and across open fields. There, on an exposed hillside, we came to a series of pits. They had evidently once been much larger, but had been filled in over the centuries by natural erosion. Berehane said that local people often found sherds of pottery here, and that his grandfather believed the pits were ancient.

Given the location and abundance of pure gold in the area, I think there's a strong possibility that these pits once formed part of Solomon's mines, but we cannot know for certain without mounting a full-scale archaeological excavation. I am sure that Samson and I came closer to knowing the truth than anyone else before.

Tahir Shah (b. 1966), born into an Anglo-Afghan family, is an explorer, author and film-maker, who lives in a Jinn-filled mansion located at the heart of a Casablanca shantytown. Always in search of the hidden underbelly of the lands through which he travels, Shah has written fifteen books – most of them grand quests for the exotic or the arcane. His written work, including *In Search of King Solomon's Mines* (2002), *House of the Tiger King* (2004), *The Caliph's House* (2006) and *Timbuctoo* (2012), has been translated into more than fifty languages.

FRANCK GODDIO
SUNKEN WORLDS

EVER SINCE I WAS A CHILD, I have been passionate about history and archaeology. Thanks to family tradition, I also had the chance to sail on the sea at an early age, and to learn to love and respect it. Looking back, it is hardly surprising that I became an underwater archaeologist.

Underwater archaeology seeks out the history buried beneath the sea. It provides us with priceless information about the way people lived, sailed and traded in centuries gone by, and explains and illuminates the meeting of civilizations and the interconnections between cultures and religions. It is a demanding discipline requiring a rigorous historical approach, an understanding of the techniques of geophysical prospecting and excavation adapted for the underwater environment, a thorough knowledge of the sea, and a range of diverse technical and even sporting skills. It is therefore impossible without teamwork. Over twenty-five years of research, the results of this teamwork reflect the enthusiasm, hard work and skill of everyone who has taken part. Our discoveries bring to light fascinating facts that complement and expand the data uncovered by archaeology on dry land.

In Asia, our excavations carried out in close collaboration with the National Museum of the Philippines have led to the study of both sunken junks and European vessels. Seven junks have been discovered, the oldest of which dates back to the eleventh century and the most recent to the late sixteenth century. Finds from these sites have built up a picture of Asian trade from its earliest growth to the arrival of Europeans in the Far East. The Manila galleon trade is commemorated by the *San Diego* and the *San José*. The *San Diego*, which sank on 14 December 1600 after a confrontation with the Dutch, played a part in the struggle between competing Western powers to control the rich lands of the East. And the *San José*, the largest galleon of its day, lost in a typhoon on 4 July 1694, provides evidence of the commerce established by the Spanish between Manila in the Philippines and Acapulco, Mexico, along the longest maritime trade route of all time. Work on these vessels has uncovered valuable data on contemporary life in the colonies, on clashes between the major colonial sea powers and on the globalization of sea trade after the age of the great discoveries, as well as on styles of naval construction.

The competition between Western powers to establish their own independent maritime trade routes is illustrated by two vessels of the East India Company. One of the most powerful companies ever formed, it controlled the sea trade between Asia and Europe, serving the political and economic might of Great Britain. The *Griffin* sank on 21 January 1761 during an attempt by the British to establish a post for trading with China in Spanish territory. The *Royal Captain* was lost in 1773 on its way to the same trading port. Both ships were loaded with tea and porcelain.

In the Mediterranean, in co-operation with Egypt's Supreme Council of Antiquities, in addition to individual ships we have located entire towns. Once centres of civilization, religion, trade and power but now submerged, these lost worlds are today being mapped and partly excavated. Beneath

After more than four centuries underwater in the China Sea, one of the canon of the *San Diego* is raised to the surface. A list dated to 1600 describing the fourteen canons taken from Manila fortress to be loaded on to the *San Diego* has been found in the archives of Seville.

the waves and sediment, we were able to locate the famed Portus Magnus of Alexandria, with its huge port structures and Royal Quarters where the legendary queen Cleopatra once lived. For centuries it was one of the most important cultural, scientific and political centres in the Western world, but before our discovery it was known only from cursory descriptions in ancient texts. Our excavations revealed extraordinary new information about this place, whose magnificence was celebrated in the writings of antiquity.

The sunken city of Heracleion, with its temple of Amun and its pharaonic port, had been the gateway to Egypt before the founding of Alexandria by Alexander the Great. But it was hidden out of sight, some 6 km (4 miles) out from the coast, beneath the sea and several metres of sediment. Rediscovered in 2001, it has now been thoroughly mapped and excavated. In its temple the Ptolemaic pharaohs, Alexander's successors on the Egyptian throne, were granted the status of universal rulers by the supreme god of the Egyptian pantheon. The mysterious city of Canopus, also submerged in Aboukir Bay and buried below the sandy sea floor, slowly gave up the secrets of its famous temple of Osiris Serapis, an ancient place of pilgrimage and centre for the celebration of the initiation rituals known as the Mysteries of Osiris.

At first, researching a site is rather like a detective story. For sunken cities, the first clues come from ancient texts which mention the existence of settlements that once stood near the coast. The next stage is to gather information on any past discoveries that could correspond with these sites. Sometimes a comparison of both sources can be productive: a town described as a thriving site many centuries ago may seem to have

I examine a stela at the site of Heracleion that was found lying face down. The inscriptions are perfectly preserved and include the name of Thonis. A 2,000-year-old enigma was resolved: Heracleion and Thonis, both mentioned in ancient texts, are one and the same city.

eluded earlier archaeologists. If no trace of its existence has ever been discovered on land, could it have been covered by the sea? A geological study of the surrounding area can validate a hypothesis of this kind. In the past, natural disasters have led to entire cities being lost beneath the waves. Confirmation marks the beginning of a long period of geophysical research, which in the case of the port of Alexandria and the cities of Heracleion and Canopus lasted six years.

With a wreck, the first task is to reconstruct a journey that took place centuries ago, using survivors' accounts, official reports, ships' logs, interrogation records, personal letters and journals or arms inventories. The

AT FIRST, RESEARCHING A SITE IS RATHER LIKE A DETECTIVE STORY.

adventure begins in archives and libraries, those storehouses of memory. Miraculously preserved, the most humble writings can, when studied and interpreted, lead to unexpected and significant discoveries. Manuscripts, often hard to decipher, must be transcribed and translated. Documents must be analysed to remove exaggerations that twist the truth or romanticize it to make the circumstances of a shipwreck more dramatic or emphasize the courage of those involved. Close study can reveal clues that may seem trivial at first but which become crucial in determining the circumstances and location of a wreck. A mention of prevailing winds, the direction of the current, a notable feature of the coastline, jotted down just before the tragedy, or a description of the place where survivors came ashore: all can be clues that guide the choice of where to search.

Once the research area for a site has been determined, a survey must be carried out, using the most sophisticated geophysical techniques available. The area indicated by the interpretation of texts and archives is

Below left A grid is set in place allowing the archaeologist to take notes and make a drawing of the excavated area.

Below right A white marble head identified as Antonia Minor, daughter of Mark Antony and the mother of the Roman emperor Claudius, lies underwater on a cushion of sand.

surveyed methodically for weeks, sometimes months, and even years in the case of urban sites. Reconnaissance dives are then made at promising locations that have been indicated by our equipment. These often bring false hopes: modern wrecks and geological anomalies register on instruments in similar ways, but such disappointments only serve to increase the pleasure of finally discovering the site that you're seeking.

An underwater archaeological excavation demands many skills. A multidisciplinary team must be set up, including archaeologists, historians, geophysical engineers, experts in restoration and conservation, divers who specialize in archaeological work, photographers, filmmakers and sailors. Gathering such a diverse group of people from different backgrounds to work underwater and live on board a boat together, sometimes for months, requires major organizational and logistical efforts. In addition, the provision of support boats, digging equipment and sometimes even remote-controlled robots or submarines for deepwater excavations often results in the setting up of a huge marine building site.

All excavations disturb a site, so during any operation it is crucial to record all the data that the most up-to-date science and technology can gather. Underwater archaeology uses the same techniques as dry-land archaeology alongside skills that are specific to the marine environment. The taking of different kinds of samples, the study of the remains of monuments, buildings and boat hulls, the recording of the relative positions of the artifacts within the site: all of these require meticulous care. Every day brings its own harvest of information, telling us a little more about the way that people of an earlier time lived, worshipped, traded, fought and sailed the seas. The support boat is gradually transformed into a floating museum of objects from another age. Conservation begins as soon as artifacts are brought to the surface, but this is just the beginning of a long process of preservation, restoration, recording and systematic study. The results are then published in journals or books.

EVERY DAY BRINGS ITS OWN HARVEST OF INFORMATION, TELLING US A LITTLE MORE ABOUT THE WAY THAT PEOPLE OF AN EARLIER TIME LIVED, WORSHIPPED, TRADED, FOUGHT AND SAILED THE SEAS.

A scientific approach does not rule out emotional involvement; on the contrary, this is a major part of any quest for knowledge. Every expedition brings its own surprises and sources of wonder. The rediscovery of the city of Heracleion in May 2001 was surely one of the high points of my life. I will never forget uncovering an intact stele of black granite, engraved with hieroglyphs, which had been lying under a wall in the great temple of

In Alexandria's Eastern Harbour, on the site of Antirhodos Island, a diver examines a section of an obelisk inscribed with a cartouche of Pharaoh Apries (589–570 BC). Another section has been discovered 560 m (1,838 ft) away, which perfectly matches this fragment.

Amun since the days of antiquity. I remained underwater admiring it until I realized that I had no air left in my tanks. In addition to its great beauty, the stele resolves a 2,000-year-old enigma by telling us that Heracleion and the city of Thonis, which some believed to be mythical, were in fact one and the same. This temple was visited by Herodotus in the fifth century BC and, according to legend, Queen Helen and King Menelaus stopped there on their journey home from the Trojan War.

It was here that I experienced another extraordinary moment. After several weeks of work with my team, we were able to witness the unique

The torso of a queen represented as Isis, carved from black stone and with inlaid eyes, at the site of its discovery in Heracleion. The statue is thought to represent Cleopatra II or Cleopatra III. Other fragments completing this piece were found scattered over an area of 350 m (1,148 ft).

underwater spectacle of three colossal statues of pink granite, of a pharaoh, a queen and the god of the Nile floods – the largest statue of a god ever discovered in Egypt – together beneath the water before they were brought to the surface. The light, filtering through metres of water, gave the scene an unearthly glow.

The city of Canopus brought us one of the world's most exquisite works of art. Arsinoë, queen of Egypt in the third century BC, is commemorated by a life-size diorite statue in the form of Aphrodite, the goddess of love, rising from the ocean clothed in a transparent tunic that clings to her graceful body. Her return to the surface was an unforgettable moment of almost unreal beauty. Yet another memorable moment was the discovery of the Naos of the Decades in the temple of Osiris Serapis. This small monolithic chapel of black granite engraved with hieroglyphs detailing the Egyptian calendar turned out to be the world's earliest astrological calendar discovered to date.

After touring in international exhibitions, these objects deserve to be preserved in a setting that is in keeping with their extraordinary adventures. It makes sense for collections that originate in an underwater excavation to be kept together, organized into coherent groups that illustrate the excavated site, and to remain permanently accessible to the public. In this way, expeditions that I have led have enriched the collections of prestigious state museums. It is always a huge source of pleasure for me to see the public admiring these objects, whose histories I know and which I have been able to touch and contemplate at leisure beneath the sea, in the silence of these sunken lost worlds.

Franck Goddio (French, b. 1947) is one of the leading pioneers of modern maritime archaeology. In 1985 he founded the Institut Européen d'Archéologie Sous-Marine (IEASM), of which he is currently President, and co-founded in 2003 the Oxford Centre for Maritime Archaeology (OCMA). For more than twenty-five years he has directed excavations on major archaeological sites including sunken cities in Egypt in the bays of Alexandria and Aboukir and historical shipwrecks in the Philippines. His work has been documented through numerous publications, documentaries and international exhibitions.

An archaeologist lights up the interior of a Naos searching for inscriptions concerning the god it used to shelter within the temple. Inscriptions on the lintel lead us to think that it was dedicated to Amun of the Gereb.

JOHAN REINHARD

INCA MUMMIES ON ANDEAN PEAKS

Searching for Inca artifacts exposed after the summit ridge had collapsed on Ampato, in 1997: Jimmy Bouroncle (right) belays Orlando Jaen while he examines the slope near the Inca burial site on Ampato's summit.

WHEN MY FLIGHT LANDED IN AREQUIPA, PERU, in late August 1995, I thought my work was over for the summer. I had located Inca ruins in Bolivia and eastern Peru that had made it one of my best field seasons ever, and I planned only a quick visit to Arequipa before returning home to the US.

Most of the ruins I had found that summer were located on mountain summits at over 5,000 m (16,400 ft). A new field of archaeology has recently developed called 'high-altitude archaeology', and its focus is on the Inca culture of 500 years ago – the only society known to make offerings on the summits of peaks over 6,000 m (19,685 ft) high. I had spent the previous fifteen years searching for Inca sites in the Andes, climbing over a hundred mountains in the process. Yet much work remained before we could ascertain the locations of all the Inca sites, let alone understand why they had built them on top of some of the world's highest mountains.

Discovery of the frozen Inca mummy known as the 'Ice Maiden' near the summit of Ampato in 1995. We found the Ice Maiden's mummy bundle lying in the open amidst ice pinnacles after it had fallen nearly 60 m (200 ft) from Ampato's summit.

SUDDENLY, TIME SEEMED TO STOP. WE WERE LOOKING STRAIGHT INTO THE FACE OF AN INCA.

I had called ahead to arrange to meet a friend of mine in Arequipa, the archaeologist José Antonio Chávez. We had worked on several mountain summits during the 1980s, but had not been to a peak together since 1991. He was as keen as I was on our continuing with excavations of high-altitude sites, and we immediately began listing the mountains we hoped to investigate the following year, in 1996.

Several of the peaks close to Arequipa had Inca sites on them, but those bordering the Colca Canyon, twice as deep as the Grand Canyon, especially attracted my interest. The inhabitants of the Colca Canyon had worshipped mountains long before the arrival of the Incas, particularly Hualca Hualca, Sabancaya and Ampato, the last being the highest in the region at 6,312 m (20,708 ft). Paradoxically, I thought that Ampato was the peak least likely to produce anything on its summit as it was permanently covered in ice and snow. However, I wanted to photograph its neighbour, Sabancaya, because it was still active – indeed it had been erupting daily for several years. Ampato was perfectly positioned for this photography, and before long my old climbing assistant Miguel Zarate and I were standing on its summit.

To our surprise, its ridge top that had previously been 10 m (33 ft) wide now measured barely 1 m (3 ft) across, a large section having recently collapsed. Within minutes we were stunned to find Inca statues sticking out of the exposed slope where a platform had been built five centuries previously. It was clear to us that artifacts must have fallen inside the crater when the ridge collapsed, and while later searching the area we spotted what looked like a mummy bundle lying on top of the ice. I had been to dozens of sites on mountain summits over the years, but I had never come across a mummy bundle on a mountain, let alone one lying out in the open.

'Maybe it's a climber's backpack', said Miguel. 'Maybe it's a climber', I replied, only half joking. As we drew closer to the bundle, my pulse quickened. Given the other items we had found, it seemed certain that it would contain something of significance to the Incas. Miguel moved it on its side for a better grip, and as he did so it turned in his hands. Suddenly, time seemed to stop. We were looking straight into the face of an Inca.

I soon realized that the mummy's face must have become exposed after its cloth covering had ripped open during the bundle's fall down the gully. The face was thus completely dried out, and our hopes of a frozen body evaporated. But when we tried to lift the bundle we were surprised at how heavy it was – close to 45 kg (100 lb). The thought struck me that there wasn't enough ice to make it so heavy, and I felt a surge of adrenaline as I realized what this meant.

Few frozen mummies had been found anywhere in the Andes and none in Peru, close to the heart of the Inca empire. Aside from the scientific value of its clothing and any artifacts with it, the mummy's intact body tissues and organs would allow complex DNA and pathological studies to be undertaken that had never before been performed on an Inca mummy. Our accidental discovery would therefore provide information unique in our knowledge of the Incas.

My mind raced with the implications. If we left the mummy behind, the sun and volcanic ash would damage it further. Obtaining an archaeological permit could take weeks, if not months, as could finding the funding to organize a scientific expedition – which would take us into the snow season. Nor could we save time by flying in with a helicopter; most helicopters could not land safely at the altitude even of our base camp.

It would have been impossible for us to lug the mummy on our backs to the closest town of Cabanaconde in a single day, but we could make it if one of the donkeys we had waiting in our base camp carried it. We could pack the mummy in ice, wrap it in the insulated pads we used to sleep on and return to town the way we had come. The pads would protect the mummy from the sun and most of the trip across the plateau would be in the chilly temperatures at 4,300 m (14,108 ft). I was aware there was no telephone in Cabanaconde and no freezer would be available to store the mummy. However, I knew there was a bus leaving the same evening we would arrive there, which would travel through the night, arriving in Arequipa at six the next morning. We could have the mummy in a freezer soon after sunrise.

ALTHOUGH IT WAS A RELATIVELY HORIZONTAL HIKE TO REACH IT, I HAD TO CLIMB AROUND STRIPS OF ICE THAT ZIGZAGGED VERTICALLY UP AND DOWN ALONG THE BOTTOM OF THE SLOPE.

The alternatives were discouraging. It was impossible to bury the mummy in the rocky, frozen ground. Covering it with ice could only be a temporary solution, and the warm weather of the coming months meant that the mummy would suffer more from exposure. Even in the best conditions it would continue to deteriorate.

There was still one problem: when I tried to pick up the mummy, it was so heavy Miguel had to help pull me to my feet. 'I'll be lucky to make it to the crater rim', I told him. Although it was a relatively horizontal hike to reach it, I had to climb around strips of ice that zigzagged vertically up and down along the bottom of the slope. An ascent of just 15 m (50 ft) required an effort that left me exhausted. After repeated falls I was bruised and panting, and I cursed myself for not bringing crampons. Once at the rim and heading downwards, instead of getting easier things got worse, and at times dangerous. Part of the slope inclined at 50 degrees, which would seem nearly vertical to a non-climber. Meanwhile, the batteries in our headlamps were giving out and falling rocks whizzed by us in the dark. Cutting footholds with his ice axe immediately below, Miguel pleaded with me to leave the mummy behind. I eventually agreed, and we left it firmly lodged among ice pinnacles at 6,000 m (19,685 ft). Without the weight, we quickly crossed the slope and descended to our tent in the dark, collapsing inside too exhausted even to eat.

Right above Excavating the Inca burial site on Ampato's summit in 1997. Jimmy Bouroncle (left), archaeologist José Antonio Chávez and Orlando Jaen (right) excavate what remains of the Inca burial site that had been destroyed when the summit ridge collapsed.

Right Archaeologist José Antonio Chávez (left) and Arcadio Mamani carefully clean dirt from pottery vessels surrounding the mummy bundle of an Inca female found in a burial site at 5,800 m (19,030 ft) on Ampato in 1997.

The next morning dawned clear. I returned to carry the mummy down, while Miguel set off down a steep scree slope. Before long we were reunited with our donkeys and on our way. By the time we reached Cabanaconde, we had been walking for over thirteen hours with only a ten-minute stop to share a tin of sardines. Later that night (and unbeknownst to the passengers) a plastic-covered bundle was placed in the luggage hold of a bus. Hours later, the mummy, still with ice attached, reached Arequipa, where she remains frozen to the present day.

Over the next few years I returned with three expeditions to Ampato, and we recovered three more mummies at an Inca site at 5,800 m (19,028 ft). Although each was unique in its way, none was as well preserved as the mummy that became famous as the Ice Maiden. Thanks to her discovery, I was able to obtain funding and undertake several expeditions in the coming years, culminating in one to Llullaillaco, a 6,739-m (22,110-ft) high volcano on the border between Argentina and Chile. It seemed only appropriate that we found three frozen Inca mummies – the best preserved in the world – at the world's highest archaeological site. At the same time, we recovered over twenty clothed statues, nearly doubling the number previously known. Perhaps just as importantly for archaeology, all were excavated in undisturbed contexts. Llullaillaco had provided us with some of the most important Inca finds ever made.

IT SEEMED ONLY APPROPRIATE THAT WE FOUND THREE FROZEN INCA MUMMIES – THE BEST PRESERVED IN THE WORLD – AT THE WORLD'S HIGHEST ARCHAEOLOGICAL SITE.

The reactions of scientists from many disciplines, not to mention the general public, made me wonder: is there anything from the past that can compare with the uniqueness, complexity and the unlimited knowledge

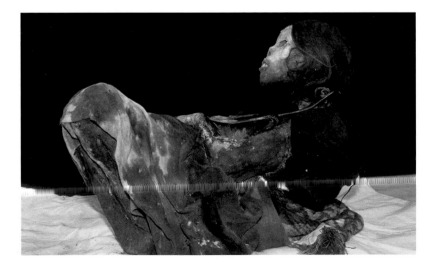

The Inca mummy from Ampato known as the Ice Maiden in the Catholic University's laboratory in Arequipa, Peru, 1995. The Ice Maiden is seen here with her outer mantel removed.

provided by frozen mummies? After all, they are not only extremely rare, they will never stop adding to our knowledge in future, since technology is constantly evolving.

The sense of accomplishment I felt from my work in the Andes extended well beyond the archaeological discoveries. While still in my teens, I had set out to study anthropology and acquire expeditionary 'tools' to help make my mark as an explorer-anthropologist. In the Andes I had been able to combine scientific disciplines such as archaeology and ethnography with everything from cinematography to mountaineering and scuba diving. I had never imagined that this would lead to decades of research in the region, but I gradually realized that the discovery of mountain mummies was only possible thanks to a path I had chosen while still a boy and now stood as a metaphor for all that I had set out to accomplish with my life.

Below left A gold Inca female statue wearing a red headdress (left) was found with an older girl, while a gold, male statue (right) was found with a boy in the burial site on Llullaillaco's summit in 1999.

Below right Examining the cloth that covered the face of a young female mummy found on the summit of Llullaillaco in 1999. The girl's head cloth had been damaged by lightning, exposing her face and a silver plaque on her forehead.

Johan Reinhard (American, b. 1943), is an Explorer-in-Residence at the National Geographic Society. His research has focused on the sacred beliefs and cultural practices of mountain peoples, especially in the Andes and the Himalaya, and on preserving the cultural patrimony of indigenous peoples. Museums have been built in three countries to exhibit the archeological finds made during his expeditions. In 1995 and 1999 Time selected his finds as among 'the world's ten most important scientific discoveries'. He has been the recipient of several awards, including the Rolex Award for Enterprise and the Explorers Medal of the Explorers Club.

FURTHER READING

POLAR

RANULPH FIENNES

Fiennes, Ranulph, *Mind Over Matter: The Epic Crossing of the Antarctic Continent* (London: Sinclair-Stevenson; New York: Delacorte Press, 1993)

Fiennes, Ranulph, *Beyond the Limits: The Lessons Learned from a Lifetime's Adventures* (London: Little, Brown, 2000)

Fiennes, Ranulph, *Mad, Bad & Dangerous to Know* (London: Hodder & Stoughton, 2007)

Fiennes, Ranulph, *My Heroes: Extraordinary Courage, Exceptional People* (London: Hodder & Stoughton, 2011)

http://www.ranulphfiennes.co.uk/

LIV ARNESEN

Amundsen, Roald, *Race to the South Pole* (Vercelli: White Star, 2007)

Huntford, Roland, *Nansen: The Explorer as Hero* (London: Abacus, 2001; New York: Barnes & Noble, 1998)

Huntford, Roland, *Scott and Amundsen: The Last Place on Earth* (London: Abacus, 2002; New York: Modern Library, 1999)

Nansen, Fridtjof, *The First Crossing of Greenland*, translated by Hubert Majendie Gepp (Edinburgh: Birlinn, 2002)

Undset, Sigrid, *Kristin Lavransdatter*, translated by Charles Archer and J. S. Scott (London: Abacus, 1995)

Vesaas, Tarjei, *The Ice Palace*, translated by Elizabeth Rokkan (London: Panther, 1968)

http://livarnesen.com/

BØRGE OUSLAND

Ousland, Børge, *Alone to the North Pole* (Oslo: J. W. Cappelens, 1994)

Ousland, Børge, *Alone Across Antarctica* (Norway: Ousland Design AS, 1997)

Ousland, Børge, *The Great Polar Journey: In the Footsteps of Nansen* (Norway: Ousland Design AS, 2009)

http://www.ousland.no/

PEN HADOW

Macrae, Rod, *The Catlin Arctic Survey* (Geo Mission, 2010)

Nansen, Fridtjof, *Farthest North* (London: Gibson Square, 2002; New York: Skyhorse, 2008)

Scott, Robert Falcon, *Journals: Captain Scott's Last Expedition* (Oxford: Oxford University Press, 2005)

http://www.penhadow.com/

MIKAEL STRANDBERG

Strandberg, Mikael, *Patagonien, 300 mil till häst* (Goteborg: Anamma Forlag, 2000)

Strandberg, Mikael, *Massajland - 100 mil till fots* (Stockholm: Alfabeta Bokförlag, 2001)

Strandberg, Mikael, *Sigge, vildhunden från Patagonien* (Stockholm: Alfabeta Bokförlag, 2001)

Vestey, Joanna, *Faces of Exploration* (London, Andre Deutsch, 2006)

http://www.mikaelstrandberg.com/

DESERT

MICHAEL ASHER

Asher, Michael, *In Search of the Forty Days Road* (Harlow: Longman, 1984)

Asher, Michael, *A Desert Dies* (London: Viking, 1986)

Asher, Michael, and Mariantonietta Peru, *Impossible Journey: Two Against the Sahara* (London: Viking, 1988)

Bovill, E. W, *The Golden Trade of the Moors* (Princeton: M. Weiner, 1994)

Moorhouse, Geoffrey, *The Fearful Void* (London: Hodder & Stoughton, 1974)

JON MUIR

Muir, Jon, *Alone Across Australia: One Man's Trek Across a Continent* (Melbourne: Penguin, 2003)

Philips, Eric, *Ice Trek: The Bitter Journey to the South Pole by Peter Hillary, Jon Muir and Eric Philips* (Auckland: HarperCollins, 2000)

Wilby, Sorrel, *Beyond the Icefall: Australia's Everest Expedition* (New South Wales: Child & Associates, 1989)

http://jonmuir.wikispaces.com/

JOHN HARE

Hare, John, *The Lost Camels of Tartary: A Quest into Forbidden China* (London: Little, Brown, 1997)

Hare, John, *Shadows Across the Sahara: Travels with Camels from Lake Chad to Tripoli* (London: Constable, 2003)

Hare, John, *The Mysteries of the Gobi: Searching for Wild Camels and Lost Cities in the Heart of Asia* (London: I. B. Tauris, 2009)

http://www.johnhare.org.uk/

ARITA BAAIJENS

Almásy, Ladislaus E., *Schwimmer in der Wüste, auf der Such nach der Oase Zarzura* (Innsbruck: Haymon Verlag,1997; reprint of the original, *Unbekannte Sahara*)

Baaijens, Arita, *First Woman A Woman Explorer In Egypt and Sudan* (Cairo: AUC Press, 2008)

Forbes, Rosita, *The Secret of the Sahara: Kufara* (London: Penguin, 1937)

Monod, Théodore, *Désert Libyque* (Paris: Arthaud, 2008)

Saint-Exupery, Antoine de, *Wind, Sand and Stars* (London: Penguin, 2000)
http://www.aritabaaijens.nl/

ROBERT TWIGGER
Bey, Ahmed Hassanein, *Lost Oases* (Cairo: AUC Press, 2006)
King, William J. H., *Mysteries of the Libyan Desert* (London: Seeley, Service & Co., 1925)
Twigger, Robert, *Big Snake: The Hunt for the World's Longest Python* (London: Gollancz, 1999)
Twigger, Robert, *Voyageur: Across the Rocky Mountains in a Birchbark Canoe* (London: Weidenfeld & Nicolson, 2006)
Twigger, Robert, *Lost Oasis: In Search of Paradise* (London: Weidenfeld & Nicolson, 2007)
http://www.roberttwigger.com/

BRUNO BAUMANN
Baumann, Bruno, *Die Wüste Gobi* (Munich: Herbig, 1995)
Baumann, Bruno, *Abenteuer Seidenstraße. Auf den Spuren alter Karawanenwege* (Munich: Herbig, 1998)
Baumann, Bruno, *Karawane ohne Wiederkehr. Das Drama in der Takla Makan* (Munich: Malik, 2000)
Baumann, Bruno, *Der Silberpalast des Garuda. Die Entdeckung von Tibets letztem Geheimnis* (Munich: Malik, 2006)
http://www.bruno-baumann.de/

RAINFOREST

GHILLEAN PRANCE
Mee, Margaret, *Margaret Mee's Amazon: The Diaries of an Artist Explorer* (Woodbridge: Antique Collectors' Club, 2004)
Milliken, William, and Bruce Albert, *Yanomami: A Forest People* (London, Royal Botanic Gardens: Kew Press, 1999)
Prance, Ghillean, and Harry Holcroft, *The Rainforest: Light and Spirit* (Woodbridge: Antique Collectors' Club, 2009)
Yungjohann, John C., *White Gold: The Diary of a Rubber Cutter in the Amazon, 1906–1916*, ed. Ghillean Prance (Oracle, Arizona: Synergetic Press, 1989)

SYDNEY POSSUELO
Angelo, Claudio, 'Prime directive for the last Americans', *Scientific American*, May 2007, 40–41
Hemming, John, *Die If You Must: Brazilian Indians in the Twentieth Century* (London: Macmillan, 2003)
Hemming, John, 'Carry on up the Amazon', *Geographical*, Dec. 2004, 59–63
Hemming, John, 'The people who shun us', *The Spectator*, December 2005, 26–27
Hemming, John, *Tree of Rivers: The Story of the Amazon* (London and New York: Thames & Hudson, 2008)
Margolis, Mac, 'A Quixote of the Rainforest', *Icaro Brasil*, June 2000, 76–82

Reynard, Nicolas, 'Amazonia: An adventure in search of the last indigenous peoples', *National Geographic Brasil*, January 2002, 123–29

J. MICHAEL FAY
Anthony, L., *The Elephant Whisperer* (London: Sidgwick & Jackson; New York: Thomas Dunne Books, 2009)
Quammen, David, 'The Megatransect' in *Natural Acts. A Sidelong View of Science and Nature*, rev. ed. (New York: W. W. Norton, 2009), 228–78
Thoreau, Henry David, *Cape Cod* (New York: Penguin, 1987)
Thoreau, Henry David, *The Maine Woods* (New York: Penguin, 1988)

WADE DAVIS
Davis, Wade, *One River: Explorations and Discoveries in the Amazon Rain Forest* (New York: Simon & Schuster, 1996)
Davis, Wade, *The Lost Amazon: The Photographic Journey of Richard Evans Schultes* (London: Thames & Hudson, 2004)
Davis, Wade, *The Wayfinders: Why Ancient Wisdom Matters in the Modern World* (Toronto, ON: House of Anansi Press, 2009)
Davis, Wade, *Into The Silence* (London: Random House, 2011)
http://www.daviswade.com/

MEG LOWMAN
Hallé, Francis, *In Praise of Plants* (Portland: Timber Press, 2002)
Lowman, M. D., *Life in the Treetops: Adventures of a Woman in Field Biology* (New Haven: Yale University Press, 1999)
Lowman, M. D. and H. B. Rinker (eds), *Forest Canopies* (Amsterdam: Elsevier Press, 2004)
Moffett, Mark, *The High Frontier: Exploring the Tropical Rainforest Canopy* (Cambridge, Mass.: Harvard University Press, 1997)
http://canopymeg.com/

MARTIN HOLLAND
Forsyth, Adrian, and Ken Miyata, *Tropical Nature* (New York: Touchstone, 1995)
Hanbury-Tenison, Robin, *Mulu: The Rain Forest* (London: Arrow, 1992)
O'Hanlon, Redmond, *Into the Heart of Borneo* (London: Picador, 1994)
http://www.heartofborneo.org/

MOUNTAIN

STEPHEN VENABLES
Venables, Stephen, *Painted Mountains: Two Expeditions to Kashmir* (London: Hodder & Stoughton, 1986; New York: Thunder's Mouth Press, 2001)

Venables, Stephen, *Island at the Edge of the World: A South Georgia Odyssey* (London: Hodder & Stoughton, 1991)

Venables, Stephen, *Everest: Alone at the Summit* (Hong Kong: Odyssey Books, 1996; New York: Thunder's Mouth Press, 2000)

Venables, Stephen, *A Slender Thread: Escaping Disaster in the Himalaya* (London: Hutchinson, 2000; New York: Thunder's Mouth Press, 2000)

Venables, Stephen, *Higher than the Eagle Soars: A Path to Everest* (London: Hutchinson, 2007)

http://www.stephenvenables.com/

CHRIS BONINGTON

Boardman, Peter, *The Shining Mountain* (London: Hodder & Stoughton, 1978; New York: Vintage Books, 1985)

Bonington, Chris, *Chris Bonington Mountaineer: Thirty Years of Climbing on the World's Great Peaks* (Fife: Diadem, 1989)

Bonington, Chris, *Quest For Adventure: Remarkable Feats of Exploration and Adventure from 1950 to 1999* (London: Cassell, 2000)

Bonington, Chris, *I Chose to Climb* (London: Weidenfeld & Nicolson, 2001)

Cave, Andy, *Learning to Breathe* (London: Hutchinson, 2005)

Murray, W. H., *Mountaineering in Scotland* (London: J. M. Dent, 1947)

Tasker, Joe, *Savage Arena* (London: Methuen, 1982; New York, St Martin's Press, 1982)

Wilson, Ken, *The Games Climbers Play* (Fife: Diadem, 1978)

http://bonington.com/

REBECCA STEPHENS

Brooks, Steve, Joanna Vestey and Rebecca Stephens, *Due South: Through Tropics and Polar Extremes* (London: Wigwam Press, 2009)

Stephens, Rebecca, *On Top of the World* (London: MacMillan, 1994)

Stephens, Rebecca, *Everest* (London and New York: Dorling Kindersley, 2001)

Stephens, Rebecca and Robert Heller, *The Seven Summits of Success* (Chichester: Capstone, 2005)

http://www.rebeccastephens.com/

HARALDUR SIGURDSSON

Sigmundsson, F., et al., 'Intrusion triggering of the 2010 Eyjafjallajökull explosive eruption', *Nature*, 468, 2010, 426–30

Sigurdsson, Haraldur, *Melting The Earth: A History of Ideas About Volcanic Eruptions* (Oxford: Oxford University Press, 1999)

Sigurdsson, Haraldur, et al., *Encyclopedia of Volcanoes* (San Diego and London: Academic Press, 1999)

KAREN DARKE

Andrew, Jamie, *Life and Limb* (London: Portrait, 2003)

Darke, Karen, *If You Fall* (Ropley: O Books, 2006)

Darke, Karen, *Boundless: An Adenture Beyond Limits* (AKreative, 2012)

Kirkpatrick, Andy, *Cold Wars* (Sheffield: Vertebrate Graphics Ltd, 2011)

Ralston, Aron, *Between a Rock and a Hard Place* (New York: Atria Books, 2004)

Yates, Simon, *Flame of Adventure* (London: Vintage, 2002)

http://www.karendarke.com

OCEAN

TIM SEVERIN

Severin, Tim, *The Brendan Voyage* (London: Hutchinson; New York, McGraw-Hill, 1978)

Severin, Tim, *The Sindbad Voyage* (London: Hutchinson; New York: Putnam, 1982)

Severin, Tim, *The Jason Voyage: The Quest for the Golden Fleece* (Leicester: Charnwood, 1986; New York: Simon and Schuster, 1985)

Severin, Tim, *The Ulysses Voyage: Sea Search for the Odyssey* (London: Hutchinson, 1987)

Severin, Tim, *Crusader: By Horse to Jerusalem* (London: Hutchinson, 1989)

Severin, Tim, *In Search of Genghis Khan* (London: Hutchinson, 1991; New York: Atheneum, 1992)

Severin, Tim, *The China Voyage: A Pacific Quest by Bamboo Raft* (London: Abacus, 1994)

http://www.timseverin.net/

HENK DE VELDE

de Velde, Henk, *Een reiziger in tussentijd (A Traveller in the Meantime)* (Delft: Elmar, 2004)

de Velde, Henk, *Een Ijskoude Doorbraak: Overwintering in Siberië (An Icecold Breakthrough)* (Delft: Elmar, 2005)

de Velde, Henk, *Nergens is ook Ergens (Nowhere is Somewhere)* (Delft: Elmar, 2010)

de Velde, Henk, *Een krijger onderweg naar huis (A Warrior on his Way Home)* (Delft: Elmar, 2011)

http://www.henkdevelde.nl/

JEFF MACINNIS

Amundsen, Roald, *The North-West Passage* (London: Constable, 1908)

Beattie, Owen, and John Geiger, *Frozen in Time. The Fate of the Franklin Expedition* (London: Bloomsbury, 1987; New York: Dutton, 1988)

Bockstoce, John, *Arctic Passages: A Unique Small-boat Journey Through the Great Northern Waterway* (New York: Hearst Marine Books, 1991)

McClintock, Francis Leopold, *The Voyage of the "Fox" in the Arctic Seas* (London: John Murray, 1859)

MacInnis, Jeff, *Polar Passage: The Historic First Sail Through the Northwest Passage* (Toronto: Random House, 1989)

Williams, Glyn, *Voyages of Delusion. The Northwest Passage in the Age of Reason* (London: HarperCollins, 2002; New Haven: Yale University Press, 2003)

JON TURK

Turk, Jon, *Cold Oceans: Adventures in Kayak, Rowboat, and Dogsled* (New York: HarperCollins, 1998)

Turk, Jon, *In the Wake of the Jomon: Stone Age Mariners and a Voyage across the Pacific* (Camden, Maine: International Marine; New York: McGraw Hill, 2005)

Turk, Jon, *The Raven's Gift: A Scientist, a Shaman, and their Remarkable Journey Through the Siberian Wilderness* (New York: St Martin's Press, 2010)

http://www.jonturk.net/

JASON LEWIS

Canfield, Jack, et al., *Chicken Soup for the Traveler's Soul: Stories of Adventure, Inspiration and Insight to Celebrate the Spirit of Travel* (Deerfield Beach, Florida: HCI, 2002)

Lewis, Jason, 'Expedition 360', in *Flightless: Incredible Journeys Without Leaving the Ground* (Melbourne and London: Lonely Planet, 2008), 137–46

Lewis, Jason, *Dark Waters* (BillyFish Books, 2012)

Smith, Stevie, *Pedalling to Hawaii: A Human-powered Odyssey* (Chichester: Summersdale, 2005)

http://www.expedition360.com/

RIVER

JOHN BLASHFORD-SNELL

Blashford-Snell, John, *In the Steps of Stanley* (London: Hutchinson, 1975)

Blashford-Snell, John, *A Taste for Adventure* (London: Hutchinson, 1978)

Blashford-Snell, John, *Operation Raleigh: Adventure Unlimited* (London: Collins, 1990)

Blashford-Snell, John, *Something Lost Behind the Ranges: The Autobiography* (London: Collins, 1994)

http://www.johnblashfordsnell.org.uk/

ROBIN HANBURY-TENISON

Branston, Brian, *The Last Great Journey on Earth* (London: Hodder & Stoughton, 1970)

Hanbury-Tenison, Robin, *The Rough and the Smooth: The Story of Two Journeys Across South America* (London: Hale, 1969)

Hemming, John, *Tree of Rivers: The Story of the Amazon* (London and New York: Thames & Hudson 2008)

Mee, Margaret, *In Search of Flowers of the Amazon Forests* (London: Nonesuch Expeditions, 1988)

Snow, Sebastian, *My Amazon Adventure* (London: Odhams Press, 1954)

http://www.robinsbooks.co.uk/

MIRELLA AND LORENZO RICCIARDI

Conrad, Joseph, *Heart of Darkness* (London: Penguin, 2007)

Naipaul, V. S., *A Bend in the River* (London: Deutsch; New York: Knopf, 1979)

Ricciardi, Lorenzo and Mirella, *African Rainbow. Across Africa by Boat* (London: Ebury Press; New York: William Morrow & Co., 1989)

Ricciardi, Mirella, *Vanishing Africa* (London: Collins, 1971)

Ricciardi, Mirella, *African Visions. The Diary of an African Photographer* (London: Cassell, 2000)

Stanley, Henry Morton, *The Autobiography of Henry Morton Stanley*, ed. D. Stanley (London: Sampson & Low, 1909)

http://www.mirellaricciardi.com/

WONG HOW MAN

Wong How Man, *Exploring the Yangtze: China's Longest River* (Hong Kong: Odyssey Productions, 1989)

Wong How Man, *From Manchuria to Tibet: A Quarter Century of Exploration* (Hong Kong: Odyssey; New York: W. W. Norton, 1998)

Wong How Man, *Voyage of Discovery* (Taipei: Commonwealth Publishing, 2007)

Wong How Man, *As River Flows* (Taipei: Commonwealth Publishing Group, 2009)

Wong How Man and Adel Awni Dajani, *Islamic Frontiers of China: Peoples of the Silk Road* (London: I. B. Tauris Publishers, 2011)

http://www.cers.org.hk/

MICHEL PEISSEL

Peissel, Michel, *Mustang: A Lost Tibetan Kingdom* (London: Collins, 1968)

Peissel, Michel, *Lords and Lamas: A Solitary Expedition Across the Secret Himalayan Kingdom of Bhutan* (London: Heinemann, 1970)

Peissel, Michel, *The Great Himalayan Passage: Across the Himalayas by Hovercraft* (London: Collins, 1974)

Peissel, Michel, *Zanskar: The Hidden Kingdom* (London: Collins; New York: Dutton, 1979)

Peissel, Michel, *The Ants' Gold. The Discovery of the Greek El Dorado in the Himalayas* (London: Harvill, 1984)

Peissel, Michel, *The Last Barbarians. The Discovery of the Source of the Mekong in Tibet* (London: Souvenir; New York: H. Holt, 1997)

Peissel, Michel, *Tibet: The Secret Continent* (London: Cassell, 2000)

UNDER SEA, UNDER LAND

GEORGE BASS

Bass, G. F., 'A Bronze Age shipwreck at Ulu Burun (Kas): 1984 campaign', *American Journal of Archaeology* 90 (1987), 269–96

Bass, G. F., 'Oldest known shipwreck reveals splendors of the Bronze Age', *National Geographic Magazine* 172.6 (December 1987), 692–733

Pulak, Cemal, 'Discovering a royal ship from the age of King Tut: Uluburun, Turkey', in Bass, G. F. (ed.), *Beneath the Seven Seas: Adventures with the Institute of Nautical Archaeology* (London and New York: Thames & Hudson, 2005), 34–47

Pulak, Cemal, 'The Uluburun shipwreck and Late Bronze Age trade', in Aruz, J., K. Benzel, and J. M. Evans (eds), *Beyond Babylon: Art, Trade, and Diplomacy in the Second Millennium BC* (New Haven: Yale University Press, 2008), 288–385

http://inadiscover.com/

ANDY EAVIS

Gunn, John, *Encyclopaedia of Caves and Karst Science* (London: Fitzroy Dearborn, 2003)

Marbach, George and Bernard Tourte, *Alpine Caving Techniques* (Allschwil, Switzerland: Speleo Projects, 2002)

Shaw, Trevor, *History of Cave Science* (Sydney: Sydney Speleological Society, 1992)

Waltham, Tony, *Great Caves of the World* (London: Natural History Museum; Buffalo, N.Y.: Firefly Books, 2008)

http://www.mulucaves.org/

JEAN-FRANÇOIS PERNETTE

Carsten, Peter, 'Deep into the land of extremes: probing Chile's wild coast', *National Geographic Society Magazine*, June 2001

Pernette, Jean-François, Richard Maire and Bernard Tourte, *The Centre-Terre Expeditions to Patagonian Karst Islands: A Historic Overview* (Texas: Proceedings of the UIS International Congress, 2009)

Pernette, Jean-François, *L'abîme sous la jungle. Aventures Extraordinaires vol 2* (Grenoble: Jacques Glénat, 1981)

Pernette, Jean-François, *Rivières sous la Pierre: Nouveau Record à la Pierre-St-Martin (BU 56)* (Paris: Fernand Nathan, Paris, 1983)

http://www.centre-terre.fr/ultima2010/presentation.html

LOST WORLDS

MARK NORELL

Dingus, Lowell and Mark A. Norell, *Barnum Brown: The Man Who Discovered Tyrannosaurus rex* (Berkeley: University of California Press, 2010)

Norell, Mark A. and Michael J. Novacek, 'Fossils of the Flaming Cliffs: epilogue', *Dinosaurs and Other Monsters. Scientific American. Special Edition*, 2004

Norell, Mark A. and M. Ellison, *Unearthing the Dragon: The Great Feathered Dinosaur Discovery* (New York: Pi Press, 2005)

Novacek, Michael J., Mark A. Norell, Malcom C. McKenna and James Clark, 'Fossils of the Flaming Cliffs', *Scientific American* 271(6), 1994, 60–69

TAHIR SHAH

Halliburton, Richard, *Seven League Boots* (Indianapolis: The Bobbs-Merrill Co.,1936)

Hayter, Frank, *The Gold of Ethiopia* (London: Stanley Paul & Co., 1936)

Prorok, Byron Khun de, *Dead Men Do Tell Tales* (New York: Creative Age Press, 1942; London: Harrap, 1943)

Shah, Tahir, *In Search of King Solomon's Mines* (London: John Murray, 2002; New York: Arcade Publishing, 2003)

Shah, Tahir, *The Caliph's House. A Year in Casablanca* (London: Doubleday; New York: Bantam Books, 2006)

Thesiger, Wilfred, *The Life of My Choice* (London: Collins, 1987)

http://www.tahirshah.com/

FRANCK GODDIO

Goddio, Franck and André Bernand, *Sunken Egypt: Alexandria* (London: Arcperiplus, 2002)

Goddio, Franck, et al., *Lost At Sea: The Strange Route of the Lena Shoal Junk* (London: Periplus, 2002)

Goddio, Franck and David Fabre (eds), *Egypt's Sunken Treasures* (Munich and New York: Prestel, 2008)

Goddio, Franck and Zahi Hawass, *Cleopatra: The Search for the Last Queen of Egypt* (Washington D.C.: National Geographic Society, 2010)

http://www.franckgoddio.org/

JOHAN REINHARD

Reinhard, Johan, *The Ice Maiden: Inca Mummies, Mountain Gods, and Sacred Sites in the Andes* (Washington D.C.: National Geographic Society, 2005)

Reinhard, Johan, *Machu Picchu: Exploring an Ancient Sacred Center* (Los Angeles: Cotsen Institute of Archaeology Press, UCLA, 2007)

Reinhard, Johan and Constanza Ceruti, *Inca Rituals and Sacred Mountains: A Study of the World's Highest Archaeological Sites* (Los Angeles: Cotsen Institute of Archaeology Press, UCLA, 2010)

http://www.johanreinhard.net/

SOURCES OF ILLUSTRATIONS

a: above; b: below; l: left; r: right

Courtesy Liv Arnesen (www.livarnesen.com) 25, 27
Ragnar Axelsson 162–63, 163
Photo Arita Baaijens 70, 71r, 72, 73, 75a, 75b
© Bruno Baumann 46, 83, 84, 85, 86, 87, 88, 89
© Mike Beedell 12, 183, 185l, 185r, 186, 187, 189
Photo Viktor Bentley 71l
© Tim van Berkel 132
Chris Bonington Picture Library: 145, 146, 147l, 147r, 148, 149; Jim Fotheringham 136, 150
Photo Douglas Botting 213
© centre-terre.fr: S. Caillault 265; P. De Coninck 262l; L. H. Fage 11b, 260; S. Jaillet 264r; D. Morales 261; J.-F. Pernette 259l, 259r, 262r, 264l; B. Tourte 242, 263
Fred R. Conrad 268, 270l, 270r, 271, 272, 273l, 273r
Photo Ian Darling 60
© Wade Davis 115, 116, 117, 118, 120
Piers Dunn 77, 78, 80, 81a, 81b
Expedition 360 Productions 170, 197, 198, 199l, 199r, 200, 201, 202
Photo J. Michael Fay 109, 110, 111l, 111r, 112, 113l, 113r
© Ranulph Fiennes 17, 18, 19, 20
James P. Blair/National Geographic/Getty Images 276
© Franck Goddio/Hilti Foundation: Photo Jérôme Delafosse 285; Photo Gilbert Fournier 281; Photo Christoph Gerigk 266, 282, 283l, 283r, 286, 287
Sebastian Guinness 241
Robin Hanbury-Tenison 212, 214, 215, 216
© John Hare 2–3, 8, 63, 64, 65l, 65r, 66, 67l, 67r
© Martin Hartley (www.martinhartley.com) 9l, 35l, 35r, 36, 37, 38
© Martin Holland 90, 129, 130, 131r, 133, 134, 135
Wang Chih Hung 228
Institute of Nautical Archaeology, photo Donald A. Frey 245, 246l, 246r, 247, 248, 249, 250
Photo Wyn Jones 152
Courtesy Christopher Knight 127

Courtesy Meg Lowman 122, 125l, 125r, 126
Jeremy Mallinson 209
Wong How Man/CERS 226–67, 229, 230, 231, 232
Steve Mann 1, 79
Photo Julie Maske 22, 23, 24
Richard Mohun 76, 82
Muir Collection: 54, 56a, 56b, 57, 58, 59; Photo Brigitte Muir 55, 62
The C. V. Starr Virtual Herbarium of The New York Botanical Garden 99
Photo Børge Ousland 14, 28, 29, 30, 31, 32, 33l, 33r
Photo Ang Passang 157
Courtesy the estate of Michel Peissel 233, 234, 235, 236, 238
© Mariantonietta Peru 48, 50, 51, 52l, 52r, 53
Photo Joanna B. Pinneo 69
Photo Krzysztof Pluskota 74
Sydney Possuelo 101, 105
Photo Ghillean Prance 93, 94, 95l, 95r, 96, 97l, 97r, 98
© Johan Reinhard 10, 288, 289, 291a, 291b, 292, 293l, 293r
Nicolas Reynard/National Geographic 9r, 102, 103, 106
© Mirella Ricciardi 4, 11a, 204, 218, 220, 221l, 221r, 222, 223l, 223r, 224
© Rupert Ridgeway 131l
Pete Round 169
Natasha Sebire 7, 165, 166, 167l, 167r
Tim Severin Archive 173, 174, 175, 176, 177
© Tahir Shah 275a, 275b, 278, 279
© Robbie Shone 254, 256, 257
Haraldur Sigurdsson 159, 160, 161l, 161r
Rebecca Stephens 154, 155, 156
© Mikael Strandberg 40, 41l, 41r, 42, 43, 44, 45l, 45r
Aundrea Tavakkoly 194
Ken Mason/Telegraph Media Group 206, 207, 208, 210l, 210r, 211
Jon Turk 190, 191, 192, 193l, 193r
Henk de Velde 178, 179, 181, 182
© Stephen Venables 139, 140, 141, 142l, 142r, 143
© Jerry Wooldridge FRPS 252, 255

INDEX